Radio in the]

MW00774417

Radio in the Movies

A History and Filmography, 1926–2010

LAURENCE ETLING

Foreword by Kenneth Jurkiewicz

McFarland & Company, Inc., Publishers
Jefferson, North Carolina, and London

Library of Congress Cataloguing-in-Publication Data

Etling, Laurence, 1945–
    Radio in the movies : a history and filmography, 1926–2010 /
Laurence Etling ; foreword by Kenneth Jurkiewicz.
        p.   cm.
    Includes bibliographical references and index.

    ISBN 978-0-7864-4949-1
    softcover : 50# alkaline paper

    1. Radio in motion pictures.   2. Motion pictures — Catalogs.
I. Title.
PN1995.9.R24E85   2011
791.44 — dc23   2011017369

British Library cataloguing data are available

© 2011 Laurence Etling. All rights reserved

*No part of this book may be reproduced or transmitted in any form
or by any means, electronic or mechanical, including photocopying
or recording, or by any information storage and retrieval system,
without permission in writing from the publisher.*

Cover images and design by David Landis (Shake It Loose Graphics)

Manufactured in the United States of America

*McFarland & Company, Inc., Publishers
    Box 611, Jefferson, North Carolina 28640
        www.mcfarlandpub.com*

To all those who have made radio
such a crazy and wonderful business.

To Jim —

In memory of the
good old days of
radio.

Larry
Christmas 2011

Table of Contents

Foreword
by Kenneth Jurkiewicz

A couple of summers ago, in "The Media in the Movies," a one-week "Special Themes" course for the School of Broadcast and Cinematic Arts at Central Michigan University, my students and I viewed and discussed four feature films in which various aspects of the media industries were depicted by Hollywood filmmakers. Two of the films we screened were about radio.

The first was Woody Allen's *Radio Days* (1987), his wistfully nostalgic coming-of-age comedy about growing up in a working-class Jewish neighborhood in the Rockaway district of New York's Queens borough during the late '30s and the World War II years, and the overwhelmingly positive impact that the omnipresent radio had on each member of the young protagonist's always bickering but forever loving and extended family.

The second film was Oliver Stone's *Talk Radio* (1988), about the last days of an obsessively driven, neurotically self-absorbed, and self-destructively hellbent motor-mouth Dallas shock jock, played by co-writer Eric Bogosian with an intensity that was matched only by his character's commercially calculated insincerity. Although these two major Hollywood movies were released barely a year apart, they depicted a mass communications industry, its practitioners, and (maybe especially) its consumers in a manner that seemed worlds apart from each other, yet in chronological terms actually represented little over a single generation. As Woody Allen's adult voiceover kept reminding his audience, commercial radio in that more naïve and less sophisticated pre-television era was a way of creating a sense of community, binding together people of different social and economic classes struggling through some very difficult times with shared fantasies, myths, and values.

No matter how illusory or shallow or artificially contrived these fantasies, myths, and values turned out to be, for the listeners of those quiz shows, big-band broadcasts, soap operas, newscasts, expert-advice programs, and kiddie

1

adventure serials, they all seemed at that moment somehow valid and deeply relevant. In direct contrast to this admittedly romantic conception of pop radio in that bygone age was Stone and Bogosian's rancidly dystopian contemporary rendition: their talk show host, with his unerring commercial instincts, promoted division instead of community, and racial hatred and class warfare instead of shared hopefulness and common purpose.

For the students in my class — some of whom, one must not forget, were studying to embark on a career in commercial radio — viewing these two films side by side proved to be a most enlightening and sobering experience, reflecting as they did a mass medium and its audience that have gone through a radical transformation in a strikingly short span of time.

This transformation is just one of many story arcs chronicled by Laurence Etling in this genuinely groundbreaking study of how the history of the radio industry — its personalities, policies, and politics — have been portrayed and refracted in the movies.

As Professor Etling reminds us here, the movies and radio had pretty much evolved concurrently throughout much of the twentieth century. Even before the advent of the talkies, the studios were able to become virtual partners with the radio networks in promoting each other's product lines in a kind of cross-promotional synergy that to a much more limited extent continues to this very day.

Indeed, throughout much of radio's Golden Age, the studios produced and the networks regularly aired long-running anthology series that consisted of radio adaptations of then-current popular movies, while Hollywood returned the favor by allowing radio stars or the characters they portrayed (Amos 'n' Andy, Fibber McGee and Molly, Henry Aldrich, the Great Gildersleeve, many others) to take visual form and continue their adventures on the nation's theater screens. How convivial and financially advantageous this relationship turned out to be can be suggested by how effortlessly many of this past century's most popular entertainers — think of Al Jolson, Burns and Allen, Jack Benny, Bob Hope, and Bing Crosby, to name only the most prominent — could move back and forth from one show biz platform to another, encompassing the vaudeville or Broadway stage, radio, the recording industry, and the movies, with their talent and reputation and iconic personas thriving in all of them.

No wonder, then, that when any aspect of the radio business was depicted in Hollywood films of the 30s and 40s, most of the time it would be in a very positive or at least thematically neutral manner. The immediacy and vitality and mysterious star-making aural alchemy of radio was celebrated and glorified in both big-budget extravaganzas and low-budget grade-B programmers, in musicals (of course), melodramas, mysteries, comedies, even Saturday matinee westerns. In almost every heart-stopping episode of the thrilling 1935 12-chapter serial *The Phantom Empire*, for example, Gene Autry had to keep breaking off from his battle to save the Earth from the evil forces of the underground continent of Mu to race back to his beloved Radio Ranch so that he could perform live on his daily radio show, since if he did not show up on time he would have been in breach of his draconian, ironclad contract and would have consequently lost not only the ranch but his livelihood as America's "Singing Cowboy." Given radio's magical properties of mass communication and its seemingly limitless potential to expand the listener's imagination, who could argue with Gene's priorities?

But there were technological and economic changes looming on the multimedia horizon that would prove more cataclysmic than anything the insidious super-scientific minions of Queen Tika's Phantom Empire could have devised. In other words, the arrival of television (among other forces) had devastating consequences for both radio's suddenly superannuated national network setup and the entrenched and complacent movie studio system. On the radio front, with the virtual collapse of national network programming, power and influence shifted to regional and local stations, while in Hollywood the five major studios began to lose their collective, once vice-like grip on all aspects of production and distribution with the rise of talent free-agency and the concomitant growth of independent production companies.

Because commercial radio in the 50s out of necessity came to rely more and more on recorded music to fill up airtime and concurrently cater to a burgeoning and increasingly affluent baby boom audience, local and regional rock 'n' roll DJs like Dick Clark and Alan Freed quickly (and controversially, as the payola scandals would delineate) evolved into powerful show biz impresarios and influential youth-culture kingmakers, becoming movie and TV celebrities in their own right. In the case of Clark and Freed, for example, while the former became best known for hosting the long-running *American Bandstand* television series, the latter starred in a short-lived series of self-aggrandizing, low-budget drive-in exploitation movies, with titles like *Mr. Rock and Roll* (1957), in which a blandly genial and avuncular Freed would invariably play both a father figure to some humble, wide-eyed neophyte trying to break into the music business, as well as a shrewd promoter-master of ceremonies for both well-known and aspiring record acts.

The ostensible rags-to-riches storylines would be simply an excuse to string together the sometimes revelatory musical performances. In many instances, in an era long before MTV, these sequences would be the only surviving filmed record of some of early rock 'n' roll's most vibrant stars at their creative heights, along with more than a few who never quite made it. These cheesy second-feature programmers may not tell us much about the recording and radio industries of that period (except perhaps inadvertently), but as cinematic time capsules of teen tastes and aspirations, they are an unparalleled treasure trove.

This particular era of American radio history, along with the romanticized image of the rock DJ as a mysterious but benign, Wizard of Oz–like background eminence presiding over the perpetual traumas and dramas of his cruisin'-for-a-bruisin' teen and pre-teen acolytes, was already a distant memory when George Lucas indelibly memorialized it in *American Graffiti* (1973). By that point, the movie's Wolfman Jack seemed as antiquated as Fred Allen, since technological advances involving (among other things) the opening up and colonizing of the FM dial fragmented the once near-monolithic boomer audience into more varied and isolated (and perhaps also more discerning and discriminating) radio listeners.

As AM's Top 40 inevitably gave way to FM's AOR (and all of its subsequent offshoots), the role of the DJ was downplayed, as was his (and occasionally her) role as a kind of binding social force. Economic necessity prodded AM radio stations away from music and into the more profitable news and call-in formats, and a new sort of radio personality began to dominate not only the nation's airwaves but the society's political consciousness: the shock jock-talk show host.

In this regard, it is mordantly instructive to compare how two of the most influential figures in modern American radio history have been portrayed in two very different kinds of biopics: In *American Hot Wax* (1978), Alan Freed (Tim McIntire, in an Academy Award-nominated performance) is depicted pretty much as a victimized martyr on behalf of the liberating energy of racial integration and youthful musical creative expression, ultimately beaten down by the uptight and mean-spirited moral and religious forces of Eisenhower-era repressiveness. In *Private Parts* (1997), Howard Stern, self-described "King of All Media," gets to play himself as an abrasive and tasteless but nevertheless charming and fearless champion of First Amendment freedoms, triumphantly overcoming every economic and political obstacle thrown down by all those hateful governmental and corporate spoilsports who would want to put limits on his raw, honest expressiveness.

As Larry Etling has shown us in this engrossing, thorough, and fascinating survey, Hollywood films have reflected the various ways in which this culture has moved from genial entrepreneurs like Freed (and his predecessors) to relentless provocateurs like Howard Stern (and his more ideologically inclined successors and competitors) with sometimes a certain amount of insight but most often with simply a desire to distract and entertain, like the personalities they were showcasing. As radio and movies begin their next transformative period in this new millennium of seemingly limitless techno-logical innovation — from synergy to convergence, so to speak — perhaps movies will be made about the adventurous romance and mysterious magic of podcasting and filesharing. But one tends to doubt it.

Kenneth Jurkiewicz is an associate professor in the School of Broadcast and Cinematic Arts at Central Michigan University, Mount Pleasant, Michigan. He has published articles and deliv-ered conference papers on subjects ranging from horror and science fiction films to rhetorical theory, and has reviewed movies for the university's public television and radio.

One

On the Air, at the Movies, and How It All Began

This is a book about radio. More precisely, as the title indicates, it is about how radio has been portrayed in films since the earliest days of the movie industry. It looks at films that have in some way depicted radio stations or the people who work in them, or those in which a radio station, broadcast, or personality plays a role in the storyline. It therefore presents a unique look at one of the most powerful media forms the world has known.

Radio has proven irresistible to filmmakers from the dawn of broadcasting and, in fact, from the birth of motion pictures. The number of titles in the filmography attests to this. One reason for radio's appeal seems to be the nature or mystique of the medium itself. Another reason may be the people synonymous with the programming heard on the airwaves over the years — the DJs and other air personalities who have, in large part, come to personify radio to the listening public. Whatever the reasons for its attraction to both listeners and filmmakers, there is no doubt that radio is unique among the mass media, and why this is so should be examined in order to understand the films discussed in the following chapters.

The Mystique of Radio

From its beginning, radio's attraction was unique and universal, for reasons not entirely explainable. Referring to himself as "the Radio Kid" because of his fascination with the medium while growing up, radio historian Gerald Nachman noted that "there was — still is — a mystique to radio unlike that of any other entertainment medium. Its intimacy amounts almost to secrecy."[1] This appeal can be traced back to radio's roots. As the medium began to take shape in the 1920s, "radio announcers and performers entered into an unprecedented relationship with the vast numbers of people who began to make up a new listening public."[2] Radio listening made the world seem, to some, "intimate, manageable, and coherent yet at the same time vast and mysterious and thrilling."[3] Stanley Elkin captured the fascination of radio in its formative years in his mordant novel about an itinerant announcer, *The Dick Gibson Show*:

> When Dick Gibson was a little boy, he was not Dick Gibson. And he could get Omaha, could get Detroit, could get Memphis; New Orleans he could get. And once — it was not a particularly clear or cold night; for that matter it may even have rained earlier — he got Seattle, Washington. He listened almost until sign-off, hoping that the staff announcer would say something about the wattage put out by the station. Then, after the midnight news but before the amen of the sermonette, the station faded irrecoverably. He'd learned never to fool with the dial, that it did no good when a signal waned to reclaim it with some careful, surgical twist a half-dozen kilocycles to the right or left. It was best to wait through the babble and static for the return of the electronic tide. Often it would come, renewed for its hiatus, its cosmic romp and drift, strongly present again after its mysterious trip to the universe.[4]

Elkin's young listener was engaged in a practice unknown to most of today's iPod and satellite radio generation: "DXing," or scanning the radio dial to find distant stations (which, due to atmospheric conditions, can be done only at night). Exactly why radio should have had this appeal is probably unknowable. One attraction was undoubtedly the music, since radio played a crucial role in introducing America to musical forms such as rockabilly, rhythm 'n' blues, and rock 'n' roll.[5] Much of the fascination might also have been attributed to other sounds coming from the speakers — the voices of the DJs and other air personalities.

While music is certainly one of the most important reasons people choose to listen to a specific station (or to radio at all) rather than the myriad of other listening possibilities, radio offers more than music. It also offers the companionship of a human voice. To many listeners, DJs define radio stations. TV viewers watch programs, but radio listeners choose "my station." It is almost certain that few newspaper readers identify strongly with, or can even name, the reporters whose stories they read (although columnists often build loyal readership). While the viewership of TV stars such as David Letterman, Jay Leno, and Jon Stewart — and Jack Paar, Johnny Carson, and others in earlier years — is measured in the millions, they are perceived mainly as entertainers, albeit hugely talented.

The DJ, however, is more like a friend who, before the advent of satellite program distribution and corporate ownership, lived in our communities (and in many cases still does). While we may admire and even idolize film and television stars, most of us realize that we cannot be like them or live like them. In fact, that is the essence of their stardom; their glamour excites and fascinates us. Not so the DJ, who, besides being an entertainer, is also a fount of information such as news of local, national, and international import, community activities, weather, and sports, sometimes with a personal interpretation. The DJ's own personality also usually comes through, and what he or she says is not part of a script writing and production process. The local DJ does not have teams of writers producing his or her on-air gags (although pre-production is often quite extensive), nor a vast supporting cast of production specialists to get the creative work to the public. Ad libs are often based on local events or activities and listener interaction is sometimes encouraged through phone calls. Romanticized, the DJ in the control room is talking one to one with listeners.

Speaking into a microphone and knowing that someone — anyone — is hearing your voice holds an attraction for a certain type of personality. To be an announcer or DJ has been considered almost a calling by some. Many who have spent years behind a microphone could imagine no other life, although they perhaps could not explain why. Radio's appeal was summed up by the Peter Downs character in the 1990 film *A Matter of Degrees*. The college station he started years before is now being sold to corporate interests.

> We started this station in 1977. First song played ... "I Wanna Be Sedated" by the Ramones. I stole that record from my brother Eddie the day I left for college. Sorry, Eddie. Anyway, thinkin' about it, in life there's stops and starts, and beginnings and endings, as we stumble through. And here we are, eleven years later. It's twelve midnight. But, uh, some kid out there has got the radio on, real low, singin' all the words to himself. He knows all the words. And that's why I can't really imagine doin' anything else. I mean, even with all the bullshit. And, uh, why I can't say goodbye, even when it's over. So I gotta put another platter on the table, let 'er spin. Peter Downs, WXOX 90.6, Providence, Rhode Island. Rock 'n' roll can save you.

The DJ therefore often feels a direct connection with the audience and derives satisfaction from just knowing that — or sometimes wondering if — listeners are "out there." In radio's earlier years, in fact, announcers often referred to "everyone out there in radioland" in referencing their unseen audiences. This connection between DJ and listener is what differentiates radio from other media. A newspaper requires the editing and vetting of stories, layout editors determine its appearance and, prior to the Internet, a complex distribution system was required (and still is, for the physical product). Television and film productions involve teams of lighting and audio experts, set designers, script writers, producers, directors, and many more, as well as elaborate physical or electronic distribution systems. All of these detract from the immediacy of the viewing experience.

Radio is much simpler in both production and distribution. In its most elemental form, one person speaking into a microphone can talk to another perhaps thousands of miles away or, in this Internet age, across the globe. Radio has a directness and immediacy not found in other media, except for television news and sports broadcasts and other live events such as telethons and concerts (all of which still require large production teams) and, of course, the Internet. It is from this directness that much of radio's unique attraction is derived. Some forms of radio, such as talk shows, provide instant audience feedback both to the show host and to other listeners, thereby involving the audience in the production of the program. Radio has undergone a transformation in recent years, and this has been effected both by technology and by the rise of huge media conglomerates, as will be discussed. But although it has been periodically reshaped by social, regulatory, and technological changes, the fact that radio remains a potent force in American society is a testament to its enduring popularity.

In radio's earliest years, air personalities were mostly singers or other entertainers, and announcers were emcees or hosts of musical programs. In the late 1930s, DJs began to formulate a new role for announcers, and a trend toward playing recorded music escalated with the demise of radio networks following World War II. Regardless of how their jobs have been defined, however, DJs and other air personalities have played a critical role in shaping the public's perception of radio. This book deals largely with the way those personalities have been depicted on screens large and small, because Hollywood has focused on them almost exclusively in the radio movies reviewed in the following pages. With occasional exceptions (managers, sponsors, engineers, writers, and others are sometimes seen), filmmakers have largely ignored almost every other aspect of the radio industry. This has probably been for dramatic reasons, such as plot and character development, to which air personalities lend themselves much more than do, for example, air time salesmen or the engineers who keep the stations on the air (DJs tend to have more colorful personalities than salespeople, writers, or engineers). A short history of radio is therefore in order, to provide a context for the discussions of the radio films in the following pages.

A Brief History of American Radio

Although historians still disagree as to what should be considered the first broadcast in the United States, radio as we now know it is regarded by many as dating to 1920 when KDKA Pittsburgh became the first station to begin continuous broadcasting.[6] Unlike most countries following World War I, successive American governments did not establish tax-supported national broadcasting systems. From radio's earliest years, the interests of broadcasters and advertisers therefore coincided, which fact is crucial to understanding both radio and many of the films in which it has been depicted.

Advertisers perceived the commercial potential of radio when it emerged in the early 1920s, and formed alliances with broadcasters to fund and promote programming.[7] The first radio commercial announcement, known then as a toll broadcast, is believed to have been heard on August 28, 1922, when the Queensboro Corporation promoted the sale of apartments in the Jackson Heights district of Queens, New York.[8] Hollywood also quickly took note of advertising's importance to radio, and commercial themes were soon being included in film plots. In *Make a Million* (1935), for example, a university president challenges the theories of an economics professor who must prove those theories correct in order to keep his job, and the professor develops a radio campaign to save the day. A sponsor argues with his wife about what kind of music should be played on their program in *What's Cookin?* (1942). Numerous other movies of the 1930s and '40s also had advertising themes or plot implications.

Since American broadcasting is advertising-based, audience size is important to radio stations, advertisers, and air personalities. Advertisers, often referred to as sponsors in radio's earlier days because they would pay for an entire program, want the largest possible audiences to hear their messages. As a result, stations try to maximize listenership size to satisfy those sponsors and generate the largest possible revenue streams from the sale of air time. Caught in the middle are the program directors and air personalities who are ultimately held responsible for the stations' success, which is most often measured by ratings.

In their simplest form, ratings measure how many people are listening to a station or program at a given time, or over a specified period of time. They do not measure listener satisfaction although it is assumed by broadcasters and advertisers alike that programs with the highest ratings are usually satisfying the most people. Over the years, numerous companies such as Hooperatings, Birch Radio, and the current dominant supplier, Arbitron Inc., have provided the radio and advertising industries with listenership figures. Low ratings have contributed to the firings of countless air personalities, program directors, and station managers.

Several screenwriters have thought to use ratings as the basis for movie plots. Some early films in which ratings played a role included *Two Against the World* (1936; a radio drama increases ratings but results in the deaths of two people); *Kentucky Moonshine* (1938; a New York radio star looks for hillbillies to bolster his sagging ratings); and *I Surrender Dear* (1948; stations begin hiring band leaders as DJs to increase the size of their listening audiences). More recent examples came in *Body Chemistry 2: Voice of a Stranger* (1992; a sex therapist is hired to increase a station's ratings); *Power 98* (1996; a talk show host kills listeners to boost his ratings); *Bare Deception* (2000; a talk show's ratings jump when listeners are killed); and *The Urban Demographic* (2005; a station switches from classical music to rap to increase its ratings).

During its formative years, American radio was largely the province of the networks, described by broadcast historian Erik Barnouw as a "Golden Web."[9] Although locally owned stations formed the backbone of the country's broadcasting system, they were often affiliated with one of the national webs such as CBS, Mutual, and NBC's Red and Blue networks. The eclectic network programming of the 1930s and '40s included variety shows (*Kraft Music Hall, The Fleischmann's Yeast Hour*); classical music (*The Palmolive Hour, Maxwell House Concert*); comedies (*Amos 'n' Andy, Fibber McGee and Molly*); quiz shows (*Quiz Kids, Kay Kyser's Kollege of Musical Knowledge*); soap operas (*Ma Perkins, The Romance of Helen Trent*); detectives (*Mr. Moto, Sam Spade*); dramas (*Grand Central Station, Dr. Kildare*); science fiction (*Buck Rogers in the 25th Century, The Planet Man*); and westerns (*The Lone Ranger, The Cisco Kid*), to name only a few genres. Since recording tape had not yet been invented, these shows were either broadcast live or recorded on transcription discs.

The foregoing titles are illustrative of the dozens of program types and hundreds of titles aired from the late 1920s through the early '50s. Numerous authors have provided details of these shows, including schedules, guest stars, and other information.[10] A review of the filmography's thumbnail descriptions reveals that Hollywood used virtually all of these program types in the radio films produced until the early 1950s. In addition to the network programs described above, a number of local shows were also heard, including news and agricultural reports, amateur talent shows, high school sports, church services, and community events.[11]

By the late 1940s, however, the end was in sight for the radio networks that had informed and comforted the country through a great economic depression and a world war. The development of television had been delayed by the onset of World War II, but the war's conclusion spawned a rapid development of that medium, which in turn would transform radio. A particularly important year was 1948, when the number of cities served by television jumped from eight to 23 and the stations serving those cities grew in number from 17 to 41.[12]

Despite a temporary government freeze on new licenses during the

Korean conflict, the nation's rapt attention soon turned to the phosphorescent blue tube. Rather, one should say most of the nation's attention turned to the emergent medium because the arrival of television marked the beginning of a new era for radio:

> With TV accepting the central network burden derived from our centralized industrial organizations, radio was free to diversify, and to begin a regional and local community service that it had not known, even in the earliest days of the radio "hams." Since TV, radio has turned to the individual needs of people at different times of the day, a fact that goes with the multiplicity of receiving sets in bedrooms, bathrooms, kitchens, cars, and now in pockets.[13]

With millions of Americans forsaking radio for the charms of television, network radio quickly became a relic of a different age and the new radio scene was not only more localized but also completely different in form:

> Commercials tended to be taken care of ad lib by the disk jockeys themselves with the help of material provided by the sponsors. The station scarcely needed a studio. News programs called for an AP or UP or INS news ticker. All of these now provided material written especially for radio. A "rip-and-read" operation could provide a news service. Such news programs were replacing commentators at scores of stations.[14]

Also at about the time that much of the nation was becoming fascinated by television, new technological forces were emerging that would change the sound of American radio forever.

The American Disc Jockey

For many years, the DJ was a uniquely American phenomenon. Due to the more commercial nature of the U.S. broadcasting system compared to those of other countries, a hallmark of American radio was greater freedom of programming. In countries with publicly funded and more tightly regulated broadcasting systems, programming was often designed to meet government-defined objectives and policies. Because of First Amendment freedom of speech considerations, American radio was considerably freer from governmental involvement, although it was certainly not unregulated, with licensing and regulatory powers invested by law in the Federal Communications Commission (FCC). In the 1960s, pirate or unlicensed radio operators tested the boundaries of governmental control in Britain and other European countries, and eventually opened radio broadcasting there to greater program freedom and, later, privatization and commercialization. Numerous movies which have depicted the pirate radio phenomenon are discussed in Chapter Two.

One product of a less-regulated broadcasting system was the DJ, who became preeminent in American radio following the arrival of television in the early 1950s. The platter-spinning air personality was hardly new to the entertainment scene, however, having been around in one form or another for well over a decade before television opened the door for the DJ's rise to prominence. The playing of music on the air dates to the advent of radio itself, since Reginald Fessenden is credited with having played music heard on a ship at sea in 1906.[15] Harold Arlin at KDKA Pittsburgh in 1920 is thought to have been the first fulltime radio announcer,[16] but the arrival of the DJ, as the term was popularized, did not occur until the 1930s. Interestingly, the airing of recorded music was frowned upon in radio's early years:

> In the birth days of radio, the playing of phonograph records on the air was largely a no-no. This disdain went back to that "quality" of live programming. In 1922 the Department of Commerce set precedent by granting preferred licenses to those who would not use phonograph records.[17]

Probably the first person to play records on the air with what was to become known as DJ ad libs was Al Jarvis at KFWB Los Angeles in 1934. He called his show *Make Believe Ballroom* and through his patter and recorded music he created the ambience of orchestras playing for dancers in a large ballroom.[18] His style and signature program title were soon picked up by others including, most famously, Martin Block in New York, and numerous *Make Believe Ballroom* shows were heard across the country in succeeding decades. In *Sing Boy Sing* (1958), Art Ford of WNEW New York hosted a show of that title, although it and the numerous other *Make Believe Ballroom* programs bore no resemblance to the Jarvis original in terms of content; they merely appropriated the famous name.

When Jarvis, Block, and others were developing the DJ's presentational style, their music and commercial announcements were recorded on transcription discs. The typical control room might contain several large turntables, which the announcer had to jockey between for the continuous playing of music and commercials. By 1949 the term "disc jockey" had been formally accepted in the industry,[19] although it had almost certainly been used before then. The turntables and other control room equipment of the era can be seen in several movies, including *Reveille with Beverly* (1943) and *Something in the Wind* (1947), both of which depicted women as DJs and are discussed in more detail in Chapter Three.

Arnold Passman claims that "jockey" is derived from the French Jacques (for peasant) and notes that one definition of the term is "to manipulate trickily."[20] Some might consider this quite apropos to the announcing profession since one of the DJ's tools of the trade is using language to create an often artificial on-air personality. In doing so, it is common for DJs to adopt pseudonyms, as Stanley Elkin's fictitious Dick Gibson did at various times:

> And one time, at KRJK, Benton, Texas — I was Bobby Spark back then — I organized my own fan club, using the name Debbie Simon as a front. I described the club's activities and made them sound so attractive over the air that before long almost two hundred teen-agers were interested in joining.[21]

Elkin's announcer used various other appellations: Ted Ellson, Marshall Maine, Ellery Loyola, Bud Ganz, I.O. Quill and, of course, Dick Gibson.

Today's DJ was made possible by a fortuitous confluence of events, including a landmark court decision. To protect musicians' incomes derived from live network performances, record companies had labeled their recordings as "not licensed for radio broadcast." Recorded music was a mainstay for the air personalities around the country who were emulating Jarvis and Block, and they began playing commercially released discs. Block himself "set the national pattern for the influential 'disk jockeys' who made hit records by bringing new popular recordings to the public's attention."[22] In 1940 the Second Circuit Court of Appeals in New York, with Justice Learned Hand presiding, ruled that copyright law protected musical performances only until the recordings were sold and that radio stations, which had purchased them legally, were thereafter free to use them as they wished.[23] The decision accelerated the use of records by radio stations across the country, which would in turn eventually kill the networks' live musical broadcasts and lead to the disbanding of costly institutions such as the NBC Orchestra. In 1942, the American Federation of Musicians, representing the artists whose livelihoods were derived from the live performances, initiated a strike against the record labels in an attempt to limit the use of recorded music by radio stations. The action was short-lived, however (about a year), doomed to failure by technological and social forces as much as by legal arguments.

Technology Changes the Radio Landscape

A hallmark of radio is the changing technology that periodically restructures the role of the DJ as well as fundamentally altering the nature of the medium itself. This is evident today in the computers that have replaced not only the turntables and tape machines used by earlier generations of announcers, but also the DJs at many stations. Shortly after the 1940 decision that opened the doors to the legal playing of recorded music on the airwaves, a new development, the transistor (transfer resistor), indelibly altered the radio industry.

Radios of the network era used vacuum tubes, whose size necessitated large receiving sets which often took a prominent place as furniture in the living rooms and parlors of American homes. Examples can be seen in many pre-television movies, especially the sports films discussed in Chapter Four in which families often gather in front of the sets to listen to various athletic matches. Radio tubes were, in fact, included in the plots of two movies, *Fifteen Wives* (1934) and *Docks of New Orleans* (1948). In these films, sound waves or music broadcast at a specific frequency shatter a radio tube filled with poisonous gas so that the radio set itself becomes a murder weapon. In those parts of rural America without electrical service, the receivers were powered by non-rechargeable external batteries.

The transistor was developed by William Shockley and other scientists at Bell Laboratories in 1947. It was a solid-state device requiring much less power than a vacuum tube and, more importantly, it was much smaller than a tube. Most pertinent to the present discussion, it made possible the tiny transistor radio, which used small internal batteries, was small enough to be tucked into a shirt pocket, and was connected to the listener by an earplug. The first transistor radio went on sale in 1953 and three years later annual sales topped three million.[24] By 1965, more than 12 million were being sold every year.[25] Listeners, especially teenagers, were freed from the cabinet radios and thus from the living rooms where the head of the household often controlled the dial.

In 1964, media theorist Marshall McLuhan observed the changing American electronic landscape and noted that teenagers had begun to manifest "tribal stigmata," to which the portable radio was a powerful contributing factor:

> Now, to the teenager, radio gives privacy, and at the same time it provides the tight tribal bond of the world of the common market, of song, and of resonance…. The mystic screen of sound with which they are invested by their radios provides the privacy for their homework, and immunity from parental behest.[26]

Besides the portable radios, another type of listening device became popular with teens. Car radios turned automobiles into sanctuaries far from parental control, both literally and figuratively, but usually not for the homework purposes noted by McLuhan. The car radio was introduced by its inventor William Lear in 1930, and by 1953 more than half of the country's automobiles, including of course those driven by teens, were equipped with them.[27] For those of legal driving age (and the many passengers who were not), the car radio provided an irresistible allure of mobility that further eroded parental control over the listening habits of the nation's teens.

Another technological advance to profoundly impact both radio and the music listening public, especially teenagers, was the 45 r.p.m. record. The 78 r.p.m. discs used prior to World War II were made of shellac and had a limited playing time. On December 11, 1948, RCA Victor brought out a new record format — the 45 r.p.m. disc. Due to their smaller size and innovative design (a larger hole in the middle), these records required a new type of player, whose appearance RCA customized to appeal to children and adults but, more importantly, to teens. The discs revolutionized not just listening but also American society itself:

> Children were becoming their own separate consumer demographic, catered to by mass production and mass marketing. Within six years the same thing would happen to the "teenage" segment of the population — in most cases the same kids. Rather than simply ease into the look and habits of their parents, these children would seek out their own clothing fashions and entertainment. The plastic 7-inch record was only the beginning.... Kids graduating into teen-hood in the 1950s would embrace their 45s because they had been weaned on the little plastic records, but they would snub ... the big bands and crooners their parents listened to.[28]

The new discs were a boon both to the radio stations which received them free from the record companies, and to the record companies which found them much cheaper to produce and distribute than the shellac discs of the pre-war years. Thus was born a symbiosis between the broadcasting and recording industries that continues to this day, for which the nation's teenagers were grateful:

> The only reliable connections that kids had to their favorite music were the ever-present radio and that diminutive disc (occasionally with a photo sleeve), doling out magic performances in small doses. They might spend hours waiting for the local jock to play a certain song, or dial the phone over and over trying to get through to the request line, which was usually busy.[29]

The new listening devices — the transistor radio, the 45 r.p.m. record player, and the car radio — revolutionized teen culture. However, at the same time these innovations were radically reshaping both radio and American society, another force was being added to the media mix which would also fundamentally alter both radio and the DJ's place in it.

The Musical Landscape Changes

In 1955, *Blackboard Jungle* hit movie screens and its juvenile delinquency theme attracted teenagers in droves. The soundtrack included "Rock Around the Clock" by Bill Haley and the Comets, "the first rock song ever to hit number one on the charts."[30] The next year, Elvis Presley appeared on the Dorsey Brothers' *Sound Stage* television show, *The Milton Berle Show* and, most importantly, *The Ed Sullivan Show*, which "pulled an astonishing 82.6 percent share of the television audience."[31] Rock 'n' roll had arrived in America.

Radio program directors soon discovered that teenagers liked to hear their favorite songs often, and pioneers such as Gordon McLendon, Chuck Blore, Todd Storz, Bill Stewart, and Bill Drake developed and refined what came to be known as Top 40 radio. In this format, playlists were comprised of a limited number of the most popular songs, rotated frequently.[32] The relationship between radio stations and record companies became somewhat incestuous when record companies found that some DJs and program directors were willing to accept financial payoffs in return for giving certain songs a coveted spot in the rotation. More frequent airplay, of course, resulted in higher sales of those song titles. "Payola" (a contraction of "pay" and "Victrola," a type of record player) was the name given to these illegal payments to DJs, and resulted in several air personalities losing their jobs when the practice came to light in the early 1960s. The influence of payola was depicted in *Telling Lies in America* (1997) and *Mr. Rock 'n' Roll: The Alan Freed Story* (1999), both of which are discussed in Chapter Three.

The most notable of the early radio DJs was Alan Freed, who was also a rock concert promoter, and the man considered to be the first to play rock 'n' roll on the air for teen audiences. Freed appeared in several 1950s movies whose simplistic plots were based on performances by teen singing idols. Bill Haley and the Comets were featured prominently in *Rock Around the Clock* (1956), whose title was derived from that of one of their hit songs. However, the first film to discuss the role of the DJ preceded both Freed and rock 'n' roll: The premise of *Disc Jockey* (1951) was the power of the DJ to make stars from unknown singers.

Radio played a vital role in the lives of American teenagers from the mid–1950s to the late '60s because many of the pre-cable TV, pre–Internet generation had limited opportunities to see their new idols perform in person. The popular bands played in concerts, of course, but many of these might have been too expensive for the average teen or held in larger centers far removed from rural listeners. Local movie houses were another possibility, and some singing stars were seen in films such as *Don't Knock the Rock* (1956) and *Go, Johnny, Go!* (1959). Numerous "beach movies" of the early 1960s also included teen idols (most famously, Frankie Avalon and Annette Funicello). Also popular was CBS-TV's *The Ed Sullivan Show* on Sunday evenings, which often featured teen heartthrobs along with a variety of other acts. But throughout the day, and particularly in the after-school and evening hours, the DJs of America provided the country's teenagers with the sounds that shaped their generation. *American Graffiti*, directed and co-written by George Lucas, illustrated perfectly the importance of both the DJ and the car radio to teens in the pre–MTV world. In this 1973 production, the legendary

Wolfman Jack was the DJ and the car radio was the music's pipeline to California teens.

Similar scenes played out in cities and towns across the country before the Vietnam war ended what seems in retrospect a much more innocent and, one may say, more romantic age. The anti-war counterculture movement of the late 1960s and early '70s also helped reshape radio to a degree by spawning FM stations which catered to that culture by playing the album rock music not heard on the heavily commercial AM band. Known as "underground" or "free form" radio, these stations were a reaction against the restricted playlist Top 40 format that epitomized much radio in the 1960s (and which was heard on the car radios of *American Graffiti*). Originally heavily drug-influenced, the music was known as "acid rock" in its earliest days, and included a variety of rock types, often with an anti-establishment or anti-war theme. The format eventually evolved into what is known today as AOR (album oriented rock), which can be heard on both the AM and FM dial.

The Radio DJ Today

As we have seen, radio is a medium given birth to, and subsequently shaped by, technology, and recent advances have largely done away with many of the functions performed by local program directors and announcers. The use of communications satellites — beginning with Telstar in 1962 — meant that radio programs, including DJ shows, could be distributed nationally much more easily and cheaply than in the network era when physical land lines were required. "Voice tracking" or pre-recording DJ shows digitally for national distribution was also greatly simplified by satellites, which replaced reel-to-reel national audio tape distribution systems used in the 1960s and '70s. Voice tracking also allowed local stations to replace many of their announcers with voices stored on computers, and the "live and local" DJs with their request lines have become an anomaly at most music stations across the country.

Deregulation of radio by the FCC in the 1980s and '90s abolished a requirement for all stations to air newscasts, which led to the abandonment of local news coverage by many smaller — and even larger — stations, severing another important link between the radio station and the community. Deregulation also permitted companies to acquire more stations than previously allowed, and huge media conglomerates emerged as larger companies bought up smaller, locally owned stations. The effect of this was to remove much program control from local hands because the decision-making processes often became centered in head offices far from the communities in which the stations' studios and transmitters were located. Group management, and programming decisions for multiple stations under single ownership, became common. The image of the local DJ as portrayed in many radio movies, spinning records for audiences of teenage listeners, has long been an artifact of an earlier age. Today's DJs compete with devices such as iPods and satellite radio for listeners' attention. Anyone with a few dollars can now become a DJ and broadcast to the world since non-terrestrial (Internet) stations are generally beyond the regulatory purview of licensing agencies in most countries because they do not use the public airwaves. Repressive regimes, of course, ban the operation of such stations and, indeed, access to the Internet itself in some instances.

The following examination of radio's relationship to the film industry will provide an additional framework for the discussions of the following chapters.

The Origins of Radio Films

Hollywood's interest in broadcasting was concomitant but not coincidental with the development of radio, which was initially perceived by the film industry as a promotional vehicle. Warner Brothers Studios founded the eponymous KFWB Los Angeles in 1925 partly as an avenue for providing publicity for its films and their stars.[33] Radio, however, was actually depicted on the silver screen before film itself had sound, and was the basis for the 1922 movie serial *The Radio King*, as some of its chapter titles indicate: "The Secret of the Air," "Warned by Radio," and "Saved by Wireless."[34] The serial, produced by the Universal Film Manufacturing Company (which evolved into the Universal Pictures Company in 1925), is believed to be lost. *Roped by Radio* (1925) was another silent film about which little is known because there are no extant copies, but the intriguing title indicates that some form of broadcasting may have been depicted. It apparently was a western which starred Art Mix, aka George Kesterson, an early western actor.[35]

Another early radio film was based on Arthur Reeve's 1926 novel *The Radio Detective*. While there are no known copies of this silent, produced by Universal Pictures in the same year the novel was published, the book provides the story outline that presumably guided directors William James Craft and William A. Crinley. Extant stills indicate that they followed Reeve's narrative, which begins with a football game followed by a "Super-Heterodyne Dance" with music by an orchestra which broadcasts from a new hotel. The super-heterodyne was a type of radio receiver whose reception in this instance was less than reliable, as Reeves explained:

The boys succeeded in making some temporary excuse, as the radio gave a squawk and Easton was adjusting, that they had better go out and make sure that the high wind that was springing up had done no damage to the outside aerial.[36]

Two shadowy figures then appear from the darkness, cut the electricity, proceed to rob the dancers, and flee in a yellow race car. Some dancers immediately head to the station to broadcast news of the robbery. The novel is informative as to the film's possible set design:

> Arrived at the great Rockledge station, one of the most powerful in America, we proceeded at once to the splendid broadcasting room with its artistic draperies and hangings, and all manner of musical instruments, mechanical voice and sound reproducers, and its library of records.... A few minutes and Kennedy was before the microphone, giving the facts of the radio robbery to be listened to by hundreds of thousands of radio fans.[37]

The reference to "radio fans" provides a clue as to the novelty of radio listening at that time. Audiences first heard an actor talk and sing in a movie theater on October 6, 1927, when Al Jolson starred in *The Jazz Singer*. Thus was made possible realistic portrayals of radio, the medium defined by sound itself. On August 24, 1929, three years after *The Radio Detective* premiered, Warner Brothers released *Say It with Songs*. This starred Jolson as prizefighter-turned-radio singer Joe Lane, who accidentally kills a man he believes is making advances to his wife. Lane goes to jail, loses his voice, and upon his release makes a singing comeback to pay for an operation so that his crippled son can walk again (and croons the tearjerker "Little Pal").

A radio broadcast played an important role in a film released by First National Pictures on February 10, 1929. *Weary River* starred Richard Barthelmess as bootlegger Jerry Larrabee, doing jail time after being framed by a rival. Encouraged by the warden, Larrabee forms a prison band with which he sings on the air. The public's appreciative response wins him an early release. His fame is short-lived, however, since he is unable to replicate his performance to the satisfaction of audiences when singing on the outside, and by the film's conclusion he again finds himself behind bars while crooning the titular "Weary River." (According to the IMDb, Barthelmess' singing voice was actually that of Johnny Murray.[38])

A month later, on March 16, 1929, Metro-Goldwyn-Mayer released *The Duke Steps Out*, a silent film starring William Haines as Duke, a millionaire's son out to prove he can make it on his own. He turns to boxing and falls in love with a co-ed named Susie (Joan Crawford in an early role), who at first wants nothing to do with him. Susie later hears a broadcast of Duke's fight and realizes she is in love with him. Thus was born the plot device, used in countless subsequent movies, of characters fortuitously hearing important information over the airwaves. Although numerous stills and posters survive, no known copies of this film exist.

As radio captured the public's imagination and became a primary source of entertainment, films with radio scenes became popular with Hollywood. The filmography includes 126 American films produced in the 1930s (at least 26 in 1937 alone) and 145 in the 1940s. However, the film industry's interest in radio lessened considerably with the arrival of television. My research uncovered only 34 American radio movie titles from the 1950s (13 of which were sports movies that included play-by-play broadcasts), and only three in the 1960s (one was a Disney TV movie and another was a remake of a British film). A resurgence of interest was apparent in the 1970s, when at least 29 radio movies were produced, followed by 35 in the 1980s and at least 58 in the 1990s. Dozens more have been forthcoming since the turn of the new century, and this includes only American productions. The first post–World War II international film for which I could find a reference was the 1951 Finnish production *Radio tekee murron*, aka *The Radio Burglary*. At least 25 foreign radio films were produced in the 1990s (including Canadian movies, many of which used American stars and radio station call letters for marketing purposes in the U.S.). Since 2000, at least 54 international films, including ten Canadian productions, confirm radio's ongoing appeal to audiences worldwide.

Early Radio Film Themes

As previously noted, music constituted a programming staple from radio's earliest years. The variety show was especially popular, as were opera (most famously, broadcasts of the Metropolitan Opera hosted by Milton J. Cross) and classical music programs, as well as alternative musical fare such as *The Grand Ole Opry*.[39] Many radio films of the 1930s and '40s drew upon this music programming by headlining established stars in either lead roles or cameo performances. These included *The Big Broadcast of 1936* (1935, with Bing Crosby, Ethel Merman, Bill Robinson and others); *The Big Broadcast of 1937* (1936, with Gene Krupa, Benny Goodman and others); *The Big Broadcast of 1938* (1938, with Bob Hope, Shep Fields, Kirsten Flagstad and others); *Sing You Sinners* (1938, with Bing Crosby); *What's Cookin'?* (1942, with the Andrews Sisters and Woody Herman); and *Reveille with Beverly* (1943, with Duke Ellington, Frank Sinatra, and others).

Another favorite type of radio program was the quiz or contest show, and these were also used as the basis for some movies, among them *Let's Be Famous* (1939, Britain; a man goes to London to start a singing career and ends up as a contestant on a quiz show); *Christmas in July* (1940; a clerk's co-workers trick him into thinking he won a radio contest); *Uncle Joe* (1941; a young woman enters a contest to help save a widow's home); *Ever Since Venus* (1944; a cook writes a song that wins a radio contest); *My Gal Loves Music* (1944; a woman fakes her way onto a radio contest show); *Take It or Leave It* (1944; sailors appear on a quiz show); and *The Jackpot* (1950; a family's life is turned upside down when the father wins a big radio contest). Many of these films depicted the effects, for good or ill, upon the lives of the winning contestants.

Some movies attempted to translate popular radio shows to the screen, with both the storylines and titles taken from the radio shows. Movies that would have seemed familiar to listening audiences included *Myrt and Marge* (1933); *Grand Ole Opry* (1940); *Nobody's Children* (1940); *The National Barn Dance* (1944); *Breakfast in Hollywood* (1946); *People Are Funny* (1946); *Hollywood Barn Dance* (1947); *Make Believe Ballroom* (1949); *David Harding, Counterspy* (1950); and *Queen for a Day* (1951). Several films worked the phrases "Hit Parade" and "Big Broadcast" into their titles to imply a radio connection although the plots often had little to do with actual radio broadcasting.

Many of the early radio films featured stars already familiar to the public from previous film appearances, such as Barbara Stanwyck (*The Miracle Woman*, 1931; *Ladies They Talk About*, 1933); Bing Crosby (*The Big Broadcast*, 1932); George Burns and Gracie Allen (*International House*, 1933; *Many Happy Returns*, 1934); Claudette Colbert (*Torch Singer*, 1933), and Ginger Rogers (*Professional Sweetheart*, 1933). Shirley Temple made two radio movies after shooting to stardom in 1934: *Poor Little Rich Girl* in 1936 and *Rebecca of Sunnybrook Farm* in 1938.

A few radio movies tried to attract audiences by capitalizing on the popularity of newspaper comic strip characters of the day, including *Palooka* (1934), which starred Stuart Erwin as the boxer Joe Palooka and Jimmy Durante as his manager, and *Blondie* (1947's *Blondie in the Dough* and 1949's *Blondie Hits the Jackpot*), with Penny Singleton as the titular housewife and Arthur Lake as the dimwitted Dagwood.

Women in Radio Films

Women were seen in many radio films in the 1930s, usually as singers or wannabe singers, or as radio station secretaries or switchboard operators. Prior to the arrival of television, the main avenues to show business fame and fortune were music, film, and radio, and the plots of numerous movies of the 1930s and '40s were based on the efforts of unknowns (such as secretaries) to become radio stars. These included *Every Night at Eight* (1935; three young women enter a radio station amateur talent contest as singers); *Men Are Such Fools* (1938; a secretary tries to seduce powerful men to get a radio show); and *Hi, Good Lookin'!* (1944; a waitress enlists the help of a DJ to start her singing career). Films such as these depicted women using radio to achieve stardom as performers (usually singers) rather than as DJs. Aside from *Reveille with Beverly* and *Something in the Wind*, virtually no women were seen operating equipment in films of that era, except perhaps holding microphones as they sang.

Three Gene Autry radio movies were notable for featuring women in different and prominent roles. In 1937's *Git Along Little Dogies*, Judith Allen played Doris Maxwell, the owner of a radio station who tricks Gene into singing on her show to seemingly support a phony oil well scheme. A similar plot was used the next year in *The Old Barn Dance*, in which station owner Sally Dawson (Helen Valkis) dupes Gene into singing on her program, thus apparently promoting tractors, which he vehemently opposes due to their effect on ranchers. In 1939, *Rovin' Tumbleweeds* featured Mary Carlisle as a radio news reporter who interviews Gene during a flood and encourages him to become involved in politics. These Autry films were unique in showing women of that period in roles other than singers, dancers, or some other type of entertainer. In fact, *Git Along Little Dogies* and *The Old Barn Dance* were the first and only movies in which women have been portrayed as radio station owners.

Rovin' Tumbleweeds was one of only a handful of films to cast women as radio news reporters. Another was *Two of a Kind* (1938), in which newspaper reporter Christine Nelson (Claire Trevor) convinces her boss to sponsor a *Newsreel of the Air* radio show in which she tries to outwit rival radio colleague Duke Lester (Cesar Romero) to get the first interview with the Dionne Quintuplets. In the spy drama *The Lady Has Plans* (1942), Paulette Goddard is a reporter sent to work for the Lisbon bureau chief of a radio network, but does little if any actual reporting. *Hi, Gang!* (1941) had soon-to-be-divorced radio reporters Bebe Daniels and Ben Lyons fighting for scoops, including in the opening scene of a peanut-rolling contest. (Unbelievably, a rival station owner is outraged at being scooped in coverage of the big race.) In *Lucky Devils*, another 1941 production, a newsreel reporter blackmails the manager of WXEW to get his girlfriend a job as a radio newscaster and she is seen reading several newscasts: "This is your woman's angle reporter, bringing you a last-minute news bulletin hot off the ticker tape." That phrase alone indicates the status of women in radio news at the time.

Far from presenting the "woman's angle," Marcia Jeffries (Patricia Neal) in *A Face in the Crowd* (1957) was a reporter for an Arkansas radio station who discovers hillbilly singer Larry "Lonesome" Rhodes and then turns him into a media star. *To Please a Lady* (1950) was the story of a romance between newspaper reporter Regina Forbes (Barbara Stanwyck) and race car driver Mike Brannan (Clark Gable), but it's a love-hate relationship. In one scene, Forbes inexplicably reads a radio newscast in which she discusses Brannan's driving. This is one of the few films besides *Lucky Devils* to show a woman reading a newscast. *In My Country*, aka *Country of My Skull* (2004), starred Juliette Binoche as Ana Malan, a white Afrikaans radio reporter who becomes involved with an African American reporter (Samuel L. Jackson) while covering South Africa's Truth and Reconciliation Commission hearings.

In the Canadian zombie movie *Pontypool* (2008), Stephen McHattie was morning DJ Grant Mazzy, a combative personality whose bad day degenerates further when the station begins receiving phone calls about townspeople behaving in strange and violent ways. A virus is being spread through the use of the English language, turning residents into zombies. Mazzy's producer Sydney Briar (Lisa Houle) coordinates the news reports of zombie activity and Laurel-Ann Drummond (Georgina Reilly) operates the equipment and ultimately succumbs to the virus. In a particularly gruesome sequence, Drummond repeatedly hurls herself at the control room window in an attempt to get at Mazzy, reducing her face to a bloody mess. Hers is a unique role because of the absence of women engineers or technicians in radio films, and Sydney Briar was one of the few female program producers to have appeared on screen.

While many films have included female newspaper and television reporters, the above descriptions indicate how rarely women have been seen as radio news reporters. Several actresses have been cast as DJs and talk show hosts, however, as discussed in Chapter Three.

Radio Films as Critical Analysis

In reviewing radio movies, one is struck by Hollywood's lack of critical evaluation of the medium. Numerous films such as *Network* (1976) and *The TV Set* (2006) have explored both the effects of television on society and the workings of the industry. Likewise, *The Last Tycoon* (1976) and *Swimming with Sharks* (1994) are but two of many titles that might come to mind when considering movies that have turned a critical eye on the film industry. Newspapers also have been examined in several films, such as *All the President's Men* (1976), *Absence of Malice* (1981), and *The Paper* (1994).

In radio's nascent years, criticism of the medium and its societal role ranged from attacks as "a source of mass culture that undercut elite cultural standards and eroded personal creativity and uniqueness"[40] to claims that radio was placing "a tremendously influential technology in the service of an extremely undemocratic minority: the captains of capitalism."[41] Certainly, radio's "proper" role was vigorously debated during the 1920s and '30s when it became apparent to most observers that it was emerging as a powerful social force. More recent criticism has focused on programming issues such as the rise of right-wing talk radio and the effects of ownership concentration on program diversity.[42] Missing from the discussions are the voices of some other media, namely film and television. It is noteworthy that few film or television writers, directors, or producers have thought in any way to critically comment on one of the most influential media forms of all time. This may possibly speak to the film industry's dismissive attitude toward radio as an essentially commercial entertainment medium without societal impact, or it may reveal a lack of appreciation of radio's historically influential role in American culture.

A few TV series have had radio settings, however, perhaps the most insightful and successful being CBS's *WKRP in Cincinnati* (1978–82). *News-Radio*, set at WNYW New York, aired on NBC from 1995 to 1999, and *Free Radio*, a series about a moronic KBOM Los Angeles morning DJ, was seen on the VH1 cable channel in 2007 and '08. The British Broadcasting Corporation had Steve Coogan as a clueless DJ in 1997's *I'm Alan Partridge*. Interestingly, all of these were comedies that portrayed many of the air personalities in a less than flattering light, and therefore any insights into radio, how it functions, or its impact are obtained through the prisms of satire and caricature.

One of the first films to cast a critical eye on radio was *Two Against the World* (1936), with Humphrey Bogart as Sherry Scott, a radio executive at the United Broadcasting Company. The ratings are floundering and Scott is assigned by the station owner to oversee the production of a play based on a twenty-year-old murder case. Gloria Pembroke (Helen MacKellar) was acquitted of murder, has remarried, and is now known as Martha Carstairs. Her daughter Edith Carstairs (Linda Perry), who knows nothing of her mother's past, is about to marry. The radio play is a smash hit but when her past is made public, the distraught Martha kills herself with a drug overdose. Upon finding the body, her husband also commits suicide. Edith storms into the office of the UBC owner, accusing those connected with the station of murder. In an impassioned statement, Scott agrees with her and turns on the owner:

> Miss Carstairs, we killed your father and mother for several reasons. I killed him and he killed him and he killed him, and all the small fry that work for UBC aided and abetted the murder to sell time on the air. That's the answer. That's the only answer there is.

The Association of Broadcasters lodges a complaint with the FCC asking for UBC's broadcast license to be lifted and Scott agrees to testify against his employer. He then resigns in disgust because of his complicity in approving the show, but not before firing his secretary to force her out of the company as well.

In *The Hucksters* (1947), Clark Gable was advertising executive Victor Norman, who returns to his job after the war. The following excerpt reflects the attitude of many listeners, and Norman's comments doubtless would be valid if used to describe the opinions of many radio listeners and television viewers today. He dictates a letter to his secretary:

> Miss Hammer, uh, take a memorandum. Mr. Kimberly. Dear Kim, for four years, I haven't been listening to the radio much. Uh, paragraph. Kim, in that time it's gotten worse, if possible. More irritating, more, uh, commercials per minute, more spelling out of words, as if no one in the audience had gotten past the first grade. Paragraph. I know how tough Evans is, and some of the other sponsors, but I think we make a great mistake in letting them have their own way. We're paid to advise them. Why can't we advise them that people are grateful for what free entertainment they get on the air? Grateful enough to buy the product that provide good shows. But ... they have some rights, Kim. It's their homes we go into. And they're not grateful to people who get one foot in the door by pretending to offer them music and drama, and then take too much time in corny sales talk. Paragraph. I want to go on record as saying I think radio has to turn over a new leaf. We've pushed and badgered the listeners. We've sung to them and screamed at them. We've insulted them, cheated them, and angered them. Turned their homes into a combination grocery store, crap game, and midway. Kim, some day 50 million people are going to turn off their radio [*snaps fingers*] snap, just like that. And that's the end of the gravy for you, and me, and Evans. Sign it "Love and kisses, Vic."

Norman eventually becomes so disenchanted with the radio advertising industry that he leaves the ad agency. The screenplay for *The Hucksters*, written by Luther Davis, was based on Frederic Wakeman's novel of the same title.

A Letter to Three Wives won Academy Awards in 1950 for Best Director (Joseph L. Mankiewicz) and Best Screenplay and was also nominated for Best Picture. University professor George Phipps (Kirk Douglas) is married to a soap opera writer (Ann Sothern) and at a party he expresses his thoughts about radio advertising to one of her guests:

> MRS. MANLEIGH: Radio writing is the literature of today, the literature of the masses.
> GEORGE: Then heaven help the masses.
> RITA: But it just serves a different purpose, that's all.
> GEORGE: The purpose of radio writing, as far as I can see, is to prove to the masses that a deodorant can bring happiness, a mouthwash guarantee success and a laxative attract romance.... "Don't think" says the radio and we'll pay you for it! Can't spell "cat?" Too bad, but a yacht and a million dollars to the gentleman for

being in our audience tonight. "Worry," says the radio. "Will your best friends not tell you? Will you lose your teeth? Will your cigarettes give you cancer? Will your body function after you're 35? If you don't use our product, you'll lose your husband, your job, and die! Use our product and we'll make you rich, we'll make you famous!"

One of the most penetrating cinematic examinations of the media was the aforementioned *A Face in the Crowd* (1957), in which radio reporter Marcia Jeffries (Patricia Neal) discovers a hayseed singer (Andy Griffith, in an absorbing film debut as "Lonesome" Rhodes) and helps mold him into a national media figure who ultimately becomes a political megalomaniac. Rhodes first becomes a radio phenomenon by dispensing homespun "aw shucks"-style humor, then discovers that his telegenic personality can bring rewards of money and political influence. The power of the media to create a popular icon was fascinatingly portrayed in a film that was entered into the National Film Registry by the National Film Preservation Board in 2008.

Talk radio's connection to right wing politics was explored to a degree in *WUSA* (1970), with Paul Newman as a liberal DJ at a conservative New Orleans station. This was the first film to introduce conservative talk radio to movie screens, but the storyline fails to fully explicate the racist motivation of the station's owner (Pat Hingle) and Newman's antipathy to it.

Woody Allen's *Radio Days* (1987), an homage to 1940s radio, clearly showed its influence on the generation that came of age during the war years. Through comedy, the film captured the fascination of radio for many in its pre-television listening audiences:

> MRS. NEEDLEMAN: I don't know what to do, Rabbi. Every night he listens to the radio. I can't keep him away. I say "Go to the beach, play in the sun, get some fresh air." No, The Lone Ranger, The Shadow, The Masked Avenger.
> RABBI: This is not good. This boy needs discipline. Radio. Tsk, tsk, tsk. It's all right, once in a while, otherwise it tends to induce bad values, false dreams, lazy habits. Listening to the radio, these stories of foolishness and violence, this is no way for a boy to grow up.
> JOE: You speak the truth, my faithful Indian companion!

Besides reflecting the attraction of radio for young listeners during the heyday of network broadcasting, the romanticized images of radio and America seen in *Radio Days* contrast sharply with those of numerous other radio films of the 1980s. Far from the innocence of *Radio Days*, many of the other '80s movies portrayed a far darker side of American society, and also a vastly changed radio industry, illustrating the transformations that both had undergone in the decades after World War II.

The year after *Radio Days* hit the country's movie screens, for example, a somewhat dyspeptic view of radio was presented by Oliver Stone when he hinted at right-wing extremism in *Talk Radio* (1988). The film was inspired by the 1984 shooting death of liberal Denver talk show host Alan Berg at the hands of neo-Nazis. Eric Bogosian was Barry Champlain, a caustic KGAB Dallas talk show host, whose confrontational style catches the attention of a syndication company with ideas of airing the show nationally. Before the plan can come to fruition, Champlain is gunned down outside the station, presumably by a right-wing fanatic although the shooter's exact motivations are not explained (but it was hardly coincidental that the film's setting was the city famous as the site of a history-altering political assassination). The movie was based on a one-man stage show developed by Bogosian, whose on-air film persona manages to be both acerbic and patronizing.

In *Betrayed*, another 1988 production, FBI agent Catherine Weaver (Debra Winger) went undercover in a white supremacist group to find the killer of controversial Chicago talk show host Sam Kraus (Richard Libertini), who was shot and killed in the radio station building by a man in a military camouflage outfit. Weaver's plans go awry when she falls in love with the farmer who heads the supremacist organization (Tom Berenger). A right-wing talk show host (Stacy Keach) headed a militant group with plans to attack the American population with anthrax in the HBO production *Militia* (2000).

Talk radio, particularly of a conservative bent, has grown dramatically in recent years to become one of the most popular formats in America and therefore would seem to offer numerous possibilities for interesting and even controversial movie storytelling. While some of the titles mentioned above included the talk radio phenomenon, no films have explored either its influence on society or the hosts' psyches. The right wing elements depicted in these movies tend toward the extreme side of the political spectrum, possibly because Hollywood's prevailing political attitudes, which have been perceived by many Americans as somewhat liberal, are not conducive to more congenial portrayals of talk show hosts. However, the popularity of talkers such as Rush Limbaugh, Sean Hannity, and Bill O'Reilly suggests that films depicting these kinds of personalities or their influence could make for fascinating viewing.

Various other aspects of radio have been examined cinematically. *Telling Lies in America* (1997), which illustrated the corrosive effect of payola on both radio and a DJ who participates in the payoffs, is discussed in detail in Chapter Three, as is *Mr. Rock 'n' Roll: The Alan Freed Story*, which showed how payola led to the downfall of the once-prominent DJ. A few more recent films have tangentially looked at radio programming. In *FM* (1978), the on-air personalities of Q-SKY Los Angeles take over the station to protest management's plans to commercialize its sound at the expense of the current music programming. Crowds gather outside the building to show their support of the DJ. The station owner arrives at the movie's end to implausibly announce that the format will remain unchanged.

Another Los Angeles station takeover occurred in *Airheads* (1994). In this instance, a rock band called the Lone Rangers (Steve Buscemi as Rex, Adam Sandler as Pip, Brendan Fraser as Chazz) sneak into KPPX Rebel Radio with Uzi-lookalike water guns to force DJ Ian the Shark (Joe Mantegna) to play their demo tape on the air. Michael McKean is program director Milo Jackson. During the takeover, Rex discovers a box of Kenny G CDs in Milo's office and the following exchange is illustrative of the effect of programming decisions:

> IAN: Speak to me! What's goin' down?
> MILO: Okay, um, we're changing formats. Sunday midnight, the station goes soft rock.
> PIP: Rebel Radio's goin' soft?
> MILO: Well, we're ... we're changin' the name of the station to, uh, The Rain. You know, "Relax to the mellow sounds of The Rain on KPPX." That, and we're being forced to re-staff.
> IAN: You're firing me? You little snake in the grass bastard! Where do you get the balls to fire me?
> MILO: This was handed down from above, Ian! I fought this thing kicking and screaming!
> IAN: You've just begun to kick and scream, you sniveling putz! I'll kill you!

Private Parts (1997) was an autobiographical look at the career of shock jock-cum-TV personality Howard Stern. Besides describing his rise to multimedia stardom in a humorous fashion, it also details his clashes with management at various radio stations when his on-air performance stretches the boundaries of established programming norms.

The Urban Demographic, aka *K-HIP Radio* (2005) is the lone contemporary movie to have seriously discussed radio programming practices. Due to declining ratings, the management of Seattle classical music station KSOF switches to an Urban Contemporary (rap) format and brings in a new program director, Bob Johnson (Rico E. Anderson), to oversee the change. Many advertisers and listeners become upset by the move due to the nature of the rap lyrics. The protest group Sista's for Justice, headed by Rea Williams (Rhonda Ray), decries the format change because of the misogynistic and violent lyrics they hear on the air. DJ Janice Green (Tiffany Haddish) hosts an on-air debate between Johnson and Williams:

> GREEN: We'll get back to y'all calls in just a minute. But Rea, tell me, what is it that rubs you the wrong way about these brothas comin' up in the rap game? Is it the fact that they're makin' money, that keeps them independent? You feel they don't deserve it, or somethin'? What's up?
> WILLIAMS: Not at all. I understand that this is a come up for a lot of the

brothas out here. I mean, somebody has to be accountable for the price they're gonna pay to come up. It just can't be on the backs of us sistas.

GREEN: Bob, is it fair to hide behind the First Amendment, or should you be responsible for the music that you program?

JOHNSON: Even if I could, I wouldn't. These people are askin' me not to play music that degrades black women, yet they can diss other people. I can never get with that.

WILLIAMS: We're askin' all black women and anyone else who's against this rap music and all the violence it causes, to boycott all the advertisers of this station. And furthermore, I've taken steps to have this station's license revoked. And anyone else against this music, please call the FCC in Washington, DC.

Statistics (2006) hinted at the power of radio to inflame opinion when satellite radio talk show host David Allen (Kent Harper) turned his program into a screed against the ills of modern society. After his house burns down, Allen begins observing the misfortunes of others and cites endless statistics about societal shortcomings such as murders, rape, burglaries and other assorted crimes ("Death is all around us, hiding in the shadows"). Vignettes depict how several people's lives have been affected by various misfortunes but ultimately, besides platitudes ("Every second of the day there are people falling in love around the world"), the statistics serve no real dramatic purpose other than to paint a grim portrait of today's urban environment. The film falls far short of presenting radio as a possible catalyst for societal change, and Harper's performance as an out-of-control talk show host contributes to its overall depressing ambience.

The "Petey" Greene story told in *Talk to Me* (2007) was a better illustration of radio's power as a societal influence. Greene, portrayed by Don Cheadle, was an ex-con who landed a job as a talk show host on WOL in the nation's capital. The language used on his first air shift causes a near riot in the station and owner E.G. Sonderling (Martin Sheen) storms into the control room, intent on firing Greene. Program director Dewey Hughes (Chiwetel Ejiofor) tries to calm down the owner:

HUGHES: Morning music, and a talk show, with the man of the people. Because WOL is a station of the people, for the people ... by the people.

GREENE: I'm the people.

Although his language is crude, his directness on matters of importance to his listeners makes Greene an icon in the community as well as Washington's most engaging air personality, and his populist political bent leads him to become a community activist.

Pirate Radio, aka *The Boat That Rocked* (2009), illustrated the power of radio to change society when unlicensed broadcasts from pirate ships off the

British coast not only entertained millions, but also resulted in structural changes to British and ultimately European broadcasting by breaking government monopolies on radio and, later, television. This movie is discussed further in Chapter Two. While the above films have illustrated various aspects of radio broadcasting and have hinted at the medium's influence, an examination of the filmography's descriptions indicates that radio films generally have lacked the exploratory dimension of the numerous cinematic depictions of other mass media. While the definitive look at the nature of radio and its societal impact has yet to be produced, *Radio Days*, *Talk to Me*, and *Pirate Radio* stand as the best examples to date.

Radio as Agent for Social Good

After analyzing the content of numerous radio movies, one might conclude that the medium has most often been cast in a negative light, but this is not necessarily the case. The films of the 1930s and '40s which showed unknowns achieving radio fame and resulting fortune certainly depicted broadcasting careers as glamorous and something to be desired.

Several movies have also portrayed radio as an agent for social good. In *Larceny on the Air* (1937), for example, Dr. Lawrence Baxter (Robert Livingston) uses radio to rail against the sellers of phony radioactive medicines, including a cure for the common cold. A New York radio producer loses his job and begins managing a small rural station to try to resurrect his career in *Behind the Mike* (1937); he finds that crooked officials have been looting the town's treasury and exposes the corruption on his station. A young woman wins a radio contest and gets her own advice program in *Safety in Numbers* (1938), then uses the show to expose contaminants in the town's water supply. *Nobody's Children* (1940) was based on a radio program in which orphaned children were interviewed on the air to help place them in foster homes. In *Hi, Buddy* (1943), a radio singer undertakes fundraisers to save a New York club for boys. DJ Al Jarvis similarly uses his show to raise money to renovate a teens' club in *Make Believe Ballroom* (1949). The title of the latter film was taken from Jarvis' radio show; the film did not portray him as creating the ambience of the titular ballroom for which he became famous and widely imitated.

Two TV movies have shown traffic reporters thwarting crime. The first was Disney's *My Dog, the Thief* (1969), a light-hearted made-for-television romp in which a kleptomaniac dog not only boosts the ratings of a traffic reporter but also upsets the plans of a pair of robbers. On a more serious note, David Janssen was Salt Lake City TV traffic reporter Harry Walker in *Birds of Prey* (1973). The former military pilot sees a bank robbery in progress and, when the criminals transfer to a helicopter, he engages them in an aerial dogfight. In the TV movie *A Cry for Help* (1975), Robert Culp was a talk show host who is quick to insult his listeners but when a caller threatens suicide he enlists the audience's help in finding her by soliciting information about her description and possible location. Comedian Dennis Miller was a Los Angeles shock jock in *Joe Dirt* (2001). During an interview he mocks the titular Dirt (David Spade), an oil well worker searching for his real parents, but the listeners rally to Dirt's cause.

Cosmic Radio (2007) involved a California station verging on bankruptcy. The owner of KZMC is about to let the station go off the air and the idealistic manager looks for a way to keep it afloat. When a nearby forest is threatened by a clear-cutting project, the station provides publicity for the environmentalists who oppose the deforestation plan. In *Changeling* (2008), John Malkovich was a radio preacher who used his show to rail against the brutality of the Los Angeles Police Department and who also aided a mother in her quest to find her missing boy.

Few films have shown investigative or serious radio news reporting. Most radio news reporters are portrayed similarly to their print counterparts — trying to scoop the competition and sometimes engaging in shady practices to do so, although a few positive examples can be found. A radio reporter infiltrated a nightclub hostess racket to uncover a white slave ring in *Missing Daughters* (1939). A reporter was sued for libel over a dramatization of a murder case and undertook an investigation to prove that the story was factually correct in *Sued for Libel* (1939). In *I Live on Danger* (1942), a radio newsman undertook a murder investigation and freed the man wrongly convicted by airing a confession from the real killer.

A more recent film that showed radio news as it comports with reality was *Our America* (2002), which was based on a true story in which two inner-city youths are given tape recorders by a public radio station and conduct interviews that paint a grim picture of urban Chicago life. They also investigate the death of a young boy who was thrown from a 14th-story window and the young reporters subsequently win a Peabody Award for the story. In *Quid Pro Quo* (2008) a radio newsman becomes interested in an unusual subject. Isaac Knott (Nick Stahl) is a wheelchair-bound public radio reporter who uncovers an underground cult of people with a psychological need to be disabled. During his investigation he meets a beautiful woman who wants to be confined to a wheelchair and the film explores not only their relationship but also the psychological makeup of people who feel the need to be disabled in some way, such as by the loss of a limb. This story was based on reality in that such a subculture exists, although the film's verisimilitude is brought into question when Knott finds a seemingly magical pair of shoes that let him rise from his wheelchair and walk.

A more realistic production was *The F Word* (2005), in which New York air personality Joe Pace (Josh Hamilton), who's about to lose his job because of an abundance of FCC indecency fines, does one last broadcast. He visits the site of the Republican National Convention to report on street protests and riots that are not getting any other media coverage. The film was produced in a docudrama style that included interviews with members of the crowds intercut with clips of Mayor Michael Bloomberg's welcoming speech to the delegates.

Although many people turn to radio in times of crisis such as the World Trade Center attack or Hurricane Katrina, television news coverage is more likely to be seen in films that include such catastrophes. Radio reporters are seldom if ever portrayed as doing any reporting, unlike television reporters who are often seen putting themselves in harm's way to cover a story. Most films in which radio is depicted as serving the public during a crisis have been zombie movies such as *The Fog* (both the 1980 and 2005 versions), *Pontypool* (2008), and *Dead Air* (2009). None of these show radio reporters on the scene; the DJs talk to listeners from their control rooms. (The small-town station in *Pontypool* airs reports from its newsman on location until he himself becomes a zombie.) The most recent Hollywood views of the importance of radio news seem to be that it may be useful in the event of a zombie attack.

Radio Films and Genre Films

In this book, the term "radio film" is used to denote movies in which some aspect of the medium is depicted, although it should be evident that the plots do not necessarily deal specifically with the radio industry or with a particular station, broadcast, or personality. "Radio film" rather than "genre" is used because of the interpretive nature of the latter term. Frank D. McConnell has noted "how very uncertain the idea of genre is, in both filmic and literary exegesis, and therefore with how great a degree of subtlety and perspicuity we need to approach it."[43] Substantial differences of opinion arise when attempting to explicate exactly what defines a genre, even the seemingly obvious such as westerns.[44] However, when one speaks of a genre, certain characteristics or conventions are implied and one definition might be:

> Stated simply, genre movies are those commercial feature films which, through repetition and variation, tell familiar stories with familiar characters in familiar situations. They also encourage expectations and experiences similar to those of similar films we have already seen.[45]

Radio films do not lend themselves to such neat categorization since they lack a common defining characteristic. Garry Whannel addressed this issue as it relates to sport films:

> Is the "sport film" even a coherent category? Sport films do not constitute a genre — they do not have a consistent set of themes, images or tropes. They do not share a characteristic style or *mise-en-scène*. Sport films do not lend themselves to being understood through concepts of "auteur".... The "sport film," then is not a genre or a style of cinema, nor the product of "auteurs," but simply a topic, which links a set of otherwise diverse texts.[46]

The same is true of radio films, which are also inconsistent as to themes, styles, and directorial interpretation. Radio scenes are used in different film genres, from westerns to crime dramas, to add excitement or to expand the audience's understanding of the screen action. In general it can be said that, like sport movies, radio films cover a range of themes and lack a consistent style that could allow them to be classified as a genre. In this book, then, there are no references to a radio film genre, but rather to radio films. Chapter Two looks more closely at the development of these films and at the most common themes that can be discerned when analyzing their storylines and characters.

Two

Cowboys, Pirates, Zombies, Murderers: Radio Film Themes

As discussed in Chapter One, radio films cannot be considered a genre because they lack consistent themes or styles. Unlike gangster, western, zombie, horror, or other identifiable film genres, radio movies are not easily categorized. In many of the films discussed in this book, radio is incidental to the main plot, or some element of radio broadcasting may be included to serve a directorial purpose such as providing motivation for a character. A character may hear important information on the radio, which spurs him or her to take some action. In *The Winning Team* (1952), for example, the wife of Grover Cleveland Alexander hears the play-by-play announcer say her husband is coming into the game as a relief pitcher so she rushes to the stadium and arrives just in time for the dramatic strikeout that ends the film. Hundreds of such ploys have been used by scriptwriters over the years, with characters often turning on a radio just as important information is broadcast, often in a newscast.

However, radio films share one important characteristic of genre films in that they are, to an extent, exemplars of the times in which they were produced. Writing of genre films, Virginia Wright Wexman has said:

> It is the popular genres that have most typified American film and given it its greatest strength and vitality.... [G]enres bear a complex relation to the society that produces them, expressing the dreams, anxieties, and ambivalences of a given era.[1]

Likewise, John Belton described film comedies as cultural dreamworks:

> To study film comedy ... is in part to look at the dreamwork of a culture's collective unconscious, to put it on the couch, and to make it speak of the forces that led to its production.[2]

The forces leading to any film production include the people who write, direct, and produce the films and who are likewise products of their culture.

In addition, the producers and financial interests which make a film possible often, although not always, attempt to appeal to popular taste so that the movie will be financially successful. Films thus become mirrors which reflect, to an extent, the times which produced them; their characters and storylines offer clues as to the nature of the cultures from whence they came. In a sense, then, movies may be considered historical artifacts of a society. Accordingly, one of the purposes of this book is to provide an unusual glimpse of American society — unique because it looks at American culture in a way never before seen, through the lenses of the filmmakers who produced the radio films discussed in these pages. When examining the plots of radio movies, one may discern recurrent themes. This chapter discusses how those themes may be reflective of the larger society. It could therefore be called the cultural evolution of radio.

Radio Stars Are Born

Before transistor radios, rock 'n' roll, and DJs there was radio, but before radio there was vaudeville. John W. Ransome is credited with using the term in the 1880s to describe the stage variety shows which consisted of singing, dancing, comedy routines, dramatic sketches and various other types of entertainment.[3] Vaudeville shows were popular in the early twentieth century, as touring ensembles traveled from state to state, performing in venues such as town halls and theaters.

Entertainers could make $2,500 to $4,000 a week doing two shows a day, with top stars such as Eddie Cantor pulling in $15,000 a week.[4] Such numbers, however, paled in comparison to the salaries offered by the new medium of radio, which could range "from $5,000 to $10,000 from commercial sponsors for thirty-five broadcasts — once a week."[5] By the late 1920s vaudeville had begun its steep and final decline in popularity for several reasons, including changing cultural tastes, the arrival of talking pictures, and "the *coup de grace* of radio."[6]

The film *On Stage Everybody* (1945) depicted the transition from vaudeville to electronic media. Michael Sullivan (Jack Oakie) is a song-and-dance man whose career is on the ropes. The owner of the Fulton Theater offers Sullivan and his daughter Molly (Peggy Ryan) $125 a week for three shows a day, and five on Saturdays, Sundays and holidays. Fulton then explains that the offer includes a weekly radio appearance, which triggers an emotional confrontation:

> SULLIVAN: Radio is the pick-ax that dug the grave for show business. Radio is what killed vaudeville. Radio has set the human race back a thousand years.

FULTON: Why, that's ridiculous. Why, radio…

SULLIVAN: Ridiculous, is it? It's the tool of the Devil, that's what it is! It's not only killed vaudeville, but it's the downfall of civilization. What used to happen? People were at the shows, they got exercise and fresh air. But now they sit home on their hootenannies, with their big ears glued to the radio!

Sullivan's opinion of the electronic medium changes dramatically later in the film, as he explains to Molly when she finds a radio in his bedroom:

It was listenin' to the World Series that really done it. There I was, the same as if I was sittin' in the bleachers, when all of a sudden it dawned on me that that little box was bringin' the whole world right here to the Rest Haven. Oh, I'm tellin' ya, you know, music, public events, even show business itself. Shakespeare was right when he said all the world's a stage, and you know what he was thinkin' about? That little radio.

Although Molly is keen to keep their song-and-dance routine going, Sullivan is sufficiently visionary to help concoct an idea that they pitch to James Carlton (Otto Kruger), the president of a broadcasting company:

Now here's what we want to do. We want to put on a show called *On Stage Everybody*. We'll go out around the country and dig up a lot of vaudeville talent and present 'em to the listening audience. It's as simple as that. Now we gotta do that, Jim! Somebody's gotta do it or there won't be any big stars tomorrow. And you know without any big stars, there's no show business.

Perhaps as a reflection of their declining fortunes following the advent of radio, vaudeville performers have always been depicted in radio films — as in *On Stage Everybody*— as being down on their luck. For example, in *Caught Plastered* (1931), two unemployed vaudevillians helped an old lady save her drugstore by remodeling it and then advertising it on the radio. *Hullabaloo* (1940) featured a jack-of-all-trades but unemployed vaudeville star who gets his own radio show and causes a panic with a fake broadcast about a Martian invasion (two years after Orson Welles' famous *War of the Worlds* broadcast). In *Spotlight Scandals* (1943), a broke vaudevillian and a barber put together a comedy routine which becomes a hit, but things fall apart when one of the duo is offered a radio job, which he accepts. It is noteworthy that in all of these films, radio is presented as being the economic salvation of the struggling vaudevillians, thus reflecting America's transition from stage to electronic entertainment.

The growing popularity of radio was a crucial factor in the nation's declining interest in live touring variety shows, as the Michael Sullivan character presciently noted in *On Stage Everybody*. Evenings at the theater became passé when the new and exciting medium of radio could bring the country's most famous entertainers into the home for the price of a radio receiver and the batteries to power it. Radio stations and especially the networks needed talent to fill their broadcast hours, and the multi-talented stage performers constituted a ready supply. Many entertainers who began their careers in vaudeville, such as Bob Hope, Milton Berle, and George Burns, successfully made the transition to radio or film. Others who were unable or unwilling to accept the new media saw their careers begin an irreversible slide into obscurity, and books about the vaudeville years are filled with names unrecognizable to anyone but historians. The same would be true later when radio stars such as Fred Allen and Walter Winchell could not adapt to television and so remain unknown to most of the Internet generation.

Americans quickly embraced the new medium of radio. By May, 1922, more than 300 broadcast licenses had been issued; by the end of the year the figure had climbed to 570, and receiving set manufacturers struggled to meet the demand for their products.[7] Because of this proliferation, radio stations often became the public face or, rather, voice of communities across the country. Owners often used their stations' call letters to reflect the nature of the communities which they served. In Stanley Elkin's novel *The Dick Gibson Show*, for example, KROP, "The Voice of Wheat," is located in Roper, Nebraska. This designation of call letters has been a common practice in radio since its earliest days and continues to the present. (In 1971's *Vanishing Point*, Super Soul is a DJ for KOW, the "fanciest station in the far west.") In addition to reflecting their communities, the early radio stations connected their listeners, particularly those in rural areas, to the glamorous world of entertainment, as explicated by Stanley Elkin:

> Filler material provoked an illusion, even at this distance, of KROP's relationship to show business. ("Now, from the sound track of Walt Disney's feature-length animated cartoon, *Snow White and the Seven Dwarfs*, the RKO Studio Orchestra plays the wistful 'Someday My Prince Will Come.' Maestro...").[8]

Hollywood soon took note of the rapidly growing popularity of radio and used the new medium in a number of ways. A frequent theme of 1930s radio films was an unknown or average person becoming a radio star, usually by singing, which undoubtedly appealed to a nation struggling with the economic realities of the Great Depression. As to the power of film, Marshall McLuhan once posited:

> The movie is not only a supreme expression of mechanism, but paradoxically it offers as product the most magical of consumer commodities, namely dreams. It is, therefore, not accidental that the movie has excelled as a medium that offers poor people roles of riches and power beyond the dreams of avarice.[9]

Many movies of the 1930s and '40s filled this dream-making role with their depictions of radio. Local radio, with its admittedly tenuous connection to show business, would have offered the avenue to riches note by McLuhan.

The only other such media possibilities were music and movies, but radio was more promising. Much of 1930s America was primarily agrarian, but while the rural audiences were excellent markets for early phonograph recordings, recording industry production was essentially controlled by music companies headquartered in Northern urban centers.[10] Few recording studios were located in the small farming communities throughout America. For several reasons, including climate and access to a variety of shooting locations, film production became centered in Hollywood following World War I.[11] The possibilities of moving there to achieve screen stardom obviously would have been so remote to most Americans in the 1920s and '30s as to constitute pure fantasy. To imagine a career in music or film therefore meant overcoming considerable obstacles, not the least of which was geography — getting to the production centers for those media.

Radio stations, however, dotted the landscape and offered a possible means of entry into the world of show business. Many local programs such as *The WSM Grand Ole Opry* in Nashville and *The Musical Clock* on KYW Chicago made stars out of the performers who appeared on them.[12] An example of the opportunities provided by the local radio station can be seen in the 1982 television movie *Rosie: The Rosemary Clooney Story*. Clooney and her sister summon up the courage to audition at WLW Cincinnati and are offered a spot as singers on *The Moon River Show* for the then-princely sum of 20 dollars a week apiece.

Decades before *American Idol* or *America's Got Talent* created media stars, radio was turning its spotlight on unknown performers through another popular type of program: amateur hour broadcasts. These were popular across the country since anyone with enough courage could perform in front of a microphone and possibly come to the attention of talent scouts who might further one's career. While most of these programs did not offer financial remuneration, some allowed listeners to vote for their favorites (presaging later TV amateur performance shows), and these unpaid appearances could have been seen by many aspiring stars as the first step on the road to far greater public recognition.

Major Bowe's Original Amateur Hour began as a local New York program in 1934 and later became one of the nation's most listened-to programs when it moved to NBC. Amateur hour shows were been portrayed in some radio films. *Millions in the Air* (1935) featured contestants striving for stardom on *Colonel Edwards' Amateur Hour*. Likewise, an eclectic group of aspirants, including a yodeler and a bird-imitating taxidermist, tried their luck before the microphone in *Here Comes the Band* (1935). Three unemployed young women with visions of singing careers performed on an amateur radio contest in *Every Night at Eight* (1935). *Cowboy from Brooklyn* (1938) included a scene in which participants appeared on *Colonel Rose's Amateurs*, a New York "gong" show whose least-talented performers were unceremoniously escorted off the stage before completing their acts. The movies' amateur talent programs were broadcast live before studio audiences, as were the actual shows such as *Major Bowe's Original Amateur Hour*.

Numerous films spoke to radio's potential as an escape from the financial exigencies of the 1930s other than through amateur hour show performances. In *Thanks for Everything* (1938), a listener from rural Missouri wins an "average man" radio contest in which his preferences for various consumer goods most closely match the average responses of the other three million contestants. He is hired to give his opinions on various products, his comments prove prescient, and *Time* eventually names him its Man of the Year. Other rags-to-riches stories were depicted in *Twenty Million Sweethearts* (1934; a talent scout discovers a singing waiter); *The Loudspeaker* (1934; a small-town railroad worker becomes the host of a national program); *One Hour Late* (1934; a radio station file clerk gets an on-air singing job); *Broadway Gondolier* (1935; a New York taxi driver becomes a singing Venetian gondolier and is discovered by a radio sponsor); *Page Miss Glory* (1935; a chambermaid becomes a media celebrity); *Stars Over Broadway* (1935; a hotel porter is heard singing and becomes an opera singer and radio star); *Mr. Dodd Takes the Air* (1937; a sponsor hears a small-town electrician singing and takes him to New York to star on his radio show); *The Singing Marine* (1937; a Marine gets his own radio show); *Cowboy from Brooklyn* (1938; a New York talent scout on vacation discovers a singing cowboy on a dude ranch); and *Men Are Such Fools* (1938; a secretary manipulates her way into becoming a radio star).

A variation on the rags-to-riches theme had hillbillies or other unsophisticated rural types being discovered and brought to the big city. Examples of these films included *The Old Homestead* (1935; a New York talent scout goes looking for rural talent); *Sing While You're Able* (1937; a singing farmer is discovered by advertisers when their car breaks down in Arkansas); *Kentucky Moonshine* (1938; a radio singer decides hillbilly singers are the answer to his falling ratings); *The Girl from Mexico* (1939; a New York talent scout goes to Mexico to find new talent); and *Melody Lane* (1941; Iowa musicians are recruited for a New York show).

Innocents could serendipitously become stars in another twist on the "unknown becomes famous" theme, as in *Poor Little Rich Girl* (1936; a child on her way to school meets vaudevillians who make her a radio star); *The Higgins Family* (1938; a housewife gets her own show when a radio sponsor stops by for dinner); *A Little Bit of Heaven* (1940; a child becomes a sensation after singing on a street radio show broadcast); and *Senorita from the West* (1945; a girl moves to New York and gets a job as an elevator operator at a radio station, and then her own show).

Such storylines undoubtedly fueled many fantasies that, with a bit of luck, an ordinary person could find fame and fortune on the radio. In most of these escapist films, the newly found stars are offered fabulous sums of money, often thousands of dollars a week, far beyond what the average movie-goer of the time could imagine ever making. In many of the films, rival stations or networks bid against each other for the services of the hot new talent, most of whom are singers and are often represented by fast-talking agents. Interestingly, although comedies and dramas were popular radio genres, none of these movies depicted unknowns being cast as actors in radio plays, or as comedians. Likewise, few if any people were seen attempting to land positions that would not lead to on-air fame, such as station managers or program directors, probably because those jobs would not have been seen by moviegoers as glamorous and therefore would not have fueled their show business fantasies. Rags-to-riches films faded in popularity with the arrival of television, the last being the appropriately titled *My Dream Is Yours*, a 1949 Doris Day musical with a Bugs Bunny dream sequence.

Criminals of the Air

Crime dramas, a popular network radio programming staple through the 1930s and '40s, also proved to be a favorite with film producers. The first title in the filmography, *The Radio Detective*, involved a robbery and the title itself indicated the attraction of crime for film plots. Murder, however, has been the most common crime in radio movies, as evidenced by the numerous "radio station murder" films that have been produced. These include someone being killed at a station, or a singer or other star becoming involved in a murder.

In one of the earliest radio films, 1933's *The Phantom Broadcast*, a radio crooner is killed because of his mob connections. Other radio station murders occurred in *Death at Broadcasting House* (1934, Britain; an actor is murdered during a live broadcast); *Take the Stand* (1934; a hated radio gossip columnist is killed); *The Woman Condemned* (1934; a reporter tries to solve the murder of a radio star); *The 13th Man* (1937; both the district attorney and a radio reporter are killed); *All Over Town* (1937; radio comedians try to solve a murder); *Hollywood Stadium Mystery* (1938; a sports reporter broadcasts a murder investigation live); *Over the Wall* (1938, a promising radio singer is framed for murder); *Danger on the Air* (1938; a station engineer tries to solve the murder of a sponsor); *Up in the Air* (1940; a singer is murdered while on the air); *Who Done It?* (1942; a radio station president is killed); *The Ghost That Walks Alone* (1944; the cast of a radio show becomes involved in a murder); *There Goes Kelly* (1945; radio station pages solve the murder of a singer); *The Inner Circle* (1946; a radio commentator is killed to shut him up); and *A Woman's Secret* (1949; a former singer confesses to killing her protégé). Despite the fact that murders at real radio stations are as rare as in any other business, between 1930 and 1950 more than 40 radio films included some form of murder involving a station or one of its employees, performers, or listeners, or had a radio detective solving or helping to solve a murder.

More modern films, including the made-for-television variety, have continued to link radio with death. *Tenafly* (1972), for example, was the pilot episode for a short-lived TV movie-of-the-week series. James McEachin was private detective Harry Tenafly, who investigates the death of the wife of a radio talk show host. *Haunted Honeymoon* (1986) was a theatrical release starring Gene Wilder as Larry Abbot, an announcer for the popular *Manhattan Mystery Theater*. He and his fiancée (Wilder's wife Gilda Radner, in her final movie) decide to get married in the castle where he grew up, and murders ensue. TV lawyer Perry Mason (Raymond Burr) defended a woman charged in the death of an obnoxious station owner in *The Case of the Telltale Talk Show Host* (1993). TV detective Columbo (Peter Falk) investigated two radio murders including the death of a radio psychologist's assistant in *Sex and the Married Detective* (1989). In *Butterflies in Shades of Grey* (1994), William Shatner was a talk show host who sparred with Columbo during the investigation of the death of his daughter's friend.

Radioland Murders (1994) was set in 1929 at WBN, a fourth American network about to go on the air. On opening night, cast members begin dying and the plot evolves into a whodunit. In *Drive Time Murders* (2001), a married Chicago morning show team investigates a theft at the Chicago Art Museum and then becomes involved in murder. *McBride: Tune in for Murder* (2005) was an TV movie-of-the-week episode with John Larroquette as a private eye investigating the violent demise of an abusive talk show host hated by almost everyone he came in contact with.

Film scriptwriters have been quite creative in connecting radio and death, and radio's unique characteristics have been used in a variety of ways in creating murder scenarios. A broadcast triggered a pistol that killed a cheating husband in *The Secret Witness*, aka *Terror by Night* (1931); a program featuring "The Electric Voice" caused a radio tube to explode, releasing poisonous gas that killed a philanderer in *Fifteen Wives* (1934); a gunshot in a radio show was used to mask a real gunshot that killed a woman in *The Fatal Hour* (1940);

a convict on death row was killed by a jolt of electricity through his head-phones as he listened to the radio in *Murder in the Big House* (1942); and another radio tube filled with poisonous gas exploded in *Docks of New Orleans* (1948). More recently, psychopaths have proven to be interesting and often deadly radio film characters, and these are discussed in Chapter Six.

Crimes such as robberies, kidnappings, blackmail, listener scams, pla-giarism, and other nefarious activities have also been used in radio movie scripts. Examples are found in *The Miracle Woman* (1931; a phony faith healer uses radio); *Rhythm in the Clouds* (1937; a songwriter cheats her way onto a show by forging another writer's name); *Racketeers in Exile* (1937; criminals concoct a religious broadcasting scam); *It Can't Last Forever* (1937; fake pre-dictions are set up by "The Mastermind"); *Sued for Libel* (1939; the director of a news show is sued in a murder case); *Mexicali Rose* (1939; sponsors are actually crooks trying to bilk an orphanage); *Where Did You Get That Girl?* (1941; a record is stolen and played on the air), and many others. More recent examples include the Canadian film *Rare Birds* (2001; a small town talk show host deliberately broadcasts a false rare bird sighting to boost tourism); *The Night Listener* (2006; a teen makes false claims about parental abuse in calls to a talk show); and the French production *Special Correspondents*, aka *Envoyes tres speciaux* (2009; radio reporters who encounter problems in Iraq file fake news reports from Paris).

Radio broadcasts have also been used by movie criminals to send messages to each other, a trick that first appeared in *The Radio Detective* (1926). A gang used radio to broadcast codes about their next robberies in *Remote Control* (1930), and in *House of a Thousand Candles* (1936) spies also used coded broadcasts to communicate. Westerns using this code device were the 1939 Gene Autry oater *Colorado Sunset* and 1942's *Ridin' Down the Canyon*, starring Roy Rogers. In *Panic on the Air*, aka *You May Be Next* (1936), robbers hijacked a radio station's remote broadcasting truck and used it to transmit information about their next job.

Radio Detectives

A particular type of crime drama involved radio detectives. *The Shadow*, *The Whistler*, and *Richard Diamond, Private Detective* were radio series fea-turing popular characters in the 1930s and '40s and film producers frequently attempted to replicate this popularity on the big screen by having a radio detective help solve murders or other crimes that baffled police. These included *Love Is on the Air* (1937; Ronald Reagan is crime reporter Andy McCaine, who investigates the disappearance of the president of the Better Business

Bureau); *International Crime* (1938; Rod La Rocque is Lamont Cranston, aka The Shadow, investigating the murder of a banker); *A Tragedy at Midnight* (1942; a radio detective finds a body in his bed); *Whispering Ghosts* (1942; an amateur detective investigates the murder of a boat captain); *Whistling in the Dark* (1941); *Whistling in Dixie* (1942); and *Whistling in Brooklyn* (1943). The latter three starred Red Skelton as radio detective Wally "The Fox" Benton, although his introductory radio scenes are brief.

Boris Karloff was the detective Mr. Wong in *The Fatal Hour* (1940; a radio broadcast gunshot masks a real gunshot). Sidney Toler played a famous detective in *Charlie Chan at the Wax Museum* (1940; Chan is lured to a museum on the pretext of participating in a radio broadcast) and *Charlie Chan in the Scarlet Clue* (1945; a murder occurs in a building housing a radio station), while Basil Rathbone was Sherlock Holmes in *Sherlock Holmes and the Voice of Terror* (1942; the detective investigates wireless broadcasts apparently originating in Germany).

In many of the radio detective movies, police are somewhat inept; despite their obvious advantage in investigatory resources, they usually arrive just in time to collar the criminals after the private eye has cracked the case. The radio detective frequently carries on a running verbal feud with the police, often a gruff captain or sergeant who is nonplussed when the case is solved. In some films, police actually follow the orders of the radio detectives or help them set up elaborate plots to snare the criminals. In many cases, the radio sleuths solve a crime but wait to reveal the culprit until they can do so on the air, at which time the police also learn the miscreant's identity. In such instances, the detective usually promotes the fact that the name of the culprit will be revealed on the air. Although sometimes threatened by police, radio detectives are seldom jailed or charged with withholding evidence. They sometimes break into offices, homes, or other buildings with impunity, and never pay a price for breaking and entering. The private eyes are always men, although female assistants or secretaries sometimes provide insights into the crimes and help gather evidence. By the late 1940s, radio detectives were losing their public appeal and disappeared from movie screens. Movie radio stations became much safer places in theatrical and television films through the 1950s and '60s since their murder rates dropped to zero until a new type of criminal, the psychopathic listener, emerged in the 1970s.

Radio Cowboys

Radio cowboys such as Gene Autry, Roy Rogers, The Cisco Kid, and Hopalong Cassidy attracted large radio audiences in the 1930s and '40s and some made the transition to the big screen. The first cowboy radio film was *The Old Homestead*, a 1935 Liberty Pictures release that included the theme of an unsophisticated unknown achieving stardom. In this instance, a New York talent scout visits a farm after receiving letters promoting a group of cowboy singers, who are persuaded to move to New York to star in a new program called *The Old Homestead*. Humorous complications arise from their attempts to adapt to big-city life and to their newfound fame. The film is perhaps most notable now for the screen debut of Len Sly, later known as Roy Rogers, as a member of the group.

Several Gene Autry films incorporated his radio show into the plot, including *Git Along Little Dogies* (1937; a surreptitious broadcast makes Gene appear to support oilmen against cattlemen); *The Old Barn Dance* (1938; Gene is duped into promoting the sale of tractors); *Rovin' Tumbleweeds* (1939; Gene gets a radio singing job to support ranchers and then becomes involved in Washington politics); *Colorado Sunset* (1939; the operator of a crooked trucking company sends secret codes in radio broadcasts); *Melody Ranch* (1940; Gene returns home for a broadcast and ends up tangling with bad guys); and *Stardust on the Sage* (1942; a radio interview is edited to make Gene appear to support a dubious mining venture).

In *Paradise Valley* (1936), a radio singer heads west and encounters a range war between sheepmen and cattlemen. The conflict is resolved when both sides discover a common love of singing around the campfire and they agree to appear together on a radio broadcast. Many of the other cowboy movies had equally simplistic plots, including *Santa Fe Rides* (1937; cowboys want to audition for a radio show to make money but other ranchers want to stop them); *Village Barn Dance* (1940; locals try to save a barn dance radio show); *Ridin' Down the Canyon* (1942; rustlers use a radio show to transmit coded information about their next job); *Twilight on the Prairie* (1944; radio cowboys head to Hollywood to make a movie but their plane makes an emergency landing in Texas); *Sagebrush Heroes* (1945; radio cowboys discover a boys' home is a front for rustlers); and *Home in San Antone* (1949; Roy Acuff and his band help track down robbers).

Many of these films included fights between villains and good guys, with the heroes, especially Autry, foiling various types of plots designed to bilk innocent people. Although murder was sometimes involved, death usually resulted from a shootout in which the villain was felled. The bad guys were usually crooks or scam artists rather than killers, although they were always male and often wore the stereotypical black hats. Humorous scenes were usually included and singing was also frequently woven into the storylines (and was *de rigueur* in Gene Autry and Roy Rogers movies).

A variation on the cowboy movie used hillbilly or other rural non-cowboy characters. Besides the aforementioned *Sing While You're Able*, there was *Kentucky Moonshine* (1938; a radio star goes to Kentucky to find new talent to boost his ratings and takes fake moonshiners [the Ritz Brothers] back to New York). The Hoosier Hot Shots, a popular hillbilly-comedy ensemble of the 1940s, appeared in several movies, including *Hoosier Holiday* (1943; the Hot Shots try to quit radio to enlist in the army); *The National Barn Dance* (1944; they help launch a national barn dance show on WLS Chicago); *Rhythm Round-up* (1945; they help a hotel owner save her business); *Lone Star Moonlight* (1946; they help save a failing radio station); and *Song of Idaho* (1948; they broadcast from a ranch).

As with radio detectives and rags-to-riches tales, Hollywood's interest in singing cowboys and backwoods entertainers faded with the arrival of television, although the Autry and Rogers films continue to be popular on cable television.

War-Themed Radio Films (I)

America's entry into World War II inspired the production of numerous war-themed radio films, many of which depicted efforts to root out Nazi sympathizers or to counter Nazi propaganda, and many involved clandestine broadcasts or coded information sent over the airwaves. The first wartime radio movie had a comedic touch. In the 1940 British production *Band Waggon*, two itinerant entertainers and radio wannabes are evicted from their squatters' digs atop the BBC's Broadcasting House. Looking for a new home, they stumble onto a secret German TV station in a castle basement, so the movie is most interesting for its early (although unrealistic) portrayal of television broadcasting.

Most of the radio war movies had more serious plots, however. *Underground* (1941) was set in Germany and involved anti–Nazi broadcasts designed to promote resistance to Hitler's war machine. *Freedom Radio* (1941) had an unusual plot in which Germany wins World War II; British Nazis control the country but patriots broadcast anti-government messages from an underground station. In *International Lady* (1941), a singer is suspected of passing along coded shipping information in her radio songs. Radio reporters help thwart Nazi spy plans in *The Lady Has Plans* (1942). In this film, undercover Nazi agents write secret plans in invisible ink on a spy's back, but a female reporter takes her place and carries phony information instead.

In *Sherlock Holmes and the Voice of Terror* (1942), Basil Rathbone played the famous detective, who is called in to investigate mysterious Nazi propaganda broadcasts that police can't trace. Authorities suspected that the wife of a patriotic American radio commentator might be a Nazi spy in *Madame Spy* (1942), but she turns out to be an undercover American agent. *Once Upon a Honeymoon* (1942) had a similar theme when the ex-stripper wife of a suspected Nazi undercover agent is also believed to have Nazi ties and to be smuggling secret codes.

In *Berlin Correspondent* (1942), an American reporter encodes secret Nazi information in his radio broadcasts. A Nazi agent impersonates an American radio reporter to broadcast propaganda in *Stand by All Networks* (1942), but the plan is eventually exposed. On the other hand, a Royal Air Force officer airs German propaganda in order to infiltrate the Nazis in *Appointment in Berlin* (1943). Nazis capture the king of a small Balkan country, using an actor to impersonate him on the radio in *The Black Parachute* (1944), but an American reporter parachutes in and frees the real king to broadcast the truth. *David Harding, Counterspy* (1950) was based on a popular radio series that aired from 1942 to 1957. In this postwar movie version, a radio commentator broadcasts misleading information and is abducted by federal agents. David Harding, the American counterspy, then relates the story of how federal agents uncovered espionage plans during World War II. As can be seen in these war-themed movies, except for *Freedom Radio*, the Nazis were always defeated and American derring-do invariably triumphed.

A couple of musical biographies with wartime themes included radio scenes. *We'll Meet Again* (1943, Britain) was the story of British songbird Vera Lynn, whose music bolstered the troops' spirits during the war; the title comes from that of her most famous song and the movie starred Lynn herself. *With a Song in My Heart* (1952) was the inspirational story of singer Jane Froman (Susan Hayward), who continued to entertain American troops despite injuries suffered in a plane crash.

Only two radio films involved the war in the Pacific. In *Manila Calling* (1942), Japanese forces capture an American radio station in the Philippines; Lloyd Nolan and Cornel Wilde are staff members who flee into the jungle and use a radio transmitter to rouse support against the invaders. *Tokyo Rose* (1946) depicted the efforts of escaped American POWs to kill the despised Japanese broadcaster.

War-Themed Radio Films (II)

Following the cessation of World War II hostilities, radio war films naturally became passé and Nazis disappeared from theater screens except for period films. Considering the wave of anti–Communist sentiment that reached its climax in the late 1950s, it is notable that the Cold War spawned virtually no anti–Communist radio films when compared to the Nazi movies of the preceding years. The House Committee on Un-American Activities was formed in 1938 and during its investigations into Communist activity in the news and entertainment industries, particularly in the postwar years, the careers of many Hollywood writers, directors, and actors ultimately were damaged if not destroyed.[13] The film community apparently had little interest in cinematic portrayals of those who threatened its members' livelihood and few anti–Communist radio films can be identified.

One such movie was *The Sickle or the Cross* (1949), co-produced by the Lutheran Layman's League, in which a Communist agent is smuggled into the U.S. disguised as a missionary to disseminate propaganda. The agent becomes so enamored of capitalism that he renounces Communism. In *Journey to Freedom* (1957), a Bulgarian journalist uses Radio Free Europe and the Voice of America to fight Communism, and *The Beast of Budapest* (1958) depicts the 1956 takeover of a government radio station by anti–Communist protestors.

Fear on Trial (1975) portrayed the postwar anti–Communist atmosphere itself. The TV movie told the story of John Henry Faulk (William Devane), a CBS radio-TV commentator whose career was cut short when he was blacklisted. Faulk hired famed attorney Louis Nizer (George C. Scott), sued the network for libel, and won $3.5 million, although he never resumed his broadcasting career. The movie won an Emmy for writer David Rintels, was nominated in four other categories, and also won a Directors Guild award for director Lamont Johnson.

A few war-themed radio movies were produced some years after the war's end. *Another Time, Another Place* (1958) was a psychological drama starring Lana Turner and Sean Connery. In his film debut, Connery is a BBC war correspondent who had an affair with Turner, an American journalist. When he is killed, she is determined to find out as much as possible about him, goes to the village where he grew up, and insinuates herself into the lives of his wife and child. In *Little Boy Lost* (1953), Bing Crosby is an American radio reporter searching for a son he fathered with a French radio singer during the war.

The Gleiwitz Case, aka *Der Fall Gleiwitz* (1961), was an East German production that dramatized the events leading to the German invasion of Poland in 1939. Nazis posing as Poles attack a German border radio station, thus justifying Hitler's invasion. *Murrow*, a 1986 TV movie with Daniel J. Travanti in the title role, began by depicting Edward R. Murrow's London bombing broadcasts to America. *Jakob the Liar* (1990) starred Robin Williams as a resident of the Polish ghetto during the Nazi regime. He inadvertently overhears a radio broadcast about a German setback, which creates hope for the ghetto residents, and his notoriety as a news source leads him to invent increasingly far-fetched stories about the war's progress, including fake news broadcasts demanded by the other residents as proof of his veracity.

Nick Nolte was expatriate Nazi propaganda broadcaster Howard W. Campbell, Jr., in *Mother Night* (1996). Campbell had in fact portrayed a Nazi sympathizer as a cover for a clandestine operation. Following the war, when he tries to resume his normal life, he is branded as a traitor by Holocaust survivors, hailed by neo-Nazis, and forced to stand trial in Israel as a war criminal. In the Czech Republic production *Protektor* (2009), a Czech journalist takes a job helping broadcast Nazi propaganda at a Prague station in order to protect his Jewish wife from being discovered. Ultimately, however, the cost of this collaboration is his marital relationship.

Given the unpopularity of the Vietnam conflict among the American public in general and the Hollywood community in particular, it should not be surprising that *Good Morning, Vietnam* (1987), in which Robin Williams starred as Armed Forces DJ Adrian Cronauer, was the only radio movie to use that particular setting. No radio films referencing the Korean conflict could be found.

Radio Pirates (I)

In most countries, to legally operate a radio station one must obtain permission from a government licensing agency that sets the terms of operation as regards broadcasting frequency, transmitting power, hours of operation, and similar considerations. In the United States, this entity is the Federal Communications Commission (FCC), whose authority is derived from the Communications Act of 1934.[14] These licensing requirements have been flouted since radio's earliest days, with illegal stations being referred to as "pirate" stations. Punishment for operating such stations varies by country. In the U.S., fines are usually imposed; an Internet search reveals that there are dozens of FCC prosecutions every year.

Internet radio stations are not licensed by the FCC since they don't use the public airwaves and any individual, organization, or interest group may operate one, subject to paying fees to a music rights licensing agency in order to operate legally. There are of course significant differences between Internet and terrestrial (over the air) broadcasting. Unlike terrestrial stations, Internet radio can be heard worldwide and there are no content restrictions. Although the FCC cannot regulate or censor broadcast content due to First Amendment limitations, it can and does impose indecency fines on terrestrial stations. A drawback to Internet radio is that the stations can generally be heard only through a computer connection to the World Wide Web, although wireless devices have been developed to allow for Internet listening on car radios and other mobile equipment.

Internet radio, however, lacks the cachet or thrill of broadcasting illegally over the public airwaves. This flouting of the regulatory rules has seemingly attracted many pirate operators and has been the basis for the pirate DJ film persona. In this, pirate station operators have much in common with the outlaws of Western movies by disregarding established legal norms and finding pleasure, fulfillment, or some other satisfaction through actions that invite societal reprisals. Pirate broadcasters can also in a sense be likened to film gangsters. "The gangster survives as long as he does against heavy odds because of his energy, cunning, and bravura"[15] and this surely describes the operators of pirate radio stations. Although lacking the gangster's inherently evil character, pirate DJs have enough cunning and knowledge to set up and operate the unlicensed equipment, possess the spirit to challenge authority and the bravura to risk the consequences of being caught (which are admittedly much less than those faced by gangsters since pirate DJs usually do not face long prison terms or possible execution).

The pirate station is an international phenomenon and the concept of thumbing one's nose at society by broadcasting outside of the law has been popular, at least with filmmakers, in numerous countries. Particularly appealing, both to American and international directors, is the mobile radio station which is usually operated from a van and which allows the pirates to more easily evade authorities. The police in these films are often portrayed as somewhat inept. Radio pirates are never easily caught and, in fact, the police chase is usually an important part of the plot. Humor is often derived from these chases and other police attempts at shutting down the pirates, who are always popular with large numbers of listeners. A common scene in pirate radio movies depicts listeners, often teenagers, enjoying the unauthorized broadcasts and cheering on the pirates as they seek to evade the authorities.

The first American pirate radio movie was a light-hearted but semi-pornographic production. *The Dirty Mind of Young Sally* (1970) starred Colleen Brennan as Sally McGuire, who broadcasts erotica three times a day on KLUV Electric Radio from her van in Los Angeles. She also takes calls from listeners while dodging the police, who are led by the aptly named Sergeant Dimwittie. Sally's goal is raising money for a kidney transplant for "Miss Susie" and the minimal storyline consists mainly of depictions of the couplings her broadcasts inspire. Her fans check their watches frequently so as not to miss her three-a-day broadcasts.

On the Air Live with Captain Midnight (1979) was a more serious film-making effort, although with a humorous tone, the title being derived from the popular *Captain Midnight* radio show of the 1930s and '40s. After being fired from his radio station internship, teenager Robin Ziegler (Tracy Sebastian) and his friend Gargen (Barry Greenberg) fiddle with the audio equipment in Ziegler's van and discover they can put their voices on the air. Gargen blurts out Ziegler's phone number for anyone to call if they can hear his voice, then hands the microphone to a startled Ziegler:

> ZIEGLER: Okay, all you wang dang sweet poontangs out there, this is Captain Midnight with some sound advice from the lovelorn.
> [*Electronic feedback over expletive.*]
> GARGEN: You can't say that! You're gonna get yourself busted!
> ZIEGLER: No, you're gonna get yourself busted, givin' 'em your name.
> GARGEN: But I gave 'em your phone number.
> ZIEGKER: You what? You dumb-ass, why'd you do that?
> GARGEN: You … you don't understand. I did it. It started out just a bunch of tubes and wires and broken parts. And I'm on the air! I'm transmitting!

Ziegler realizes the power they have discovered when his phone begins ringing incessantly with listeners' calls. By sweet-talking a friend into a midnight trip to the electronics store where she works, more sophisticated equipment is installed in the van. Captain Midnight is on the air, playing music and ad libbing as he drives around Los Angeles. Complaints about interference and obscenities soon roll in from listeners to other stations, however, and an FCC field agent (John Ireland) arrives to engage in a cat-and-mouse chase with the pirates.

In *Born in Flames* (1983), a unique take on the pirate radio concept, lesbian feminists operate two New York City pirate stations to help push their radical agenda. The low-budget independent film is set ten years after the election of a socialist government. However, the new government is not progressive enough for these feminists, so they undertake actions to further the cause of more economic and political freedom for women. Besides broadcasts on Radio Regatta, including a rapping DJ named Isabel, and Phoenix Radio, operated by black militants, they organize street protests and demonstrations. The film used a docudrama approach with numerous street scenes and interviews using hand-held cameras. Two dramatic actions occur in the movie's final twenty minutes. Four armed feminists enter the building of the CBS-TV affiliate on the evening of a presidential address to the nation, overpower the lone security guard, and force the control room operators to interrupt the broadcast with a radical videotaped message. Then, at the film's end, feminists drive two stolen rental trucks to the World Trade Center and take a briefcase of explosives to the top. In an eerily prescient scene, as a TV reporter delivers an anti-socialist editorial, an explosion at the base of a TV tower atop the Trade Center sends smoke billowing skyward.

The appeal of pirate radio to teenagers as seen in *On the Air Live with Captain Midnight* was again evident in *Pump Up the Volume* (1990). Nerdy high school student Mark Hunter (Christian Slater) discovers the joys of clandestine broadcasting after arriving in Arizona from New York. Unbeknownst to his classmates and even his parents, he operates a pirate station in the basement of his home. Going by the name Hard Harry, his ad libs are filled with sexual innuendo and he becomes a hit with the high school crowd. Things take a serious turn when a depressed teen sends Harry a note with his phone number; Harry calls him on the air, and the listener says he's contemplating suicide. The DJ can provide no answers to the teen's problems and it is later announced that he has followed through on his suicide threat. A local TV station picks up the story, the FCC is called, and students rally to support Harry. The DJ loads his equipment into his father's Jeep and, with his girlfriend at the wheel, leads the authorities on a merry chase. Although the pursuit ends in his arrest, Harry has spawned a slew of imitators who take to the airwaves as the film's final credits roll.

Women of the Night (2000), directed by Zalman King of cable TV's *Red Shoe Diaries* fame, was another soft-core pornography production, this time with pretensions of storytelling art. Shawnee Free Jones is a beautiful blind DJ whom assistants drive through the streets at night in an 18-wheeler. She broadcasts tales of lust and betrayal, including stories of her own unfortunate upbringing, and Sally Kellerman takes a turn behind the microphone as well. The meandering plot is ultimately nonsensical because the stories are presented visually and thus the DJ's verbal descriptions would carry no meaning to anyone actually listening to her radio broadcasts. The film is, essentially, a series of erotic scenes connected by the DJ's narration.

Another FCC chase ensued in *Radio Free Steve* (2000), a B-movie with a budget so low it took several years to complete. The action in the futuristic saga occurs in Texas several years after World War III. The FCC has shut down all private radio stations, replacing them with the Emergency Broadcasting System. In a landscape reminiscent of *Mad Max*, Radio Free Steve (Ryan Junell) broadcasts from a van equipped with radio equipment, eluding mutant albino vampires and an FCC assassin.

The story of *Pirate Radio* (2009), aka *The Boat That Rocked* in its original British release, was based on ships such as Radio Caroline that operated illegally off the British coast in the 1960s. By broadcasting from international

waters, they were beyond the reach of British authorities. Philip Seymour
Hoffman, Bill Nighy, and Rhys Ifans were among the actors portraying eccentric air personalities on Radio Rock, as the film's vessel is named. Their unlicensed broadcasts create such a stir that the government moves to shut them
down. Kenneth Branagh is Sir Alistair Dormandy, and the government's attitude is revealed in his comments about Radio Rock: "They are a sewer. Dirty,
irresponsible commercialism, and low morals." While the government eventually passes legislation providing jail time not only for the pirates but also
for those who listen to them, it takes a North Sea storm to capsize the pirate
ship and put it off the air. The film's climax comes when fans rescue the DJs
from a watery death. *Pirate Radio* was panned by critics and largely ignored
by audiences after its British release and was re-titled and re-edited for its
American debut. The film was lauded mostly for a soundtrack which included
many of the top rock hits of the 1960s.

Radio Pirates (II)

The pirate radio station is a worldwide phenomenon. The enduring and
international popularity of pirate operators is evident when considering the
number of such films that have been produced in numerous countries over
the decades. In fact, the pirates were first seen in a 1935 British film titled,
appropriately, *Radio Pirates*, in which three young men start an underground
station to make money by playing music. Police bust up the operation, the
boys flee, and the chase scene culminates with their capture at Big Ben. Since
then, pirate radio operators have continued to capture the imagination of
people around the world, or at least the imagination of filmmakers from
numerous countries.

British teen idol Cliff Richard and his friends started a pirate station in
The Young Ones, aka *Wonderful to Be Young!* (1961). Their favorite club is in
danger of being replaced by a new office building and Nicky Black (Richard)
records a song to raise money to save their hangout. But to make money from
the song, the teens need radio airplay so they start a pirate station which they
operate from a fruit cart they wheel through the streets of London. The authorities can't seem to track them down and in fact an officer buys some fruit from
the cart harboring the hidden equipment. Richard, backed by The Shadows,
was one of Britain's top pop singers through the 1960s and was knighted in
1995 for his contributions to music.

Greek teenage boys ran afoul of police when they started competing
pirate stations in *Vasika ... kalispera sas* (1982). Conflict arises when different

groups try to operate on the same unlicensed frequency and then their girlfriends become involved in the dispute. The Norwegian production *Piratene* (1983) was the story of unemployed teenagers who operate pirate station Radio Feskslog from a van. They play rock music and exhort the authorities to take action to alleviate joblessness among young people. Their constantly changing location helps them avoid the authorities and at one point they take to a boat with their transmitting equipment. Police give chase, TV reporters pick up on it, and their disbelieving parents watch the event unfold live on their living room TV sets.

Radio Corbeau (1989) was an updated version of 1943's *Le Corbeau*, in which venomous letters filled with lies and half-truths were sent to residents of a village, causing suspicion and dissension as they turned on each other. In this version, the unauthorized Radio Raven is operated by someone unknown, broadcasting accusations of various misdeeds about the townspeople. Police and a local newspaper journalist try to discover who's behind the pirate station.

Young Soul Rebels, a 1991 British film, was unusual for its depiction of openly gay characters and sexual situations. Chris (Valentine Noyela) and Caz (Mo Sesay) are DJs on East London's pirate station "Soul Patrol P-Funk." The movie opens with an interracial homosexual encounter in a park that results in the murder of a gay black man. With the police less than interested in solving the crime, the DJs set out to find the murderer of their friend. The film is an engrossing look at race relations and sexual attitudes in England at the time of Queen Elizabeth's Silver Jubilee. In the Yugoslavian *Black Bomber* (1992), a fired DJ is aided by a wannabe punk rock singer in starting a pirate station, and ends up dodging not only the police but also a machine-gun-wielding psycho who takes exception to the DJ's music.

In *Rude* (1995), a Canadian production, a black female DJ introduces stories of urban life in Toronto. With explicit language and sexual situations, the film is comprised of three stories strung together by the DJ's narration. As with *Women of the Night*, the stories would be incomprehensible to anyone listening on the radio and lacking the visual depictions. The DJs in both of these films are thus virtually superfluous, serving only to set the stage for the erotic scenes to follow and to explicate their meaning for the viewer.

The Polish film *Kalozok*, aka *You or Me* (1999), starred Attila Kiraly as Pipi and Viktor Bodo as Max, two young men who operate a pirate station in a van with the assistance of their friend Marta (Karina Krecskes). The minimal storyline has the pirates playing their favorite songs until Pipi decides to get a job at a real radio station; a plot twist sees both boys become interested in a female neighbor. In the Brazilian production *Uma Onda No Ar*, aka *Some-*

thing in the Air (2002), four friends start the pirate station Radio Favela as a voice for the people in their Belo Horizonte shantytown neighborhood. Based on a true story, the film depicts the ambience of the *favelas* and the authoritarian control the police exert over the residents.

Johnny Was (2006) told the story of Johnny Doyle (Vinnie Jones) who forsakes his violent Irish world to take up residence in the London slum of Brixton. He connects with a former pal, recently released from prison, and becomes involved in a plot to disrupt the Northern Ireland peace process with bomb attacks. One of his neighbors is a Rastafarian DJ (former heavyweight boxing champion Lennox Lewis), whose music provides the movie soundtrack.

Norwegian pirates returned to the screen in *Radiopiratene*, aka *The Radio Pirates* (2007). The young man Karl Jonathan (Anders Hermann Clausen) moves with his father and sister Sisseline (Helene Gystad) to their father's hometown. The village is designed to protect children in every possible way: All sharp building corners are padded and youngsters must wear helmets when bicycling and elbow pads in the playground. In an abandoned building, Karl and Sisseline find some old radio equipment which broadcasts on the same frequency as the official station and use it to air their anti-establishment views about the town's stifling culture.

The plot of the Welsh movie *Flick* (2008) was unusual, to say the least. The action begins in 1960, when insecure teenager Johnny "Flick" Taylor (Hugh O'Conor) fatally crashes his car into a river after being ridiculed at a party for asking a popular girl to dance. Brought back to life forty years later by pirate radio broadcasts of 1950s music ("Radio Rockabilly, the pirate station that just wouldn't die"), he returns to live with his mother who, being senile, doesn't realize he's been gone, and to take revenge on those who humiliated him all those years before. He also wants his dance with the beautiful blonde. Faye Dunaway is Lieutenant McKenzie, a one-armed Memphis cop brought in for some unexplained reason to help local police discover who's been knocking off the now-middle-aged victims. Richard Hawley is pirate DJ Bobby Blade, whose rockabilly music on the soundtrack helps create a retro-1950s ambience for the movie.

Comedown (2010), a pirate radio movie with a twist, tells the story of young people who agree to set up a replacement transmitter for the London pirate station Skank. The station operator offers cash and drugs if the gang can install it atop an abandoned apartment building, but little does anyone know that it is inhabited by a psycho who will kill anyone who invades his territory. The plot entails a deadly game of cat and mouse within the eerie darkness of the empty building.

Zombies and Aliens

Zombies have fascinated filmmakers since the earliest days of moviemaking. The term can be traced back to at least 1819 in referring to the walking dead, and the concept of a *corps cadavres* originates in the voodoos of Haiti.[17] Their first film appearance was in 1932's *White Zombie*, which starred Bela Lugosi as a voodoo sorcerer.[18]

Zombies have appeared in several radio films, beginning with John Carpenter's *The Fog* (1980). Zombie sailors emerge from the sea off the California coast to avenge their deaths a century before and Adrienne Barbeau is the DJ who helps guide townspeople to safety in a church from her control room atop a lighthouse. A 2005 remake of the same title was co-written and co-produced, but not directed by, Carpenter, with Selma Blair in the DJ role. Both films are discussed in more detail in Chapter Three.

California was the scene of another zombie attack in *Night of the Comet* (1984). Southern Californians gather for "comet parties" to celebrate a celestial flyby, but the visitor from space wipes out most of the residents except for those who have somehow been shielded by metal walls, which in this case includes Valley Girl sisters Regina (Catherine Mary Stewart) and Samantha (Kelli Maroney). Hearing a DJ on the radio, they make their way through the deserted streets only to find that the voice is coming from prerecorded tapes and that a hunky truck driver has also taken refuge in the station. Samantha decides to have some fun as a DJ:

> And, here's some other changes. Most of you guys had finals this week? Huh, later! They're history. The legal drinking age is now ten. But you will need ID, let's be real. I'll be takin' requests for all you teenage comet zombies on the hitline. That's 555–4487. Get it? 555-H-I-T-S.

The sisters later attract the attention of scientists who also managed to survive and who want to test the girls' blood to develop a possible serum, although they also seem to have some sinister ulterior motives.

Zombi 3, aka *Zombie Flesh Eaters 2* (1988), was an Italian production set in the Philippines, with the actors' English dialogue dubbed in. The body of a terrorist is infected by a chemical and when the corpse is cremated, the smoke carries a virus to the rest of the population, turning them (and the island's birds) into zombies. In a characterization reminiscent of the original *Vanishing Point*, an uncredited actor portrays blind DJ Blue Heart, who dispenses ecological advice between songs. He tries to guide his listeners to safety as the militia cordons off and kills the zombies but the film's ending reveals that he has also become infected, thus becoming the world's first and only zombie DJ.

Movie radio stations became a refuge from zombies in two 2008 films. *Pontypool* was a Canadian production with Stephen McHattie as morning man Grant Mazzy and Lisa Houle as his producer Sydney Briar. The station receives phone calls about residents of their small community behaving oddly, rioting, and speaking in strange tongues. It turns out that a virus which has turned them into zombies is spread through the use of the English language, which of course makes the radio station their logical target. *Pontypool* differs from other zombie movies in that the creatures do not appear until quite late in the film and the tension builds through the news reports that Mazzy airs and the phone calls that Briar makes to her relatives. Mazzy and Briar escape by playing innocuous Muzak-like songs, communicating with each other through written notes, speaking French, and airing nonsensical sentences. French-Canadian soldiers arrive to control the English-language-driven zombies.

The same year that zombies attacked the Pontypool radio station, a virus also caused the living dead to storm a station in Leadville, Colorado, in *Day of the Dead*. Flesh-eating hordes fill the streets as a young man named Trevor Cross (Michael Welch) and his girlfriend flee to the KXWT building, where several others have also sought safety. Trevor uses the station to broadcast appeals for help but, unbeknownst to Trevor and his girlfriend, some of those who took refuge at the radio station have been infected with the virus and eventually mutate into zombies. Unlike *Pontypool*, *Day of the Dead* has a high blood-and-gore quotient as Trevor's army sergeant sister Sarah (Mena Suvari) leads a group of rescuers to the station, blasting away at the walking corpses in their path.

In *Dead Air* (2009), Bill Moseley was Logan Burnhardt, the host of the late-night talk show *Heartburn* on KCBP Los Angeles. Once again the population turns into zombies, this time as the result of a terrorist attack on the country through the release of a virus at sporting events and public gatherings. The radio station's TV monitors show street riots in cities everywhere, but Burnhardt defies orders to switch to the Emergency Broadcasting System and continues his live broadcasts to explain what's happening. The staff moves to lock down the building but not until zombies and terrorists both manage to get inside. As with other zombie radio movies, broadcast appeals for help are useless, although listeners continue to call in reports about what's happening on the streets. A terrorist forces Burnhardt at gunpoint to broadcast a Muslim nuclear threat to foment more religious hatred, and zombies battle terrorists in a climactic scene. The film ends weakly when the zombies inexplicably start dying off and scientists are reported to be optimistic about developing a serum.

Besides zombies, aliens have fascinated filmmakers since moviemaking's earliest days. Some of the first filmmaking attempts, such as *The Astronomer's*

Dream (1898), included images of outer space.[19] *Aelita* (1924), *Metropolis* (1927), and *Things to Come* (1936) helped establish the genre as a favorite with audiences worldwide, and aliens have appeared in a few radio films. In *Spaced Invaders* (1990), Martians landed in a rural community at the same time the local station decides to air Orson Welles' famous *War of the Worlds* program as a Halloween feature. The humor, such as it is, arises from the invaders being mistaken by residents as children in Martian costumes because they're only about four feet tall. The same year, another weak production was *Invasion of the Space Preachers*, in which aliens tried to take control of the world by posing as radio evangelists in a small backwoods town.

One of the strangest story concepts translated to any screen, large or small, was the basis for *Bad Channels* (1992). Paul Hipp was "Dangerous" Dan O'Dare, a DJ who's just returned to the air after a six-month FCC suspension due to his on-air antics. The owner of KDUL in rural Pahoota has discovered that the station can broadcast at 50,000 watts because it has the unique clear channel frequency of 666 kilohertz. It is thus the only station in America to broadcast on the undesirable 666 frequency (666 is the "mark of the beast" in the book of Revelation), which is not used in actual broadcasting. O'Dare is known for creative stunts such as locking himself in chains and playing polka music for days on end. The film's action begins when an alien with a large head arrives, looking to capture human females in bottles to study them. When the visitor bursts into his control room, O'Dare describes what's happening but the listeners think it's just another of his gags. Then local women begin to disappear because the alien can remotely zap and transport them back to the station to capture them. With a waitress, nurse, high school band musician, and TV reporter (former MTV VJ Martha Quinn) bottled up in his control room, O'Dare discovers that the aerosol spray Germasol is the only effective weapon to repel the invader.

David Alan Bache was talk show host Dale Sweeny in *I'll Believe You* (2007). That's also the title of his all-night show on WMEL Melbourne, Florida, because it deals with conspiracy theories, paranormal phenomena, and other assorted lunatic fringe topics. ("So all you weirdos, wackos, and conspiracy freaks, when they call you crazy, you call me.") Listeners are so few in his time slot that the show is about to be cancelled until one morning a caller speaks in an unintelligible language. Sweeny takes the call seriously and tries to have the message interpreted, then two strange federal agents show up to question him and he becomes convinced that he's been on the receiving end of the first extraterrestrial communication.

In *Dead Signals: The Jonathon Moon Chronicles* (2008), Michael Bailey Smith was the titular Moon, aka "The Prince of the Paranormal," who hosts a talk show about paranormal activities. During a broadcast marathon he discovers that an alien which has been killing people in the desert is now using his broadcast signal to track him down.

Radio Film Biographies

Besides the fictitious stories of unknowns becoming famous radio singers that were so popular in the films of the 1930s and '40s, some radio films have depicted the careers of real musical artists. *We'll Meet Again*, the British film about the life of Vera Lynn, was probably the first such musical biopic. Others with varying degrees of factual accuracy included *The Fabulous Dorseys* (1947), about the careers of bandleaders Jimmy and Tommy Dorsey. Their first radio broadcast ends in a squabble over how to play their music; in real life the brothers eventually split due to professional differences. *With a Song in My Heart* (1952) starred Susan Hayward as singer Jane Froman and depicted her radio appearances. Ruth Etting's career was detailed in *Love Me or Leave Me* (1955) with Doris Day as the torch singer whose gangster connections helped launch her career with her own radio show.

Lady Sings the Blues (1972) starred Diana Ross as Billie Holiday in a film that, while panned by critics at the time of its release, provided some insights into American racial attitudes of the 1940s. A scene depicted the cancellation of Holiday's network radio premiere performance because Southern stations refused to carry it for racial reasons. *Bound for Glory* (1976), on the other hand, was acclaimed by critics and moviegoers alike, won two Academy Awards and was nominated for four more. The movie followed the career of folksinger Woody Guthrie, who first gained national attention on radio in the 1930s, with David Carradine as the singer. *Rosie: The Rosemary Clooney Story* was a TV movie with Sondra Locke as the singer, and the voice of Clooney herself dubbed in. It depicted not only the singer's rise to stardom both on the radio and as a recording artist ("Come on-a My House"), but also her mental breakdown.

La Bamba (1987) was the Ritchie Valens story, starring Lou Diamond Phillips as the rocker and illustrating how radio helped make his signatory tune a hit, with Jeffrey Alan Chandler as Alan Freed. The following year, the tale of another Hispanic star was told in *Break of Dawn*. Oscar Chavez was Pedro J. Gonzales, a singer who turned his radio appearance into a career as the first Hispanic DJ in Los Angeles; he later became a community activist. *Cadillac Records* (2008) told the Chess Records story as it depicted the career of Etta James (Beyonce Knowles) and showed how DJs helped popularize rhythm 'n' blues. Finally, plans for *The Goree Girls* were announced in 2010.

Produced by and starring Jennifer Aniston, it's the true story of a women's band that was formed in a Texas prison in the 1940s and achieved national stardom via radio broadcasts.

Two radio films have depicted the lives of country music personalities. *Louisiana* (1947) starred Jimmie Davis, a country music composer and singer ("You Are My Sunshine") who went on to become the governor of Louisiana. Also in 1947, *Hollywood Barn Dance* told the story of Ernest Tubb from his boyhood days on a Texas farm to the titular radio show that brought him national fame.

Besides musical biographies, the lives of many sports legends have been played out on screen, and radio has been an important part of these films in helping to create ambience and build tension during the athletic contests. Play-by-play broadcasts are often used for these purposes, as is discussed in Chapter Four. Biographies of well-known sports heroes came into vogue in the years immediately following World War II, beginning with 1948's *The Babe Ruth Story*. This was followed by film biographies of Jackie Robinson, "Dizzy" Dean, "Satchel" Paige, and Grover Cleveland Alexander. *The Story of Seabiscuit* (1949), *Seabiscuit* (2003), and *The Harlem Globetrotters* (1951) also included radio scenes. Boxing biographies became popular in more recent years. The first modern biopic with blow-by-blow descriptions was *Ring of Passion* (1978), a TV movie account of the Joe Louis-Max Schmeling heavyweight championship fights of the 1930s. Rocky Marciano, Jake LaMotta, Jack Dempsey, and Primo Carnera have also been profiled, either on the big screen or in made-for-television movies with radio broadcasts.

Despite the fact that radio personalities, at least in the pre-satellite era, could well have been described as interesting, unusual, and even eccentric, few have been portrayed on film. The various movies that starred Alan Freed are discussed in Chapter Three. Although it begins with his wartime radio broadcasts from London, the TV movie *Murrow* (1986) dealt mostly with Edward R. Murrow's years at CBS-TV, with Dabney Coleman as network president William S. Paley. *Good Morning, Vietnam* (1987) was the highly entertaining story of Adrian Cronauer's career as an Armed Forces Radio DJ, with Robin Williams as Cronauer. *Private Parts* (1987) chronicled the rise of shock jock Howard Stern from his start in college radio through his ascension to the self-described position as "King of All Media," while *Talk to Me* (2007) depicted the career of Washington DJ and talk show host "Petey" Green, with Don Cheadle in the lead role. Considering the number of larger-than-life characters who have populated the radio industry over the years, these offerings should be considered slim. Chapter Three looks more closely at how DJs have been portrayed on film from their emergence in the late 1930s to the present.

Three

Alan Freed, Rock 'n' Roll, and the American DJ

Marshall McLuhan once referred to radio as being "a subliminal echo chamber of magical power."[1] Following the decline of network radio after World War II, the magician wielding that power became the DJ, "the servant and sorcerer of this media mix."[2] The radio DJ has become firmly entrenched in the public's consciousness as an important fixture of American mass media.

While satellites and computers may have greatly changed the way DJs perform in the control room, the perception of McLuhan's "tribal drum of radio"[3] persists in the way radio stations and DJs have been portrayed on film. Despite the widespread use of non-radio listening devices such as iPods, the DJ remains a popular figure on movie and television screens, as evidenced by the number of movies which have included on-air personalities in either leading or supporting roles. Countless other films have made mention of DJs or radio stations, or have included scenes of listening to DJs. This chapter examines the ways in which DJs have been depicted in both American and international films and also looks at the verisimilitude of some of these depictions.

In the following pages, unless otherwise noted, "DJ" refers specifically to those air personalities who actually introduce songs interspersed with chatter. Both in cinema and in real life, the DJ may operate the equipment or in some instances may sit in a studio or booth while an engineer or operator manipulates the controls. In years past, control room equipment included the audio console (known as a "board" in industry parlance), turntables, tape machines of various types, and microphones. Today, CD players or computers have replaced the turntables and tape machines although the audio console remains (as, of course, does the microphone). The term "disc jockey" is sometimes used interchangeably with the more generic "announcer," "air personality," "jock," "shock jock," or even "talk show host." The latter takes calls from listeners, usually on specific topics. "Shock jock" is also an ambiguous term, referring either to abrasive DJs who also play music or to talk show hosts who specialize in delivering outrageous commentary or insulting callers.

Early DJ Films

As outlined in Chapter One, the man recognized as likely the first to spin records in the manner that would come to define radio DJs in later years was Al Jarvis at KFWB Los Angeles in 1934. Probably the first film to feature a DJ playing records, released some nine years after the debut of Jarvis' *Make Believe Ballroom*, was *Reveille with Beverly* (1943). Prior to this, radio announcers in movies usually introduced singers or orchestras and sometimes read commercials or doubled as wisecracking emcees. This was the era of live broadcasting, when network programming dominated the airwaves and radio films of the 1930s and '40s predominantly featured live orchestras and singers. In the earliest radio films, becoming a "radio star" therefore usually referred to achieving success as a singer rather than as an announcer. The latter, aside from the wisecracking emcees, were usually handsome men with rich baritone voices.

Reveille with Beverly starred Ann Miller, who later found fame on Broadway as a singer, dancer, and actress. The title refers to Beverly Ross, a radio switchboard operator, record store clerk, and part-time announcer who gets her own show when she becomes popular with soldiers who call the station with requests. The film includes performances by Duke Ellington, Count Basie, Bob Crosby, the Mills Brothers, and others. After Ross introduces them, she sets the turntable in motion, the music begins, and the camera zooms in on the spinning disc, which is followed by a transition to the live performers.

Hi, Good Lookin'! (1944) was the next movie with a DJ, in this case, Joe Smedly (Fuzzy Knight), although he is as much entertainer as DJ. Smedley spins records, sings, and tells jokes, and his studio contains a piano as well as turntables and microphones. His role is a minor one, however, as he serves merely as the vehicle by which unknown singer Kelly Clark (Harriet Hilliard) is introduced to the public. Clark becomes a hit with listeners and thus an unknown performer achieving stardom, seen in so many early films, again becomes the basis for a story.

Another female DJ appeared on film in 1947. Deanna Durbin was WFOB announcer Mary Collins in *Something in the Wind*, a screwball comedy of misplaced identities. She is mistaken for her aunt and offered a bribe by the family of a recently deceased millionaire with whom Collins is believed to have had an affair. As the film opens, Collins wraps up her morning show by singing her theme, "The Turntable Song." The movie includes several songs by Durbin, an operatically trained singer, including a duet with Metropolitan Opera tenor Jan Peerce.

In *I Surrender Dear* (1948), a film of particular interest because it reflects the post–World War II transformation of radio, Gloria Jean was singing DJ Patty Nelson. The end of the Big Band era and network broadcasting is in sight, and the manager of KXIW Los Angeles, R.H. Collins (Douglas Wood), is disturbed because other stations are hiring bandleaders as DJs to spin records rather than lead orchestras. The ratings of the other stations have soared while KXIW's programming still consists mainly of the orchestral music that is rapidly declining in popularity. Collins summons the program director into his office.

> COLLINS: Rogers, do you ever read the trade papers? Look at this. "Disc jockeys replacing live programs. Five top bandleaders go disc jockey. Crooner inks million dollar deal." Every station in the country's jumping on the band wagon. And what are we doing? Nothing! We're asleep, Rogers, fast asleep. Bradford in New York has added twelve new accounts since he put on Jack Eigen at the Copacabana. Listen [*Collins turns on the radio*].
> EIGEN: Hello, ladies and gentlemen. This is your Broadway and Hollywood reporter and recorder, Jack Eigen, speaking from the Copa Lounge, located in the famous Copacabana, 10 East Sixtieth Street in New York City [*Dissolve to Eigen at table with WINS mic*]. Yes, we're on the air right now from the Copa. We speak with the famous who visit here, give out with some Broadway and Hollywood news, and we do answer phone calls. It's a nice program for nice people. Looking around right now I see Mr. Frankie Carle, one of the nation's top bandleaders, sitting at a table here. Will you come up, Frankie, please? By the way, Frankie Carle's recording of "The Anniversary Song" is one of the top sellers from coast to coast and we just happen to have a record of "The Anniversary Song" with us. Just happen to have … you don't happen to have a Victrola there, do you, Frankie? [*Eigen interviews Carle with "The Anniversary Song" playing in the background. Dissolve to Collins' office.*]
> COLLINS: I'll let you figure out how many housewives are listening to him. Philips in Chicago has added fifteen new accounts since he put on Dave Garroway [*Dissolve to Dave Garroway at NBC mic; he ad libs and introduces a record. Dissolve to Collins' office*]. There isn't a station in the East that hasn't a big name spinning platters. Why, it's the greatest thing to hit radio in years!

Because of these changes, the job of elderly announcer Russ Nelson (Robert Emmett Keane) is in jeopardy. Meanwhile, his daughter Patty, who wants a singing career, auditions for bandleader Al Tyler (David Street), wins the job and lies to Russ in order to join Tyler's band under an assumed name. Tyler is later hired as a DJ at KXIW, replacing Nelson, unaware that Patty, who has since left his band, has joined her father as co-host of his radio show. The father-daughter team has boosted the ratings, which presents a dilemma for the station manager, having hired Tyler as their replacement. Everything ends on a happy note, however, when Tyler, Patty, and Russ agree to work together on the program with Tyler's band supplying the music and Patty and Russ sharing the announcing duties.

I Surrender Dear is interesting for several reasons. Disc jockeys introduce records in one of the first cinematic appearances by actual DJs rather than actors portraying air personalities. More importantly, the film illustrates the growing popularity of recorded music in radio and foreshadows the end of live bands as a programming staple, although in the final scene Tyler's orchestra is introduced by Patty and Russ and, as with *Something in the Wind*, Patty is as much singer as DJ. The film also continued the earlier transitional device, used in *Reveille with Beverly* and *Something in the Wind*, in which the DJ's song introduction is followed by a close-up of the spinning record, which then dissolves to a live artist, who then performs the song. The Frankie Carle interview also presages the role of air personalities in promoting records and recording artists, a practice that would culminate in payola scandals some twenty years later.

In 1949 the original DJ, Al Jarvis, made his movie debut in a production titled, not surprisingly, *Make Believe Ballroom*, in which he portrayed himself. He conducts an on-air contest for teenagers to help them buy and renovate a diner, which becomes a popular hangout for the teen crowd. The movie employs the earlier technique in which the DJ starts the turntable in motion and the spinning record dissolves to a live performer. The film included popular recording artists such as the King Cole Trio, Kay Starr, Frankie Laine, Jimmy Dorsey and several more, all of whom were former guests on Jarvis' radio show. *Reveille with Beverly, Hi, Good Lookin'!, Something in the Wind, I Surrender Dear*, and *Make Believe Ballroom*, while illustrating the increasing use of recorded music in radio, had more in common with the radio films of earlier years than with the DJ movies that would follow; all relied upon live music as the main form of musical entertainment. But Hollywood soon took notice of the arrival of television, which would revolutionize radio and doom the live performances that had been its foundation since its earliest years.

Just as *I Surrender Dear* presaged the end of network programming and the coming of the DJ, so *Disc Jockey* (1951) reflected the growing popularity of television. It opens with a debate among bandleader Russ Morgan, announcer Mike Richards (Michael O'Shea), and radio advertiser Chris Marley (Jerome Cowan) about an article in *Variety* in which the author opines that radio audiences are declining because of television. Marley argues that his advertising fees should be halved because of smaller audiences while Richards claims that radio is responsible for his success. The minimal plot entails a talent scout trying to get his client a recording contract and radio singing job, but the film includes a cameo appearance by Los Angeles DJ Gene Norman as well as nightclub performances by, among others, George Shearing and Sarah Vaughan. Despite its fluffy plot, *Disc Jockey* indicates that the film community had taken note of television's growing appeal to the American public.

The dawn of the television age saw a waning of Hollywood's interest in radio, which is evident by examining the number of American radio films produced in the early 1950s: 13 films were released in 1949 as network radio began its decline (six of these were sports movies with play-by-play broadcasts); nine were released in 1950 (three were sports movies); six in 1951; five in 1952 (three sports movies); five in 1953 (four sports movies); one in 1954 (a sports movie); one in 1955 and one in 1956. Thus, throughout the 1950s, play-by-play broadcasts of various sporting events, rather than DJs, were the focus of radio films. Not until the 1970s would large numbers of radio movies again be seen on movie screens.

The DJ Becomes the Radio Star

With the decline of network radio, recorded music took over the nation's airwaves and by the mid–1950s DJs were becoming stars to the nation's teenagers, some with popularity rivaling that of the singers whose records they introduced:

> Deejays also staged teen talent shows, teenage guest deejay hours, and record hops.... Deejays joined forces with jukebox music operators in Detroit in 1955 and 1956 to stage more than sixty teen-oriented talent and variety shows and record hops, drawing a total of more than 100,000 teens.[4]

So to millions of teenagers, the demi-gods of their emerging culture were the radio DJs. Perhaps because of Hollywood's interest in the popularity of the new rock 'n' roll music, or possibly due to an awareness of the emerging teen culture, DJs became the main characters in some radio films of the 1950s. These films, however, continued to feature live performances rather than music from records.

The first of the new DJ films starred Alan Freed, generally considered the first DJ of the modern (rock 'n' roll) era. *Mister Rock and Roll* (1957) was Freed's fourth film but the first in which he appeared as a DJ. The storyline is so thin as to be virtually non-existent; the movie consists mostly of performances by Chuck Berry, Little Richard, LaVern Baker, Clyde McPhatter and other early rockers. The formative nature of the new musical genre is evident by the inclusion of Lionel Hampton's big band and country singer Ferlin Husky. The movie is notable, however, for including Freed's claim to have invented the term "rock and roll" (prior to its linguistic transformation to include a truncated "and"). In the film, the editor of *World Magazine* has published a number of articles critical of the music and its effects on the country's youth and Freed responds on the air:

> FREED: All your wild claims, Joe Prentiss, about rock and roll running into trouble, about rock and roll corrupting our children with a primitive beat, all these claims are not only false, they're punches aimed below the belt. You know as well as I, Joe Prentiss, that no one cooked up rock and roll as a means of turning a quick dollar. Rock and roll just happened, and I was there when it happened. Yes, if I'm guilty of anything, I'm guilty of being present at the birth of rock and roll, music which is the honest, spontaneous expression of today's youth — its restlessness, its craving, and its sentiments. And this birth took place three years ago in a little record shop in Cleveland. At the time, I was a disc jockey on a local station... [*Dissolve to record store scene and Freed talks to teens about the records they're buying. Cut to Freed as a Cleveland DJ and he introduces Little Richard, who sings "Lucille"*].
> FREED: Man, that Little Richard really rocks. If it rocks, if it rolls, you're gonna hear it right here, because we're gonna send you with that rock and roll beat [*Dissolve to present day*].
> FREED [*over montage of spinning records and dancers*]: Those few simple words, rock and roll. A new name for music we've had around for decades. And then it really started to rock. Why? No one will ever know for sure. Anything as far-reaching as a new musical phase spreading like the wind is mighty difficult to analyze. It just happens. And I just happened to be there when the first breezes started blowing up a storm. "Rock and Roll Coronation Night" in Cleveland convinced me that the music with the beat had really come into its own [*Dissolve to studio with "Rock 'n Roll" [sic] sign and Freed is introduced*].

Although Freed claimed to have coined the phrase "rock 'n' roll," its origination with him is debatable at best due to the euphemistic term "rocking and rolling" which had been in the rhythm 'n' blues vernacular long before Freed's arrival on the music scene.[5] However, Freed unquestionably popularized its use. Other than Freed's appropriation of the signature phrase that would define a musical genre, and for the performances of early rock stars, there is little memorable about *Mister Rock and Roll*. It also used the earlier transition device of a spinning turntable dissolving to live singers.

Freed also starred in *Go, Johnny, Go!* (1959), although primarily as a concert promoter and emcee. The film includes some radio scenes as Freed seeks the anonymous winner of his talent contest. Other Freed appearances included *Rock Rock Rock!* (1956), *Rock Around the Clock* (1956), and *Don't Knock the Rock* (1957), which are not discussed here or included in the filmography because his roles were those of a concert promoter and emcee rather than a DJ.

Two other versions of Freed's story have been produced. *American Hot Wax* (1978) was loosely based on his career and starred Tim McIntire, whose first words into the microphone were, "This is Alan Freed and this is rock 'n' roll." The film covers only Freed's New York years and explicates both teenagers' infatuation with early rock and the influence of the DJ in creating a musical hit. In public Freed is bombarded by singers' requests to play their records, and adoring fans hover at the radio station door. While including performances by Chuck Berry, Jerry Lee Lewis, and other stars, the movie passes lightly over Freed's personal life, which included a battle with alcoholism. The film ends with the police shutdown of a rock concert he promotes — riots had actually occurred earlier in Cleveland and Boston — but makes no reference to a payola scandal that ended Freed's career in 1959. Jay Leno, in his second film appearance, has several scenes as Freed's chauffeur. *American Hot Wax* recreates the ambience of the rock 'n' roll years as few other films have done, save perhaps 1973's *American Graffiti*.

In the 1999 production *Mr. Rock 'n' Roll: The Alan Freed Story*, Judd Nelson was a more introspective personality who narrates his feelings by voiceovers throughout the film. The TV movie deals at length with Freed's personal life, including his marriage to dance instructor Jackie McCoy (Madchen Amick), his alcoholism, and the job stresses that constantly threaten to tear their marriage apart. The film begins in Cleveland and covers Freed's rise to fame in New York, including his acceptance of a check from a Roulette Records promoter to finance his first house. It includes the payola scandal and his subsequent firing from WOR (WLOR in the movie) and Freed's final words into a microphone: "And just remember, rock 'n' roll is here to stay. Thanks for listening." In reality, Freed married three times and died in Palm Springs, California, of problems related to alcoholism five years after pleading guilty to criminal bribery charges. He was one of the original inductees into the Rock and Roll Hall of Fame in 1986.[6]

Some of Freed's contemporaries made cameo appearances in *Sing Boy Sing* (1958), the story of a teenager who was raised by his grandfather, a fundamentalist preacher. Tommy Sands is Virgil Walker who, despite his religious upbringing, becomes a singing idol. Pushed by aggressive managers, Walker's songs are played on several New York radio stations, and real-life DJs Art Collins, Bill Randle, and Biff Collie are seen in less-than-realistic control rooms introducing his singles.

The DJ Persona Evolves

While the Freed films and *Sing Boy Sing* showed that Hollywood had not completely forgotten the radio DJ, there were few indications that filmmakers were aware of the transformation radio was undergoing in the 1960s due to the popularity of the Top 40 format and, later, the emergence of the counterculture underground FM radio. One film stands out, however. *The Courtship of Eddie's Father* (1963) was evolutionary in that its depiction of radio was more consistent with real broadcasting than had yet been seen on a movie screen. The plot was based on radio station personalities but did not revolve around music and there were no live performances. DJ Norman Jones (Jerry Van Dyke) is a roué whose antics with his adoring female fans are a major distraction for his boss, program director Tom Corbett (Glenn Ford). Beautiful young women congregate outside the control room and Jones' risqué ad libs are a constant headache for Corbett. Although the Jones character is not a major one, his behavior makes for a humorous subplot and his is one of the first realistic portrayals of the DJ as the role is commonly considered today. The film is most notable for the casting of Ron Howard as Corbett's eponymous son, whose plan to find a spouse for his divorced father drives the plot. Howard went on to much greater fame as TV's Opie in *The Andy Griffith Show* and *Mayberry, R.F.D.* and later became an acclaimed director and producer. The movie also spawned a TV series of the same title, with Bill Bixby as Tom Corbett and Brandon Cruz as Eddie.

One of the more unusual radio films of any era was originally produced in Britain in 1964 as *Just for You*. It was re-edited with additional material added and released in the U.S. as *Disk-O-Tek Holiday* in 1966. The simplistic plot has wannabe singing stars Casey Paxton and Katherine Quint trying to get some airplay for their single. The original production included a British DJ and several popular musical acts of the day such as Freddie and the Dreamers. The edited version featured American air personalities, including WITH Baltimore's Bob Foster, whom the wannabe stars visit in his crude and unrealistic-looking control room and manage to trick into playing their song on the air. Then it's off to Philadelphia, where the duo hits up WIBG's Hy Lit, who hosts a teen TV dance party, and then on to Boston where popular announcer Arnie "Woo Woo" Ginsburg does a live remote broadcast on WMEX. This originates from a TV studio, so Ginsburg doubles as a TV dance show host, using some of the unusual sound effects that were his radio trademark. All three DJs introduce singing acts who then perform, so that stylistically the film resembles the earlier Alan Freed movies. However, despite its B-movie production values, *Disk-O-Tek Holiday* offers a glimpse of real DJs at work, albeit briefly and not always in their natural radio habitat. Since few films have used actual air personalities to portray DJs, *Sing Boy Sing* and *Disk-O-Tek Holiday* are rarities.

The paucity of radio films evident in the 1950s became more pronounced in the following decade. Only three such American movies were made in the

1960s: *The Courtship of Eddie's Father, Disk-O-Tek Holiday,* and *My Dog, the Thief,* a Disney TV movie about a traffic reporter and the St. Bernard who saves his job by boosting his ratings while foiling thieves. The Top 40 revolution that changed the sound of AM radio in the 1960s and included some of the most colorful DJs the business has known went unnoticed by Hollywood, as did the FM underground scene with its own wildly disparate air personalities. Years later, *American Graffiti* and *The Boat That Rocked* provided a nostalgic look-back at this decade, which included some of radio's most remarkable years. However, none of the 1960s DJs, whether from Top 40 or the equally fascinating underground FM radio, commanded as much attention as did Alan Freed in the radio films of the 1950s.

The 1970s brought a renewed interest by filmmakers in radio with at least 30 American productions being seen on theater or television screens. Although many of these were sports movies with play-by-play broadcasts, at least 19 included DJs or other air personalities. The first was *Play Misty for Me* (1971), with Clint Eastwood as the bookish Dave Garver interspersing jazz with poetry and other readings. The title was drawn from the request of a female listener for him to play Errol Garner's "Misty." The film introduced the psychopathic listener to viewing audiences and is discussed at greater length in Chapter Six.

The next DJ movie was *Vanishing Point* (1971), an "existential chase [that] was a big drive-in hit and remains a cult favorite."[7] It was interesting for several reasons. First, it had one of the great cinematic chase sequences; in fact, the plot is little more than an extended chase as a former race car driver and cop named Kowalski (Barry Newman) is hired to take a Dodge Challenger from Colorado to California. He is soon set upon by police and the rubber begins to fly. Most noteworthy for radio fans is the performance of Cleavon Little as the DJ Super Soul. Aided by a police scanner, Super Soul is Kowalski's guide and, indeed, soulmate along the Southwestern highways:

> And there goes the Challenger, bein' chased by the blue, blue meanies on wheels. The officious traffic squad cars are after our lone driver, the last American hero, the ... the electric Centaur, the demi-god, the super driver of the Golden West! Two nasty Nazi cars are close behind the beautiful lone driver, the police numbers are gettin' closer, closer, closer to our sole hero in his soulmobile. Yeah, baby, they about to strike, and they gonna git him, smash him, rape ... the last beautiful free soul on this planet!

Vanishing Point also featured an outstanding musical soundtrack with songs by Jerry Reed, Mountain, Big Mama Thornton, and others. Finally, its eclectic and fascinating characters included a pair of gay hitchhikers (Anthony James and Arthur Malet), a snake-handling prospector (Dean Jagger), a revivalist preacher with the appellation J. Hovah (Severn Darden), a nude blonde motorcycle rider (Gilda Texter), and a brief uncredited appearance by John Amos as Super Soul's control room engineer.

A 1997 TV version of *Vanishing Point* lacked the impact of the original, a not uncommon phenomenon of made-for-television movies. The remake had Viggo Mortensen as driver Jimmy Kowalski — rather than the more mysterious one-named Kowalski of the original — and Jason Priestley as his cross-country DJ guide. In this telling, Kowalski agrees to drive the Dodge Challenger from Colorado to Salt Lake City to pay for a hospital birth for his expectant wife. He is stopped by police and an altercation leads to a threat of jail time but, due to his wife's medical condition, the driver can't risk it and flees with the police in pursuit. News of the chase is picked up by a DJ at KBHX, who turns it into a political spectacle:

> Oh, you will love this, citizens. This is America, circa 1996. The Federal Bureau of Investigation has joined in the hunt for our man in the Challenger, Kowalski. Now, what business does Big Brother have sending a hi-tech helicopter after a mere speeder, you may ask? Why, our new anti-domestic terrorism statute, of course. Driving too fast now makes you a threat to the well-being of our great republic. People, the Bill of Rights is as forgotten as the Dead Sea Scrolls.

Rather than a lone figure who captures the public's imagine in his desert flight, this Kowalski soon has wide support as a national KBHX Challenge Watch is formed, and the driver calls the DJ to explain the financial problems that are his motivation for fleeing. He uses night vision goggles to help evade police, which also detracts from the solitary nature of the chase.

In the original film, Kowalski meets his end by driving the Challenger into a roadblock of road graders on the California border. As the smoke clouds from the collision waft over the gathered onlookers, including a TV crew, Kim Carnes' *Nobody Knows* offers the viewer time to contemplate the tale just told. In the TV version, however, a cheering crowd awaits the driver, Kowalski learns that his wife has died in childbirth, which provides the motivation for his fiery crash, and police open fire on the Challenger as it speeds toward the roadblock. The DJ then spells it all out for the audience:

> It's estimated that the Challenger, riddled with more than 200 bullet holes, hit those bulldozers at over 185 miles an hour. No one could have survived that impact. But no body was ever found. So what happened to Kowalski? The authorities say he's dead, vaporized in the explosion. Some witnesses swear they saw him bail out and escape with the help of allies in the crowd. Still others claim that he and his daughter are now livin' somewhere out west. I don't know. But it's somehow reassurin' that even in this computerized, bar-coded era of databanks and thumb prints, at least a few mysteries still remain.

Unfortunately, the DJ's explanation robs the film of its mystical quality, as do the hi-tech nature of the chase, the DJ's political comments, and Kowalski's explanation to the national audience. The TV remake, while true to the original script, thus lacks many of the elements that made the original engrossing.

Slipstream, a 1973 Canadian production, was the first film in which the DJ's role itself was the focus of the story rather than being incidental to the main plot. From a remote farmhouse on the Canadian prairies, Mike Mallard (Luke Askew) broadcasts to a national audience. Listeners are attracted by the solitary nature of the DJ, who is described as having a large following. Things begin to fall apart, however, when a group of young people arrives by airplane to seek out the reclusive announcer. Kathy (Patti Oatman) decides to stay with Mallard when the others leave, and this ultimately leads to Mallard's undoing. As Kathy makes increased demands upon the DJ's time and attention, he must choose between his relationship with her and the work that has defined his life. The film's title is derived from a Van Morrison song and *Slipstream* delineates the conundrum of countless young DJs torn between the commitments of their personal lives with those of the demanding and time-consuming profession of radio.

A landmark of sorts, being a breakthrough directorial effort by George Lucas four years before *Star Wars*, *America Graffiti* (1973) starred Richard Dreyfuss, Ron Howard, Cindy Williams, and Harrison Ford as 1960s California high schoolers ready for one last fling at their senior prom. A box office smash, due partly to a soundtrack featuring dozens of the top hits of the day, it used the gravelly voice of legendary DJ Wolfman Jack to punctuate the AM radio airwaves. A touching scene comes toward the end of the movie when Curt (Dreyfuss) ventures into the radio station, hoping to get the Wolfman to play a request. The announcer denies being the famous air personality and plays a prerecorded tape of the Wolfman taking a request. He then offers the teen some advice, along with a thought on popsicles that neatly sums up the DJs life. Curt is uncertain as to whether he wants to leave for college:

> WOLFMAN: I can't talk for the Wolfman, but I can tell you one thing. If the Wolfman was here, he'd say "Get your ass in gear." The Wolfman comes in here occasionally, bringing tapes, you know, to check up on me and whatnot...
> CURT: Yeah.
> WOLFMAN: ... and the places he talks about that he's been. The things he's seen. And it's a great big beautiful world out there. And here I sit, sucking on popsicles.
> CURT: Why don't you leave?
> WOLFMAN: I'm not a young man any more. And ... Wolfman gave me my start in the business. And I like it.

Numerous air personalities appeared on-screen in 1978's *FM*. Mother (Eileen Brennan), Prince (Cleavon Little), Doc Holiday (Alex Karras), and Eric Swan (Martin Mull) take over Los Angles station Q-Sky to protest management's decision to fundamentally alter the programming by playing more commercials. The humor is ribald and the movie is believed to have provided the inspiration for the CBS-TV series *WKRP in Cincinnati* that debuted the same year and ran until 1982. The movie paints a fairly realistic picture of radio in the mid–1970s and the characters are believable. The ending is weak, however: Crowds of Q-Sky's boisterous fans gather to support the DJ takeover, then the owner arrives to announce that because of the show of support there will be no programming changes after all. While dramatically satisfying, it does not comport with the realities of broadcasting, because it is unlikely that such a decision would be made in this manner.

A Manhattan DJ helps make heroes of two runaway girls in *Times Square* (1980). Tim Curry is Johnny LaGuardia, whose WJAD control room overlooks the titular area:

> There are a million stories in the big city. People say I have a bird's eye view perched up here, night after night, looking down into the throbbing, pulsing, mainline veins of the city. Looking right down into the heart of the beast.

Pamela Pearl (Trini Alvarado) is a street girl with an attitude who meets the middle-class and nerdy teen Nicky Marotta (Robin Johnson) in a psychological evaluation ward at the New York Neurological Hospital. The girls flee the institution in a stolen ambulance, which is newsworthy because Nicky's father has just been appointed commissioner in charge of cleaning up sleazy Times Square. LaGuardia picks up on the news and uses his microphone to broadcast information about the search for the missing girls, who have formed a punk rock duo called The Sleez Sisters. The publicity turns the fugitives into folk heroes and the film culminates in a packed Times Square concert in which Pearl performs atop a theater sign for the cheering crowd.

The Great American Traffic Jam, aka *Gridlock* (1980), told the story of Los Angeles drivers who become ensnarled in one of the city's legendary traffic tie-ups. Commenting on and finding humor in the situation is "Senor Smooth," a DJ at KPSA. The voice of the unseen announcer is that of Howard Hesseman, known to TV viewers of the day as Johnny "Dr. Fever" Caravella in *WKRP in Cincinnati*. The formulaic and clichéd patter is typical of that heard from DJs on hundreds of stations over the years. The film begins with the announcer's voice over opening credits and aerial shots of freeways:

> It's seven o'clock on Monday morning and all I can say is "My brains are falling out!" This is K-PASA radio and you've got the one, the only, Senor Smooth. Here at KPSA, the mercury's holding steady at a crisp 81 degrees, and if you live 'til noon, look for the expected high of— hold on to your roll-ons — one hundred and three. Air quality, you ask? Somewhere just below chunky. So try not to breathe unless it's absolutely necessary. Hey, the old Senor knows my amigos wanna stay healthy. Right? So if you must jog, I suggest you slip into some scuba gear.

Remember, the freeways are light so don't get uptight. You've got to drive to stay alive. Los Angeles, this one's for you! [*Music up*].

In one of his most forgettable performances, Donald Sutherland starred as Nick the Noz in *Gas* (1981), a spoof of the gas shortages of the late 1970s. He does the show from a helicopter and, as with *The Great American Traffic Jam*, the saga begins with opening credits over shots of busy freeways.

> EARTHMAN: You're listenin' to the 553, WGAZ, where hot rocks are at home, your GAS station, with the bopper in the chopper. Speakin' of the bopper, heeere's Nozzle!
> NOZ: You're all right, you're okay. You got the Nozzle, Nick. Hi, Earthman, you're in safe hands now. This is Nozzle Nick Noto, comin' to ya from his favorite air chair, the bopper chopper, WGAZ. Six-fifty in the a.m., a beautiful morning up here in the sky, but when I look down at the city you live in, Earthman, my heart just fills with despair, 'cause all I see are lines and lines, and you can't sort any of them, Earthman, 'cause they're full of cars. Day 22 of your very own, very local gas crisis. Wow!

Short of production values and lacking a coherent script, the film included appearances by some respected actors such as Susan Anspach and Sterling Hayden, and featured the screen debut of Howie Mandel.

Gilbert Gottfried was DJ Johnny Crunch in *The Adventures of Ford Fairlane* (1990); his appearance is brief because he meets an untimely end through electrocution while on the air. The rest of the movie is taken up with the search by rock 'n' roll detective Ford Fairlane (Andrew Dice Clay) for a mysterious woman and his uncovering of nefarious goings-on in the recording industry. *Zoo Radio* (1990) depicted various antics of brothers engaging in a ratings war to win their father's inheritance. In many of the radio films of the 1990s and 2000s, DJs were replaced on theater and television screens by other types of air personalities, most often talk show hosts.

Good Morning, Vietnam (1987) was Robin Williams' first major film role following his success on TV's *Mork and Mindy*, which ended five years earlier. Portraying real-life announcer Adrian Cronauer, his performance is particularly memorable in a lengthy scene in which he is introduced to Armed Forces Radio listeners. A wild mélange of ad libs and song introductions, it was improvised by Williams and established the offbeat nature of the character who drives the military brass to distraction. The power of the DJ as an entertainer has never been more forcefully presented.

In *Telling Lies in America* (1997), Kevin Bacon was Billy Magic, a DJ at rock 'n' roll station WHK Cleveland in 1961. Bacon's performance captures the essence of the itinerant DJ of the pre-computer era in an on-air performance complete with sound effects and jingles. Teenager "Chucky" Jonas (Brad Renfro) visits the station after winning Magic's radio contest and becomes enchanted with the DJ. He dreams of also becoming a DJ, but learns a hard lesson about life when he finds that the secret to Magic's financial success is payola, the practice of taking cash for playing records on the air. This is also Magic's downfall; the film echoes the career of Alan Freed and many other DJs of the late 1950s and early '60s. It also demonstrates the influence of the DJ upon young male listeners inspired to enter what they considered a magical world of entertainment by emulating the voices of the DJs coming from their radios.

Another 1997 release was *Private Parts*, an autobiographical film about Howard Stern, starring the DJ and portraying his rise through college and small-market radio to stardom in New York. It depicts both a young man's struggle to achieve success in radio and his clashes with management as he continually pushes the envelope while developing his shock jock persona. Employing a voiceover narration by Stern, its script accurately portrays the commercial radio world of the 1970s and '80s. Like *FM* and *Slipstream*, it reflects the tension that often exists between a station's management and its creative on-air performers.

A few films have translated the performances of real announcers to the screen. *Breakfast in Hollywood* (1946), based on a popular Los Angeles morning show starring Tom Breneman, detailed the efforts of women to appear on his eponymous show. Breneman introduces performers such as Andy Russell and Spike Jones, who perform live; the DJ also interviews members of the mostly female audience. Additional segments tell the stories of some of those who appeared on the show and how those appearances affected their lives.

American Graffiti prominently featured the voice of Wolfman Jack, who also appeared in a scene near the end of the movie. The plot of *The J-K Conspiracy* (2004) involved a missing encyclopedia volume and the antics of the morning crew of KGB San Diego (Dave Rickards, Shelly Dunn, and Cookie "Chainsaw" Randolph). Control room chatter, recreations of on-air jokes, and a cameo appearance by sportscaster Bob Costas round out the filmsy plot. *El Vacilón: The Movie* (2005) included numerous "bits" from popular Hispanic morning DJs Luis Jimenez and Moonshadow. Their show, *El Vacilón de la Manaña* (*The Morning Goof-Off*) on New York's Mega 97.9 was popular at the time the film was released. The plot, such as it is, begins with the team deciding to make a movie, but the idea never develops beyond the conceptual stage and the humor is mostly sophomoric, with various bodily functions providing the basis for many of the jokes.

Real air personalities have occasionally been cast as movie DJ characters, perhaps in the director's belief that they would lend an air of realism. (Two drawbacks of using actors as DJs is that their scripted ad libs often don't sound completely authentic and the actors playing the DJs also sometimes lack the authoritative vocal delivery gained by real DJs from years behind the microphone.) Real-life DJs who have been seen in films include Jim Ladd as himself in *On the Air Live with Captain Midnight* (1979), Chris Ryan as the pirate DJ Caligari in *American Nightmare* (2002), and Ryan Cameron as a wannabe stand-up comedian in *Jinx'd* (2000). The low-budget *Wash It Up* (2003) and *Ski Trippin'* (2005) also featured rap DJs in cameos. No real-world female DJs have made the transition to the movie screen.

The DJ as Hit Maker

Radio has historically played a key role in the promotion of both new and established musical artists because of its symbiotic relationship with the record industry. The numerous films of the 1930s and '40s in which unknown performers strive for a chance to be heard on the radio attest to the power of the airwaves. Radio as music starmaker was portrayed as early as 1937, in *Rhythm in the Clouds*. In this film, an unemployed songwriter cheats her way onto a radio show by forging another writer's name on her song. In *Where Did You Get That Girl?* (1941), a composer and a musician become famous when their record is stolen and played on the air. The plot of *Disc Jockey* (1951) was based on the premise that radio could turn an unknown singer into a star, and *Disk-O-Tek Holiday* contains several humorous scenes as teen wannabe stars try to maneuver DJs into playing their song.

The payola scandals of the early 1960s, which have continued in various forms and degrees of influence to the present day, illustrated the importance of radio airplay as a music promotion tool. Record companies were prepared to spend significant sums of money to ensure their songs would be heard on the air and the corruptive influence of payola was depicted in *Mr. Rock 'n' Roll: The Alan Freed Story* and *Telling Lies in America*. One of the story elements of *American Hot Wax* involves the consistent efforts of would-be singing stars to inveigle Alan Freed into spinning their discs on his show.

Several other movies have also shown the relationship between the radio and recording industries. Disc jockeys promoted records in numerous films, including *That's the Way of the World* (1975). Harvey Keitel was a record producer assigned against his wishes to a less-than-talented band. Included in the record label's promotion is an interview with a lecherous New York DJ who seems more interested in connecting with the band's female singer than with promoting their single. Disc jockeys played a key role in *Outlaw Blues* (1977), in which Peter Fonda (as country singer and ex-con Bobby Ogden) is on the run from the law again after assaulting another singer, while at the same time promoting a hit single through interviews with country DJs. He manages to duck out of the stations just before police arrive with lights flashing in futile attempts to collar him.

In *La Bamba* (1987), Ritchie Valens' eponymous song becomes a hit partly because of DJs Alan Freed (Jeffrey Alan Chandler) and Ted Quillin (real-life DJ Rick Dees). The premise of *Airheads* (1994) is that an unknown band needs airplay to make their song a hit, so the group takes over a Los Angeles station and holds the DJ hostage until he plays their tape. In *Dill Scallion* (1999), a school bus driver becomes a country music star through a combination of much luck and minimal talent. The titular Scallion (Billy Burke) becomes incensed and storms out of the station when, after interviewing him, a DJ plays a bootleg version of his hit. *Sueno* (2005) was the story of a Mexican immigrant (John Leguizamo) whose road out of his lower-class life was an amateur talent contest sponsored by a Los Angeles radio station. *Cadillac Records* (2008) was Hollywood's version of the Chess Records story, focusing on the career of Etta James (Beyonce Knowles), with Adrien Brody as Leonard Chess. DJs were crucial to the label's success by giving the then-unknown Chess artists their first exposure.

Women Behind the Mike

Female announcers were uncommon in radio's early years, although a few occasionally were heard.[8] Donna Halper has surmised that one reason for this may have been the medium's technological roots. Many of the first radio receivers were homemade, and hobby magazines of the 1920s recommended electronics mostly to male consumers. "Advertisements stressed the benefits of learning the new technology; girls, if portrayed at all, were typically shown watching in amazement as brother and father built something together."[9] Other barriers to women developing any kind of announcing career included, for many years, ambivalence about working women in general, and being heard on the air in particular. Magazine articles in the 1930s were critical of women in any radio role except behind the scenes.[10] Some critics in radio's early years argued that the voices of men were inherently more pleasant on the air than those of women. For whatever reason, by the 1930s virtually no female voices were heard on the nation's airwaves.[11]

While women DJs were not common until the late 1960s and early '70s, the 1950s did see the arrival of a limited number of radio personalities such as Martha Jean "The Queen" Steinberg, Zilla Mays, and Vivian Greene.[12] Some of these pioneers were African American women who played rhythm 'n' blues music. Until the late '50s, however, most on-air radio jobs for women were limited to hosting homemaker shows or other programs oriented toward female audiences.[13] These roles are typified in the movie *The Higgins Family* (1938), in which a housewife gets her own radio show and discusses household products. Female announcers are notably absent from *The Deejays*,[14] Arnold Passman's seminal work on the DJs of the 1950s and '60s, indicating their lack of influence in the industry. Many station managers felt that few listeners wanted to hear women on the air and WHER Memphis, with an all-female air staff, was a novelty in 1955. An attempt at attracting women listeners by using only female announcers and billing itself as "a thousand beautiful watts," WHER was the brainchild of Sun Records founder Sam Phillips and remained on the air until 1972.[15]

Reveille with Beverly thus represented a breakthrough of sorts in 1943, although its plot reflected society's attitudes of that time toward women. In an early scene, two soldiers hear Beverly on the air and make a bet about whether she is good looking. And, while Deanna Durbin is presented in a strong role as platter spinner Mary Collins in *Something in the Wind*, the film takes a subtle dig at women announcers when, as she signs off her morning show, Collins refers to being "in search of a sponsor," implying that a show hosted by a woman might have difficulty attracting advertisers. Not explained is how a morning show would ever be aired without sponsors. Also, as she sings her theme song, Collins lounges across the equipment in a sensual semi-prone position with her feet nearly caressing the turntable.

Another type of sensuality, or at least sexuality, was on display in the 1970 soft-porn and low-budget *The Dirty Mind of Young Sally*, the next film to feature a female DJ. It starred Colleen Brennan, known to adult film devotees as Sharon Kelly in fare such as *Lady by Night* and *Street Heat*. Here she's the voice of a pirate station operating from a van and the suggestive lyrics of the songs she plays serve to further motivate the libidos of her listeners.

Another Brennan was seen on movie screens in 1978 when Eileen Brennan created the role of Mother in *FM*. Mother's character hints at an aging hippie persona, her nickname apparently referencing the Mother Earth figure of the Woodstock generation, which her first screen ad-lib reinforces:

> This is Mother talkin' to ya. Mother, with whom it all began. I held ya close, I tucked ya in, I took ya all the way back home. Now, I am sayin' "rock-a-bye baby." The Prince is due up next with another fabulous payday champagne celebration from Sky Radio, 7–11 FM, Los Angeles.

FM was probably best known for its offbeat characters and became something of a cult hit among radio announcers at the time. In 1980, John Carpenter's *The Fog* brought another strong female presence to theaters, with Adrienne Barbeau as DJ Stevie Wayne at KAB. Besides playing music, she conveys information about weather and sea conditions from her control room atop a lighthouse overlooking the California community of Antonio Bay. As the village celebrates its hundredth anniversary, it is visited by a mysterious glowing fog which brings with it zombie sailors seeking revenge for the campfire that lured them to their deaths a century earlier. Wayne's voice on car radios guides some of the townspeople to safety in the church.

The Fog was remade in 2005 with Selma Blair as Stevie Wayne. Although displaying a somewhat stronger air personality than Barbeau's as the film opens, this Wayne ultimately becomes another victim of the zombies. As she flees, Wayne's car grinds to a halt in the enveloping mist, presumably because of the fog's supernatural power. She is trapped inside as the vehicle crashes off a cliff into the water and, although Wayne escapes, she joins other survivors scrambling for refuge in the lighthouse housing the radio station. Rather than being an authoritative voice of guidance, Blair's Wayne is a weaker character in her actions, demeanor, and dialogue. Both films were co-written by John Carpenter and Debra Hill; Carpenter directed the original and co-produced the remake.

Jamie Lee Curtis, star of the 1979 *The Fog*, returned in another radio film, *Love Letters* (1983), as Anna Winter, the host of a classical music program on listener-supported KLAS. Her gentle nature is established in her first radio scene, in which she mimics playing a piano on the audio console as a classical piano is heard in the background. Winter has psychological problems, and after her mother's death she finds letters revealing an illicit affair. The discovery triggers an abiding passion by Winter for such an affair of her own so she becomes involved with a married photographer (James Keach). Wracked by guilt but unable to end the relationship, Winter becomes emotionally distraught when her lover breaks off the relationship to save his marriage. A female air personality of a distinctly different type was also seen in 1983's *Born in Flames*, which was discussed further in Chapter Two. An early feminist film, it featured a black lesbian DJ named Honey as one of several militants operating pirate radio stations to push for a socialist revolution in the U.S.

The next female film DJ was Caroline Williams in *The Texas Chainsaw Massacre 2* (1986). Williams was "Stretch" Brock, an air personality at a Dallas rock 'n' roll station who tapes listeners as they make requests and thus records the deaths of two college students whose call is interrupted by a chainsaw-wielding psycho named Leatherface. Texas Ranger "Lefty" Enright (Dennis Hopper) arrives to investigate and agrees to let Brock air the recording, which triggers a visit to the station by Leatherface and his partner Chop-Top. Although Leatherface virtually destroys the station with his chainsaw, he spares Brock, who follows him to his underground hideout. Enright arrives and the film devolves into an orgy of blood and mayhem as the Texas Ranger and the psychos engage in a battle of chainsaws, with Enright wielding his like pistols.

In 1990, Canadian actress Genevieve Bujold was Rachel Roux with the on-air name "Coyote" in *False Identity*. Having left Atlanta for a job at KLEX in California, the host of *Coyote's Rhythm 'n' Blues* is upset with the station management about her lack of programming freedom. At a flea market she finds a Purple Heart medal and decides to investigate the story of its honoree for a Veteran's Day program she has been assigned to produce. Her search leads her to Ben Driscoll (Stacy Keach), a Vietnam vet with amnesia who has returned home after being released from prison for a crime he can't recall committing. The pair's investigation becomes complicated when it stirs up an old murder case that involves the town's leading family. The script suffers from Coyote's use of the badly dated phrase "out there in radioland" in addressing her audience. According to IMDb, the radio scenes were filmed at KPFK in North Hollywood.[16]

Night Owl (1993), a TV movie set in New York but shot in Toronto, was unique in that the female DJ is never seen. Her mysterious voice takes over a station's airwaves by unexplained means, causing several male listeners to leap to their deaths from high places. Jennifer Beals portrays a woman trying to prevent the same fate from befalling her husband, but the movie founders on the implausibility of its plot premise.

Grosse Pointe Blank (1997) had Minnie Driver as DJ Debi Newberry at WGPM in Grosse Pointe, Michigan. Both her career and her life are interrupted by the arrival of former boyfriend Martin Blank (John Cusack) on the eve of their high school reunion. Unbeknownst to her, Blank is now a hit man on assignment while simultaneously dodging another hit man and federal agents. Debi is on the air when Martin first reappears in her life, and she is so nonplussed that she stumbles through a song introduction and the record "wows" at the start because it has not been cued properly. The dark comedy centers on their relationship as Debi grapples with the choices she must make about her future and whether it will include the former boyfriend for whom she still has feelings.

Molly Ringwald's Anne Winslow was an announcer at classical music station WZIN Philadelphia in *Requiem for Murder* (1998), but her on-air scenes were brief. The film falls into the psycho listener category, since murder victims have been listening to her show and the press dubs them the "Mozart murders." Winslow becomes the object of affection of a serial killer and the plot revolves around the police investigation into the murders and a detective's efforts to prevent Winslow from becoming another victim.

Women of the Night (2000) featured pirate station DJs Shawnee Free Jones and Sally Kellerman in a film long on bare flesh but short on a coherent storyline. The announcers serve mainly to set up stories that are then told visually. The verisimilitude of the movie is not helped by having the pirates broadcast at night from an 18-wheeler packed with expensive equipment.

Despite the casting of women as DJs discussed earlier, Hollywood has generally been more interested in depicting them as talk show hosts, and the list of these films is quite lengthy: *Don't Answer the Phone!* (1980; a psycho strangles women, calls a talk show host and then stalks her); *Choose Me* (1984; a radio sex therapist has psychological problems); *Midnight Magic* (1987; a talk show psychologist has an affair); *Body Chemistry 2: Voice of a Stranger* (1992; a radio psychologist encourages a listener to act out his sexual fantasies); *Sexual Response* (1992; a radio sexologist has an affair with a sculptor); *Straight Talk* (1992; an Arkansas woman accidentally becomes a Chicago talk show host); *Ring of the Musketeers* (1992; a beautiful blonde love doctor becomes a modern-day Musketeer); *Dangerous Touch* (1994; a radio sex therapist's promiscuous behavior leads to blackmail and murder); *When the Dark Man Calls* (1995; a talk show host is stalked by the man convicted of murdering her husband); *Midnight Confessions* (1995; the host of a radio sex talk show becomes the target of a psycho who kills prostitutes); *The Truth About Cats and Dogs* (1996; the veterinarian host of a talk show for pet lovers suffers from low self-esteem and becomes involved with a listener); *The Night Caller* (1998; a listener becomes obsessed with a talk show psychologist); *Shattered Illusions* (1998; a psycho stalks a talk show host and her sister); *Mad Song* (2000; a radio therapist tries to help a troubled teen while struggling with her own emotional problems); *Bare Deception* (2000; ratings for a sex talk show skyrocket when a listener is killed); *The Midnight Hour* (2000; a woman hosts a talk show to find her sister's killer); *You Belong to Me* (2001; a radio psychologist helps police track down a serial killer); *Deranged* (2002; a radio psychologist goes psycho when her show is cancelled); *Sinful Desires* (2002; a talk show host becomes the victim of a stalker); *A Lover's Revenge* (2005; a talk show host is stalked by a caller's husband); *A Valentine Carol* (2007; a talk show host is visited by the ghost of her former mentor and relives experiences with past boyfriends); and *The Accidental Husband* (2008; a radio love doctor discovers she's a married woman due to a prank by friends).

Some of these movies were made for television and a few could be considered soft-porn. Sexual or relationship problems abound in them, as does violence. As the titles indicate, many obviously portray the announcers as victims of stalkers or as having some kind of psychological disorder.

African American DJs

Black DJs have been heard on the nation's airwaves since at least 1932.[17] The first station to feature all black-oriented programming was WDIA Memphis in 1947[18]; a burgeoning black radio industry through the 1950s was made possible by the improving post-war economic climate for African Americans.[19] With the growing popularity of rap and hip-hop in the 1990s, black DJs were heard in greater numbers across the country. In cities with large African American populations, black formats such as Urban Contemporary are often at or near the top of the ratings conducted by Arbitron Inc., the company that measures radio listenership. DJs of color, however, have been scarce on movie screens.

Although it had a running time of only about 42 minutes and did not depict DJs playing records, mention should be made of *Stars on Parade* (1946). It was noteworthy for its rare all-black cast and the appearance of African Americans in roles other than those in which they were then usually cast, such as maids, gardeners, and other hired help, or as singers and dancers. In this movie, WLAT owner Johnny Bennett (Milton Wood) returns from military service to find that his station's only advertiser, the Glow-Tan Cosmetic Company, is canceling its account. Bennett and his sister Jane (Jane Cooley), who co-owns the station, line up a group of talented musicians to perform a special concert in hopes of persuading the sponsor to continue advertising. Of course, the broadcast is successful and Glow-Tan signs up for more commercials. While mostly a musical, the film is unique for showing African Americans as station owners and sponsors as well as the singers and musicians who perform in the concert.

Despite the racial changes that made radio a more hospitable industry in the 1950s, African American DJs did not appear in a radio movie until 1957, when *Jamboree*, aka *Disc Jockey Jamboree*, featured numerous announcers introducing teen singing stars. The minimal plot involves a teenage couple striving for a hit record. The unrealistic radio studio sets are laughably similar (DJs sit at a microphone with station call letters in identical layouts displayed on a plain background wall). However, two popular black DJs appeared: Robin Seymour of WKMH Detroit and Jocko Henderson of WOV New York. The self-proclaimed "Ace from Outer Space," Henderson was one of black radio's pioneers and made this film appearance wearing the spacesuit he donned in real life when promoting music concerts.

The DJ who preceded Clint Eastwood on the air at KRML Carmel in the psycho listener thriller *Play Misty for Me* (1971) was James McEachin, an African American actor playing Al Monte ("Hey, hey, hey, you're diggin' the master jock of solid rock, Sweet Al Monte!"). The first truly memorable performance by an African American DJ was Cleavon Little's turn behind the microphone as the blind Super Soul in *Vanishing Point*, described earlier. In *Melinda* (1972), a low-budget Blaxploitation movie with a vengeance theme, Calvin Lockhart was finger-snapping, jive-talking Frankie J., a DJ at KJLH Los Angeles. An early scene has Lockhart signing off his morning show; the rest of the film centers on his campaign to avenge the death of his girlfriend at the hands of the white mob and he spends little time at the radio station.

Cleavon Little returned to the screen in 1978 as The Prince, one of the offbeat but believable characters in *FM*. In his introductory scene, he's accompanied into the control room by two white girls, either topless or naked in a brief shot, and describes them to Mother as "a couple of, uh, stereo assistants who so charitably agreed to give The Prince a hand on the show tonight." Gregory Hines, one of America's finest dancers, turned in an authentic performance as late-night DJ Jim Sheppard in the TV movie *Dead Air* (1994). He takes harassing phone calls from a listener who has also been stalking him, and who apparently commits a murder while on the phone with him.

Another 1978 film to prominently feature a black DJ was *Thank God It's Friday*. The iconic disco movie was set amidst the twirling globes and strobe lights of a disco nightclub and captured the essence of the disco craze, as radio DJ Bobby Speed (Ray Vitte) struggles to perform his first remote broadcast in the frenetic disco atmosphere. Wannabe singing star Nicole Sims (played by real-life disco queen Donna Summer) is determined to seize the opportunity to demonstrate her vocal prowess, and the Commodores also put in an appearance. The 1990 college radio film *A Matter of Degrees* opens with black DJ Wells Denard (Wendell Pierce) behind the microphone and also includes an appearance by Gilbert McCauley as Roger, the host of *Reggae Bloodlines*. This movie is discussed in more detail later in this chapter.

The Warriors was more than a little controversial when released in 1979 because gang violence greeted its opening at some theaters.[20] Directed by Walter Hill, the film's story was based on the struggles of a Greek mercenary army led by Xenophon to return home following a battle in 401 B.C.[21] In this telling, a New York gang fights its way back to its home turf in the Bronx through the hostile territories of rival groups after a gang summit ends in violence. In addition to its notorious opening in some movie houses, *The Warriors* also stirred controversy with its shots of a DJ who talks to the Warriors to guide them home. African American actress Lynne Thigpen is never seen full face, but only in extreme close-ups of her mouth and the microphone. Both Hill and Thigpen disclaimed any underlying racial motivation for her unusual portrayal and, according to Hill, "the super close-ups was something that happened just on the set. I kept saying, 'Go closer, go closer.'"[22]

A similar DJ portrayal came in the Canadian film *Rude* (1995), in which a black woman (actress Sharon Lewis) is seen primarily in close-ups of the mouth and microphone as she narrates stories of life in urban Toronto. In this instance, however, the movie's opening scene provides an establishing wide shot of the control room, its equipment, and the announcer.

Levitation (1997), described by an IMDb reviewer as "a confused, meandering film, the meaning of which the makers couldn't explain at gunpoint,"[23] detailed the search of Acey Rawlin (Sarah Paulson), an orphaned and pregnant young woman, for her birth mother. Along the way she encounters Downbeat, the host of KROV's blues show *Downbeat 'til Dawn*. Ernie Hudson's performance as the DJ is entirely believable, his baritone voice and smooth delivery epitomizing the intimate style emulated by countless announcers in the blues format. Ultimately, however, the fact that Rawlin can levitate is irrelevant both to her character and the already feeble plot.

A serial killer film, *Outside Ozona* (1998) realistically portrayed small-town radio, with blues musician Taj Mahal as Dix Mayal, a DJ bitter at being forced to play country music and also not particularly enamored of his social surroundings. He threatens to walk off the job when the replacement announcer (the owner's son) fails to show up for the midnight air shift. Dix is persuaded to stay by manager Floyd Bibbs (Meatloaf). The film is unusual for the casting of musicians in the lead roles, but both bring off convincing performances. The movie captures the angst of many DJs trapped in the small-town radio life as Dix angrily leaves the control room and heads down the hall for the exit as his air shift ends.

> BIBBS: What am I supposed to do, Dix? Cito was supposed to cover 'til sunrise.
> DIX: Get Rhonda to do it.
> BIBBS: Rhonda? Are you crazy? Rhonda ain't no radio personality.
> DIX: It doesn't matter, Floyd, ain't nobody out there listenin' to that old shit anyway.
> BIBBS: That ain't true. KWOK goes across the Red River into five states.
> [*Dix opens the door to leave*].
> BIBBS: Dix! I'm beggin' ya. J.W. ain't too happy with me lately. Slippin' ad sales and all. He's losin' faith in me as a station manager. Dix. I can't lose this gig. Please [*Dix pauses, returns to control room, opens the mic*].
> DIX: Well, boys and girls, looks like Dix is gonna be with ya all through the night one more time. And that means we're goin' to have to dip into Big Daddy's personal bag of oldies but goodies [*Puts CD in player, rock music up*]. First one goes out to my boss, Junior Craven, and all the rest of you beer-guzzlin,' tobacco-chewin' hillbilly dipshits out there.
> RHONDA: Can he say that?
> BIBBS: He just did.

High Freakquency, aka *Da Station* (1998), was a low-budget movie about a Los Angeles station with an Urban Contemporary format. Of interest mainly because of its mostly black cast and an early depiction of contemporary African American DJs, its minimal plot includes an overbearing manager, antics of the various DJs and listeners, and a concert promoted by the station. In *Jinx'd* (2000), obnoxious DJ Ryan Lawson tries to launch a career as a stand-up comedian but ends up in front of an audience of redneck white supremacists. In *The Midnight Hour* (2000), Derrick Bishop was a college DJ named Pepper who has a couple of turns at the microphone before a beautiful blonde DJ arrives for her air shift.

Eight Legged Freaks (2002) was the tale of spiders transmogrified into giant mutants by a chemical spill in the mining town of Prosperity, Arizona. Among those fleeing the arachnids is paranoid announcer Harlan Griffith (Doug E. Doug) on KFRD Freedom Radio, which operates from a trailer on the edge of town and is described by Griffith as "the only source for the inside dope on government conspiracies, space aliens, and up-to-the minute reports on when they plan to invade." The DJ, who has an innate and inexplicable fear of alien anal probes, flees to safety with some townspeople to a mall and then to a web of mining tunnels beneath the community.

8 Mile (2002) was the story of the rapper Jimmy "B-Rabbit" Smith (Eminem), struggling to make it in the music industry in his home town of Detroit. A humorous scene occurs when Smith takes his demo to a radio station and sees his purported girlfriend making out with a man in another studio. A confrontation erupts while the DJ — Bushman, a real-life Detroit air personality — conducts an on-air interview, oblivious to the violent scene being played out behind him as Smith attacks the interloper. The scene used a reconstruction of the studios of WJLB-FM, a popular Detroit Urban Contemporary station.

T-Roy (Terrence Howard) was both a DJ and a talk show host in *Love Chronicles* (2003). He co-hosts a talk show on WKN Love Radio with his girlfriend Sara (Paula Jai Parker) and intersperses sexy music with phone calls about relationship issues. Sparks fly when author Monifa Burley (Robin Givens) appears as a guest, mostly because of Sara's disgruntlement with T-Roy's apparent interest in the beautiful author. Listeners stir up the conversation by calling in to discuss their relationship issues, and T-Roy and Sara often find themselves at odds in the ensuing conversation. Givens was well known to many radio listeners as Howard Stern's long-time sidekick on his controversial radio show.

Car wash girls dreamed of singing careers while being entertained by KJMZ Dallas rap DJs in *Wash It Up* (2003). Urban youths won a ski trip contest sponsored by Philadelphia's Power 99 FM in *Ski Trippin'* (2005), with the putative humor derived from the juxtaposition of African American young people vacationing in a mainly white ski resort. The comedy is weak, however, as they are never seen on the slopes and the storyline, such as it is, features various bedroom shenanigans.

In *K-Hip Radio*, aka *The Urban Demographic* (2005), KSOF Seattle abandons classical music in favor of a rap format. During the opening credits a newscaster is heard reading stories about black crime and violence in Seattle's inner city and then the narrator's voice justifies the change of formats: "Our research indicates that the growth of the urban format has tremendous potential in a market of this size." Thus are the urban format and its listeners subtly linked to street crime, although the station management is white and the main plot line entails protests in the black community against the format change (black protesters chant "rap is crap") as well as protests by advertisers. A black female DJ, a rarity on film, is heard on the new station when Tiffany Haddish plays Janice Green. Rico E. Anderson as program director Bob Johnson is another infrequent casting of an African American actor in a position of authority.

Academy Award winner Don Cheadle (*Hotel Rwanda*) gave a highly praised performance as "Petey" Greene in *Talk to Me* (2007). Greene was an ex-con who became a radio star and community activist in Washington DC in the 1960s. Cheadle's performance is a sensitive portrayal of a man struggling to cope with both alcoholism and the toll of fame. While he failed in an attempt at television stardom through an appearance as a stand-up comedian on *The Tonight Show*, he found his niche on radio and used his show to espouse the causes of the common man in the nation's capital. The film included depictions of other black DJs: Cedric the Entertainer as "Nighthawk" Bob Terry and Vondie Curtis-Hall as Sunny Jim Kelsey. Chiwetel Ejiofor was WOL program director Dewey Hughes, who gave Greene his first opportunity for radio stardom. Finally, a unique performance should be mentioned: CCH Pounder as Fran Ambrose in 1990's *Psycho IV: The Beginning* (the film is discussed in more detail in Chapter Six). It is noted here because of the appearance of an African American woman as the host of her own program, *The Fran Ambrose Show*. The only other similar portrayal was Paula Jai Parker as Sara, the co-host of a talk show in the previously-discussed *Love Chronicles*.

The College Scene

College radio has a history as long as the medium itself. One of America's first college stations began in 1911 with transmitter experiments under the call letters 9XM at the University of Wisconsin. On January 13, 1922, the Federal Radio Commission issued a broadcasting license to the university for station WHA.[24] Today most college stations' licenses preclude them from airing commercials and, with some exceptions, most are FM stations whose announcers are students and whose programming runs to an eclectic mix of musical genres seldom heard on commercial radio. Freed from the constraints of ratings and commercial considerations, and often playing music outside the mainstream, college stations tend to be considerably less structured, both on the air and off, than their commercial counterparts.

Some university stations are affiliated with National Public Radio and have professional staffs and announcers, augmented by students. These stations frequently play classical, jazz, blues, folk, and other types of music rarely heard on commercial stations. They often have professional and respected newsrooms to provide news and public service programs such as interview shows, in-depth news investigations or documentaries, election night coverage, and other kinds of mainstream programming. The free-wheeling atmosphere of most college stations would seem to afford ample opportunities for interesting stories but, while the college scene has been the setting for dozens if not hundreds of movies,[25] only a few have included radio, other than play-by-play broadcasts of sporting events such as football games. In many of these films, the college setting is only tangentially related to the plot, and verisimilitude of the stations' operations is frequently lacking.

Girls Nite Out (1982) was a slasher movie in which someone kills the mascot of Dewitt University's basketball team, then dons his bear suit and outfits it with knife blades in the paws. The action takes place on the evening of a scavenger hunt as co-eds fan out across campus, following on-air clues provided by a DJ with the moniker "Kaiser" (Larry Mintz) on campus station WDVX. As students begin dying from slashed throats, Kaiser receives mysterious clues from an anonymous caller. Hal Holbrook is campus security chief Jim MacVey, who desperately tries to track down the psycho killer.

In *A Matter of Degrees* (1990), the radio station is central to the plot. Students at WXOX in Providence, Rhode Island, try to keep their non-commercial station on the air with pledge drives, which they hate. They are typical of the offbeat personalities found at many campus stations and become upset when weapons manufacturer Orbital Technologies announces plans to build a research center on campus. The students are further outraged when the company offers to fund a new broadcasting facility which will entail a change of format from the alternative music they have been playing and which provides the beat for the film's soundtrack. This exchange exemplifies the difference between college and commercial radio:

PETE: Who you competing with, Aubrey? We're not a commercial radio station. We don't have to kiss advertisers' ass, we don't have to worry about ratings, either. That is an unrealistic attitude, you gotta pull in ratings to be taken seriously in this country.

AUBREY: Pete, we can place more people in the industry if we can give them some genuine commercial experience.

PETE: Experience? What the fuck do you know about experience? You can get a goddamn monkey to cycle the top ten! We're playin' music on this station that isn't heard anywhere else on the radio.

To protest the station buyout, some students interrupt their graduation ceremonies by broadcasting an anti-capitalist message over the public address system from the station's control room. Ultimately their protestations fall on deaf ears. *A Matter of Degrees* was shot on location at Brown University in Providence.

Burning Annie (1994) was the story of an insecure young man who spends much of his spare time at the college station. In an unusual plot premise, Max (Gary Lundy) believes his life has been ruined by his forced exposure to Woody Allen films by his parents. In particular, he has developed an obsession with *Annie Hall*, which he feels has had drastic negative effects on his social and romantic lives. Max narrates his problems to the viewer from the control room and the dialogue is interspersed with scenes of his various relationship problems.

The previously discussed 1997 Howard Stern biopic *Private Parts* included the shock jock's start at Boston University station WTBU. ("My name is Howard Stern on *The Howard Stern Experience* and if you love music, you'll love Deep Purple on T-B-U.") The brief scene depicts the type of tribulations experienced by many neophyte announcers when first learning to use the control room equipment when a stack of tape cartridges comes crashing down onto a turntable as he struggles to cue a record due to his first-time on-air anxieties.

In *Urban Legend* (1998), another campus slasher flick, students began dying in a variety of ways, each corresponding to an urban legend tied to past events at the small New England university. Sasha Thomas (Tara Reid) was a late-night DJ at WZAB ("You're under the covers with Sasha at WZAB, the voice of Pendleton University"), with a penchant for broadcasting weird sound mixes. The bodies pile up and eventually Sasha finds herself alone in the station with the unidentified psycho. Thinking quickly, she turns on her microphone and her screams for help are heard by the listeners but, unfortunately for her, they think it's another one of her sound collages and she falls victim to a bloody ax murderer who has done in several of her classmates.

More campus mayhem came to the screen in *The Midnight Hour*, aka

Tell Me No Lies (2000). Alex Sheppard (Amber Smith) gets a job hosting a late-night music-talk show on a Santa Barbara college station so she can track down the killer of her sister, also a student. Sheppard apparently never attends classes and the film contains the requisite amount of B-movie nudity. It is discussed in more detail in Chapter Six since it also falls into the psycho listener category.

First Time Caller (2002) was a Canadian production with a college station control room as the setting for much of the dialogue. Caesar (John Catucci) is a young man whose girlfriend goes away to college for a year. When she returns with a new boyfriend, Caesar finds himself at loose ends and his attempts at starting new relationships meet with failure. Enter Julie (Catherine Rossini), the host of the all-night *Small Talk* show on an unidentified station. Caesar begins calling Julie regularly, she breaks up with her boyfriend, and the film has a predictably happy ending. Although the station is identified as being at a college, the campus is never seen and Julie never attends classes or engages in any other activities usually associated with college life. A control room filled with candles adds little to the authenticity of the call-in discussion scenes.

Two young men became involved with student-run station Alice Radio in *Lavorare con Lentezza*, aka *Working Slowly* (2004). The film is set in 1976 Bologna and reflects the disaffectedness of Italian youth at the time. The two men agree to work for a local hoodlum by digging a tunnel underneath a bank vault. While working they become enamored of Alice Radio and its anti-establishment, anti-capitalist political views, and live unedited telephone calls from listeners. They eventually begin working at the station until a police raid shuts it down. The film was inspired by the real Alice Radio that took to the airwaves for a few months in 1976–77.

College Radio Sucks (2008) was made on a shoestring budget by film students at San Jose State University. Kurt (Bobby August, Jr.) and Trevor (Riley Kempton) work at university station KSJS-FM. When a local commercial station announces a contest in which it will hire one new air personality per year, they become determined to win. Hijinks ensue when Kurt's girlfriend decides to win the contest herself. The KSJS scenes were shot at the university station of the same call letters, which lends a strong sense of realism.

The Omniscient Announcer

"Omniscient (om nish' ent), adj. 1. having complete or unlimited knowledge, awareness, or understanding; perceiving all things."[26]

Some films have presented air personalities as omniscient so that they may comment on the action, directly address the movie's characters, or provide useful information to the lead character(s) over the airwaves. The first movie to use a DJ in such a fashion was 1971's *Vanishing Point*, in which Super Soul addresses the driver Kowalski by name to guide him across the roads and highways of the Southwest on his trek to California:

> Person to person call for Kowalski. Person to person call for Kowalski. Can you hear me, Kowalski? This is to conform you of the latest developments. Correction to my last delivery. All the main doors are closed except one. This one opens to Sonora.

Kowalski, of course, hears all of Super Soul's broadcasts as the DJ never talks to him in the middle of a chase or when the driver is otherwise engaged. As discussed earlier, the 1997 made-for-television remake of *Vanishing Point* lacked much of the appeal of the original and one reason for this was the absence of an omniscient DJ in the TV movie.

In *The Warriors*, the Lynne Thigpen DJ character is not identified on the air but is a presence throughout the film although seen only sporadically. She comments on the gang's trek through hostile territory and, according to Billy Weber, one of the film's editors, "She became like a Greek chorus for the movie, always telling us where they were, how much farther they had to go."[27] She talks directly to the gang:

> All right, now, for all you boppers out there in the big city, all you street people with an ear for the action, I've been asked to relay a request from the Gramercy Riffs. It's a special for the Warriors. That's that real live bunch from Coney, and I do mean the Warriors. Here's a hit with them in mind [*Music up "Nowhere to Run"*].

The DJs voice is omnipresent although it comes from a studio of which the viewer sees the barest of set dressings: a turntable, audio console, and a tape machine. Close-ups of the equipment, hands, mouth, and microphone, bathed in red and orange, create a surreal atmosphere that contributes greatly to the ambience and strikes a discordant note when intercut with the gang's street scenes. Close observation, however, reveals that few members of the Warriors or other gangs carry radios, so the omniscient effect of the DJs comments was largely mitigated.

DJ Johnny LaGuardia (Tim Curry) acted as the voice for the runaway girls in the 1980 movie *Times Square*. He not only talks to them but also apprises the listeners of the condition of their life in the Times Square area, and the runaways gradually come to trust him to a degree. They perform as the Sleez Sisters on his show and also send him a letter which he reads to Pamela Pearl's father on the air:

> Quote. Dear Daddy. I not kidnapped. I am me-napped. I am soul-napped. I am

Nicky-napped. I am happy-napped. Doctors, lawyers, Indian chiefs, we are looking after ourselves, and having our own Renaissance. We don't need anti-depressants. We need your understanding. Unquote.

Ultimately, the girls believe LaGuardia has betrayed their trust when he helps the authorities track them down.

Do the Right Thing (1989) was written, directed, and produced by Spike Lee, who also appeared in it as the character Mookie. It examines the relationships, often tense and ultimately violent, between the white, Asian, and African American residents of Brooklyn's Bedford-Stuyvesant district. It opens with the voice of morning DJ Senor Love Daddy (Samuel L. Jackson) on We Love Radio 108 FM, "from the Heart of Bed-Stuy." The station's control room overlooks the street, thus affording Senor Love Daddy a fine view of its unfolding proceedings. The DJ's comments are reflective of the outside events and his music resonates the mood of the various scenes. After the film's climax in which an Italian pizza parlor is destroyed by an angry mob of African American youths, the DJ surveys the scene of carnage from his control room:

> My people, my people. What can I say? Say what I can. I saw it but I didn't believe it. I didn't believe it, what I saw. Are we gonna live together? Together, are we gonna live? This is your Mister Senor Love Daddy talkin' to you from We Love Radio, 108 FM on your dial.

The announcer's voice provides the film's coda as it floats out over the street scene of the aftermath of the firebombing of the pizza restaurant. The camera pulls back in a long shot that reveals the rhythm of street life resuming after the tragic events that have left a young man dead and racial relations frayed.

Woody Harrelson's talk show host character Charlie Frost was at least prescient if not omniscient in *2012* (2009). Operating from a ramshackle trailer, Frost warns about the world's coming demise due to a rare planetary alignment: "It's the apocalypse. End of days. The judgment day. The end of the world, my friend. Christians called it the rapture, but the, the Mayans knew about it, the Hopis, the, uh, the I Ching, the Bible." Proven correct, Frost refuses to flee to safety when given the chance to escape the pending cataclysm and meets a spectacular end when Yellowstone Park erupts in balls of fire. He reports to his listeners with a portable backpack transmitter, "I have goose bumps, people. I wish you could see what I'm seeing, people. I wish you could be here with me! Oh, baby! Hah, hah. Bring it on! Always remember, folks, you heard it first from Charlie!" The broadcast is cut short when Frost is engulfed by a wall of flames as the film's main character, Jackson Curtis (John Cusack), escapes in Charlie's trailer.

On the Air Everywhere: International Films

The DJ persona is universally popular, and air personalities, either DJs or talk show hosts, have appeared in films from every continent. DJs from various countries were seen introducing singing stars of the day in 1957's *Jamboree*, aka *Disc Jockey Jamboree*. Represented were Germany (Werner Goetze, Bayerische Rundfunk Munich; Chris Howland, KOLN Munich), Britain (Jack Jackson, ATV London; Jack Payne, BBC London), and Canada (Keith Sandy, CKEY Toronto; Gerry Myers, CKOV Ottawa). Interestingly, they were dressed much more formally than the DJs of today and, except for Jocko Henderson (the "Ace from Outer Space" in his spacesuit), all wore suits or sports jackets and ties.

Glasgow morning personality Alan "Dicky" Bird (Bill Paterson) coped with his girlfriend walking out and taking most of their possessions just before Christmas in *Comfort and Joy* (1984). Written and directed by Bill Forsyth (*Local Hero*, 1983), this charming film is surely the only movie whose plot arises from a dispute between rival Italian ice cream companies. Bird finds himself in the crossfire of a territorial war that turns violent as he struggles to resolve his personal problems. The film was nominated for a British Academy of Film and Television Arts Award for Best Original Screenplay.

Other DJ films include *Barocco* (1991, Italy; a student becomes involved with a late-night DJ); *En el aire* (1995, Mexico; the music an aging DJ plays causes him to reflect upon his former hippie lifestyle); *Love Serenade* (1996, Australia; sisters become enamored of a morose DJ who moves in next door, with fatal consequences); *Radio Samurai* (Australia, 2002; a fired DJ tries to get his job back by staging a rock concert); *The Day Silence Died* (1998, Bolivia; a DJ creates havoc in a small town by starting a radio station to let residents air their grievances with each other); *Frau2 Sucht HappyEnd* (2001, Germany; a lonely DJ looks for love on the Internet); *Halbe Treppe* (2002, Germany; a DJ has an affair with his friend's wife, changing all their lives); *Radio Star* (2006, South Korea; a sullen former rock singer is forced to become a small-town DJ as a way back to the big time); *Il mattino ha l'oro in bocca* (2008, Italy; a biopic about Italian DJ Marco Baldini); and *Radio: Love on Air* (2009, India; a DJ tries to resolve personal problems after his marriage fails).

A few foreign movies have included female DJs, such as the intriguingly titled *Fatty Girl Goes to New York* (*Cicciabomba* in its 1982 Italian release). In this film, an obese DJ is teased and taunted by other teens but wins a contest in which the prize is a trip to New York for a glamour makeover. The transformation is so complete that no one recognizes the erstwhile air personality upon her return, and she takes revenge upon her former tormentors. *Kokkuri*

(1997) was a Japanese film with an opaque plot in which teenage girls, one of whom secretly hosts a midnight radio show, unleash strange forces through a Ouija board.

At least three Indian films have featured women behind the microphone. In *salaam namaste* (2005), a DJ has an on-again, off-again relationship with a chef in Australia. *Lage Raho Munna Bhai* (2006) was a true Bollywood production set in Mumbai in which a gangster falls in love with the beautiful host of *Good Morning, Mumbai*. He wins a station contest, one of the prizes being an on-air interview with the DJ. He poses as a professor to impress her and humorous complications arise when he gets his own talk show which becomes a hit as he dispenses advice given to him by the ghost of Mahatma Ghandi. *Radio: Love on Air* (2009) was a meandering story about the personal travails of a Mumbai DJ. He continues seeing his former wife even after meeting another woman who becomes his on-air partner and later his new wife.

A Russian DJ was seen in *Piter FM* (2006). Masha (Ekaterina Fedulova) works at a Saint Petersburg FM station. While planning for her upcoming wedding she drops her cell phone, which is retrieved by a young architect, and there follows a series of missed encounters as he tries to return it. In the process, Masha rethinks her plans both for her marriage and for her life.

In 2009, another Japanese DJ appeared in *Hikidashi no Naka no Love Letter*, aka *Listen to My Heart*. Mai had a fight with her father four years before and has not spoken to him since. Now she finds out he has died, and shares her true feelings about him with her listeners, with the story of the relationship told in flashbacks. Also in 2009, the South Korean movie *Hello My Love* provided an interesting plot twist. Ho Jeong (Jo An) eagerly awaits the arrival of her boyfriend from two years of studies in France. They had plans to marry, but the DJ finds her returning fiancé is gay which, naturally, throws her life into turmoil.

Other international films have shown both men and women as talk show hosts. These include *City in Panic* (1986, Canada); *Midnight Magic* (1987, Canada); *Sexy Radio* (1987, Italy); *Frequent Death*, aka *Frequence meurtre*, aka *Murder Rate* (1988, France); *Stadtgesprach*, aka *Talk of the Town* (1995, Germany); *Magic in the Water* (1995, Canada); *99.9—The Frequency of Terror* (1997, Spain); *Les Gens qui s'aiment* (1999, France); *Entre las piernas*, aka *Between Your Legs* (1999, Spain); *El chacotero sentimental: La Pelicula* (1999, Chile); *You Belong to Me* (2001, Canada); *Rare Birds* (2001, Canada); *The Night Watchman* (2002, Canada); *First Time Caller* (2002, Canada); *Sexphone & the Girl Next Door* (2003, Thailand); *Escuela de seduccion* (2004, Spain); *Master of Airwaves* (2004, Russia); *Love Talk* (2005, South Korea); *Private Moments* (2005, Britain); *A Lover's Revenge* (2005, Canada); *3 Guys, 1 Girl, 2*

Weddings (2006, France); *A Valentine Carol* (2007, Canada); *The Aquarium*, aka *Genenet al asmak* (2008, Egypt); *Speeding Scandal*, aka *Kwasok Scaendeul*, aka *Scandal Makers* (2008, South Korea); *Radio Love* (2008, Spain); and *Pontypool* (2009, Canada).

Verisimilitude of DJ Movies

Radio movies have displayed varying degrees of realism and accuracy; as this relates to sports broadcasting is discussed in Chapter Four. Some directors seem to have done considerable research to accurately portray stations, control rooms, and the handling of equipment by the announcers and operators. Other films display rudimentary sets, and equipment operations are often not professionally depicted.

Control room and studio set designs vary widely. Some movies were shot at real radio stations or accurately replicated an actual station's facilities. These include *False Identity* (KPFK North Hollywood); *The Upside of Anger* (WRIF Detroit); *8 Mile* (WJLB Detroit); *Captive Audience* (WFNX Boston); *College Radio Sucks* (KSJS San Jose); *A Matter of Degrees* (WXOX Providence); *Ski Trippin'* (Power 99 FM Philadelphia); *The J-K Conspiracy* (KGB San Diego); and *El Vacilón de la Mañana* (Mega 97.9 New York).

In films such as *The Gladiator*, *The Warriors*, *Militia*, *Ring of the Musketeers*, *Cherish* and many others, directors have made little effort to create the ambience of an actual station, but rather suggest a control room or studio. The DJ or talk show host is seen with a microphone, audio console, and perhaps a tape machine or some other equipment in the background, often with an "on air" light and the station call letters affixed to a sign. Leaving the rest of the set dark obviates the need for a more expensive set and usually indicates a low-budget production. In some cases, however, such as *The Warriors*, the minimalism contributes to the film's ambience, in this case through the use of light and color as well as focusing the viewer's attention on the DJs mouth with extreme close-ups.

When control rooms or studios are created, they are often done so in a less than realistic fashion. In some films, such as *Ladies of the Night* and *High Freakquency*, aka *Da Station*, flashing lights in some unidentifiable piece of equipment imply an attempt to create a control room setting, but with little accuracy because the equipment does not accurately reflect that used in real stations. Large reel-to-reel tape machines are also frequently used to add realism and the reels are usually in motion, often for no apparent reason. Due to digital technology, such machines are becoming rarer in real stations. In some movies, such as *FM*, *Talk Radio*, and *Talk to Me*, studios and control rooms were constructed with such an attention to detail that a very realistic impression of an actual radio facility is created.

Probably the most telling aspect of control room equipment operations, as regards realism, is the handling of records and most films fail in their depictions of this. In the real world of radio, especially the Top 40 format, silence or "dead air" is a cardinal sin and a DJ who consistently allowed dead air between records would not long be employed. The computers and programming software used today make this a relatively rare occurrence, but many radio films were set in the days when turntables and records were the norm. To avoid dead air, records must be "cued" by manually moving them backwards and forwards on the turntable (listening carefully while doing so) until an exact amount of space is set between the needle and the first note of the music. When the turntable is then set in motion, the music begins with neither a "wow" (playing off speed while the turntable gets up to full speed) nor dead air. Cueing records properly was an art quickly acquired by neophyte DJs and an example of doing it properly was shown in *Telling Lies in America*. In *Grosse Pointe Blank*, Debi Newberry is so startled by the arrival of Martin Blank that she accidentally wows the record.

The most egregious movie error depicting the use of records is when the DJ announces a record's title, lifts the turntable arm, sets the needle on the record, then puts the turntable in motion. This is unrealistic because preparing records in this fashion would result in several seconds of dead air, which is unacceptable in professional radio. This type of turntable operation was seen in *Disk-O-Tek Holiday*, *The Warriors*, *Girls Nite Out*, *Body Chemistry 2: Voice of a Stranger*, *Love Chronicles*, and several other films. In *Bad Channels*, Dan O'Dare used an automatic turntable in which the player drops the disc onto the platter and then moves the stylus onto the disc. These players were not used in radio stations because they do not allow for the tight cueing of records to avoid dead air. *Private Parts* depicted student Howard Stern having problems cueing a record at the Boston University station, due to his nervousness at being on the air for the first time. This was not unknown in college and small market radio stations.

Other turntable misadventures were also possible, and some have been used to humorous effect in movies. One of these is the stylus sticking in a record groove, repeatedly playing the same phrase. This happens in *On the Air Live with Captain Midnight* and *Love Serenade*, a 1996 Australian film. In the latter, the DJ solves the problem with a kick of his foot to the turntable as he relaxes in his chair behind the audio console. In *Good Morning, Vietnam*, Adrian Cronauer (Robin Williams) begins to play a record at the wrong speed, another common mistake, although one usually made mostly by inexperienced announcers; he recovers with a brilliant ad lib.

In *FM*, a humorous scene depicted both the sensitivity of announcers to the dangers of dead air and a DJ's ability to ad lib his way out of trouble. Q-Sky's engineer, Bobby Douglas (Jay Fenichel), yearns to become an announcer and finally gets a chance to read the news. However, DJ Eric Swan (Martin Mull) is deep in a reverie when the newscast ends and Bobby rushes frantically into the control room:

> BOBBY: You're on! You're on! You're on the air right now, you're on, I mean on! I'm done with the news, I'm finished! It's my first broadcast! Come on, Eric...
> SWAN: Bobby, for how long? For how long...
> BOBBY: I don't know, a minute, two, three, five...
> SWAN: Okay, just shush [*Turns on mic*]. What you were just listening to, ladies and gentlemen, was side one of Marcel Marceau's new hit single. Well, it's not a hit yet, but we think it will be. And don't forget, you heard it here first on Q-Sky FM. Now back to something a little more traditional. This is Eric Swan [*Music up*].
> BOBBY: All right, it was very good. I mean, it was very, very ... it was brilliant.
> SWAN: Bobby, I can only do that once.
> BOBBY: Yes, I know that.
> SWAN: And you can only do that once.

Marcel Marceau was the famous French mime, probably the world's most accomplished pantomime artist. Radio films often contain errors which could be noted by viewers familiar with radio broadcasting. In *The Texas Chainsaw Massacre 2*, "Stretch" Brock works at KOKLA, although American radio stations have a maximum of four call letters. In *Gas*, the announcer refers to 553 WGAZ, although no such frequency exists because AM radio frequencies end in zero. In *Bare Deception*, KTLK is said to be at 440 on the dial, although AM radio frequencies go no lower than 540.

Although possibly true in earlier years, the use of cigarettes in control rooms as seen in many movies would not be allowed in real stations today. Although smoke curling around microphones is visually interesting, radio stations now adhere to the same anti–smoking policies as most other types of business and the smoking DJs or talk show hosts seen in *The Fan*, *Laser Moon*, *Statistics* and other movies would be anachronisms today. In fact, the David Allen character in *Statistics* is warned by the program director to stop smoking, but continues to do so anyway. Many stations banned smoking in control rooms and studios years ago due to its deleterious effects on the equipment, especially microphones. So, while it may serve dramatic purposes, portraying a DJ or talk show host as a chain smoker does not comport with today's radio station operations.

Since turntables and tape machines have been replaced by computers in the country's radio stations, future film depictions of DJs must necessarily change. Unless the movie is set in an earlier period, DJs will no longer be seen putting discs onto turntables and the ubiquitous background tape machines likewise will probably disappear. Numerous films of recent years, including *Piter FM, The Fan, The Accidental Husband, salaam namaste,* and *Naughty or Nice,* showed computers being used in control rooms, which contributed to the verisimilitude of the overall ambience.

Despite the technological and regulatory changes that have transformed the job of DJs in the past several years, however, the number of titles included in this chapter indicate no diminution of the DJ's popularity among film-makers in America or elsewhere. Although the screen depictions of air personalities at work will likely change as directors become more aware of the nature of radio and radio station control rooms today, it seems likely that DJs will continue to be portrayed as interesting and evocative characters.

Four

82 Years of Radio Sports Broadcasting on the Screen

Besides the elements of music and news that constitute much radio programming, two other program types should be considered in any discussion of radio films. These are sports and religion, both of which have come to assume considerable importance in American society in addition to their financial impact on both the radio and television industries. This chapter examines sports radio films, while religion is discussed in Chapter Five.

The conjunction of sports and religion is of particular interest because of the role that each plays in American society today. Whether watching games or playing them, "Americans are consuming sports on a scale unprecedented in history."[1] Some have argued that sports is a form of religion, due to their underlying commonalities: worship aspects (particularly in the television age, which has elevated sports stars to near-deity status in the eyes of many), the excitement and sense of community that each generates, the use of "sacred space" for both athletic contests and religious ceremonies, the ritualistic dress or costumes used by participants in each, and so on.[2] Indeed, religious elements of athletic contests can be traced to ancient times (contests in honor of Zeus, Apollo, and Poseidon), through the Middle Ages (jousting contests at Easter and Christmas festivals), to the nineteenth century (athletic contests between Evangelical colleges).[3] The "character building" aspect of athletic endeavors at educational institutions, often cited as a justification for spending large sums of money on athletic programs, also has religious overtones.

No one can deny the influence of religion on sports. It is particularly evident when watching athletic events on television, where one will often see players praying before football games, genuflecting after scoring touchdowns, and crossing themselves while stepping up to the plate in baseball or before and after a boxing match. In post-fight interviews, boxers often bear witness to their religious faith before answering reporters' questions. More

102

than three decades ago, author James Michener noted that numerous NFL teams carried their own chaplains with them and most held religious services before games.[4]

Evangelical religious beliefs predominate in American sports, as reflected by the formation of organizations such as the Fellowship of Christian Athletes and Athletes in Action.[5] *Sports Illustrated* writer Frank Deford coined the term "sportianity" in referring to the sports-religion nexus that "combines locker room slogans, Old Testament allusions to religious wars, athletically slanted doctrines of assertiveness and sacrifice, and a cult of masculinity, backed up by cherry-picked Bible verses prescreened to ensure that they don't conflict with sport's reigning orthodoxies."[6] *Facing the Giants* (2006), outlined in Chapter Five, epitomizes the relationship between religion and athletics: A high school football player finds that his faith in God is rewarded by success on the field, and Biblical references permeate the dialogue.

Another commonality between sports and religion is the role the media play in each. (The roots of religious broadcasting are discussed further in Chapter Five.) The various Christian radio formats today are numerous, varied, and growing,[7] and any number of televangelists reach worldwide audiences through cable and satellite television as well as terrestrial TV stations. The popularity of sports in America has been attributed as well to radio's development as a social force, since "it was with the emerging electronic medium of radio that sports really caught fire."[8]

The media have long had a symbiotic relationship with sports, especially of the professional variety, and the phenomenal popularity and growth of sports in the United States is largely a product of this relationship:

> Virtually every surge in the popularity of sport has been accompanied by a dramatic increase in the coverage provided sport by the media. Furthermore, each surge in the coverage of sport has taken place during a period in which the mass media have sharply increased their penetration into the nooks and crannies of American social life.[9]

The growth of radio parallels that of sports. WWJ Detroit claims to have aired the first radio sportscast, probably in 1920.[10] The first baseball broadcast was heard on KDKA Pittsburgh on August 5, 1921, with Harold Arlin doing the play-by-play announcing.[11] Ad hoc networks were formed for the descriptions of football games, the World Series, and boxing matches. For many years, radio fight broadcasts were recreated by announcers using information from Western Union "tickers" with crowd sounds and other ambience supplied by sound effects producers, and the same legerdemain was performed for baseball games prior to the advent of live network hookups. The creation of these tickers is demonstrated during a boxing match in *Palooka* (1934). Baseball play-by-play became a summer listening habit for millions of Americans in the 1940s when numerous stations used programs such as Mutual Broadcasting's *Game of the Day* to fill their schedules.[12]

Radio has also been crucial to local teams' efforts to forge strong bonds with their fans. The broadcasting rights of local games in most team sports are usually highly prized, especially in smaller cities and towns where large numbers of the population closely follow the high school or college teams whose games are unlikely to be seen on television. Listenership to game broadcasts also helps boost the ratings of local stations and thus makes these broadcast rights valuable as vehicles for the sale of commercial time.

A key component of successful local sports broadcasting is the announcing team, whose members usually live in the community and are extremely knowledgeable about the players and coaches of the various teams, often interacting with them outside of the games. *Possums* (1998) illustrates the importance of both a sports team and its announcer to a small town. The announcer for a high school football team continues to broadcast fictitious games after the program is disbanded, because of the team's importance to his town. Ridiculed at first by the residents, the broadcasts capture the imagination of the populace.

The rapidly increasing popularity of radio sports in the 1920s created a demand for a particular type of announcer, one who could convey a sense of excitement to the listeners. After listening to a football game on radio, James Michener concluded that "the announcer's job was to create suspense, sustain tension, and give the listener the feeling that he had participated in a game which had been decided only in the final seconds."[13]

One early sportscasting specialist was Graham McNamee, who "had a great voice and a flair for the dramatic."[14] McNamee appeared briefly as himself in the 1934 film *Gift of Gab*, and was depicted by actor Dayton Lummis in a baseball broadcast booth in *The Winning Team* (1952). Other real-life sportscasters appearing in films were Ted Husing of CBS, seen in *Mr. Broadway* (1933) and *To Please a Lady* (1950), and Bill Stern of NBC, perhaps most famous as the host of *The Colgate Sports Newsreel* on radio; he appeared in *The Pride of the Yankees* (1942) and *Here Come the Co-eds* (1945). The techniques of sports broadcasting developed for radio by these pioneers would later be adopted by generations of television announcers:

> McNamee and his partner, Phillips Carlin, came up with the two-man system of sportscasting still in use — one to call the action and the other to fill in the color commentary, spell him at the mike, and give the play-by-play guy somebody to banter with, like a couple of informed fans in the stand. McNamee and Husing influenced a generation of sportscasters — excitable enthusiasts — as well as those who came after them.[15]

But the influence of radio on sports in America went beyond the announcing styles of the first play-by-play announcers:

> Radio's experience with sports exercised a powerful influence upon early television coverage of sports.... Club owners, league commissioners, and college authorities often approached the new medium of television based on the knowledge they had gained dealing with radio broadcasts of sports.[16]

Radio thus changed both organized sports in America and the way Americans perceived sports, as would the production techniques — and vast amounts of advertising money — of television in later years. But besides providing countless hours of entertainment over the decades, radio and television transformed sports and American society itself.

Radio Sports on Film

The popularity of radio sports might have been predicted on July 2, 1921, when ringside reports of a boxing match between Jack Dempsey and George Carpentier were sent by telephone transmitters as an experiment. Given boxing's popularity in the 1920s, it should not be surprising that pugilistic play-by-play was a key plot element in one of the first movies to include a reference to radio, the 1929 silent *The Duke Steps Out*, described in Chapter One.

Athletic endeavors lend themselves well to film and the number of sports-themed movies runs into the hundreds. One reason sports is attractive to filmmakers is undoubtedly the nature of athletic competition. Many films, regardless of the sport portrayed, depict an underdog facing a heavily favored opponent or overcoming seemingly insurmountable odds to reach a championship game or match. The protagonists usually triumph or occasionally are magnificent in defeat. Such films often explicate numerous obstacles the players, either individually or collectively, must overcome to reach their goals. Many sports films celebrate the triumph of the human spirit or, in some cases, demonstrate how character flaws can lead to an athlete's demise. The downside of fame is often depicted, as is the pressure to win and the negative effects this can have on the human psyche and interpersonal relationships.

It is true, as pointed out by Nora Sayre, that the plots of most sports movies are predictable, since the star can seldom lose an important game or contest early in the film, storylines tend to be melodramatic, the dialogue is often cliched, and "most of these pictures distill a very native brand of sentimentality and brutality, an essence of syrupy sadism."[17] These comments seem especially applicable to made-for-television films, with "biopics" being particularly susceptible to sentimentality. Of course, the plots of biographical pictures hold few surprises since the careers that make their subjects attractive for the small screen are usually well known. The challenge of developing an interesting or original biographical interpretation also faces the directors of films intended for theatrical release, although they are less constrained by the advertising (commercial breaks) and time considerations that shape the structure and plot of television movies.

Sports-themed films often include radio play-by-play descriptions, usually of the most important matches or their most compelling moments. These serve several purposes. First, the announcer provides information that places the contest into context for the viewer, as in *The Express* (2008), the story of Syracuse University football star Ernie Davis. The climactic event is the 1960 Cotton Bowl game, for which the announcer sets the scene as the players take the field amidst the roar of the crowd:

> With a phenomenal record of 10 and 0, Ben Schwartzwalder's Fighting Orangemen of Syracuse, ranked number one in the nation, take the field here at the historic Cotton Bowl in Dallas to face Darrell Royal and the second-ranked Longhorns of Texas.

An announcer can also explain to the viewer the importance of what is being seen. *Glory Road* (2006) tells of the Texas Western University Miners' drive to the 1966 national basketball championship. Play-by-play descriptions explicate what is happening, as in this description that provides information the viewers may be unaware of:

> ANNOUNCER: And Jo Jo White extends the Jayhawks' lead to five.
> COMMENTATOR: But more importantly, right now Kansas has all the momentum.
> ANNOUNCER: And it looks like Coach Haskins is going to go to his bench. He's calling for Willie Cager. And Cager, of course, missed half the season with heart problems, but the Miners sure could use a lift right now.

Broadcasts can also contribute to the ambience of a movie scene. *We Are Marshall* (2006) depicts the aftermath of the 1970 plane crash that killed virtually the entire Marshall University football team. The radio announcer conveys the excitement of the touchdown that gives Marshall its only win of the 1971 season, against Xavier University: "Touchdown! Touchdown! I can't believe it! I can't believe it! Marshall has won!"

Radio descriptions often illustrate the importance to, and impact of a game on, the listening audience, as in the 1983 TV movie *Dempsey*, with Treat Williams as the heavyweight champ. Jack Dempsey's parents listen to the broadcast of his 1926 loss to Gene Tunney:

> Still trying to land the one punch that will save his fight. But Tunney won't let Dempsey near him! Dempsey is still on his feet! Ten rounds of punishment! The

champ is still standing, but it's over, ladies and gentlemen, it's over. And there's the bell. Ladies and gentlemen, we have a new heavyweight champion of the world — Gene Tunney!

Sports movies often include such home listening scenes, usually with close-ups of the faces of the listeners and of the radios to which they are paying rapt attention. This also helps convey a sense of the excitement and tension the contest is generating.

Although numerous films have included play-by-play accounts, the filmography lists only those in which the announcer is seen calling the action. In some, such as *The Mighty Ducks* (1992), play-by-play is included only as a voiceover and, as in most cases, the announcer is not named either during the film or in its credits. More recent movies have depicted televised games, with fans watching at home or some other location, often a bar. Movies with only television broadcasts have not been reviewed for this book, although they are numerous. Various sports have been portrayed on film with play-by-play narration, including boxing, football, basketball, hockey, horse racing, auto racing, wrestling, and even a bicycle race and a regatta boat race.

Probably the first movie to employ a play-by-play account of an athletic event was the 1931 Mascot Pictures serial *The Galloping Ghost*, which began with the broadcast of a college football game. Movie serials were popular in the 1920s and '30s and were shown in weekly episodes of about fifteen minutes, each episode ending with a cliffhanger to lure audiences back the following week. *The Galloping Ghost* runs for 12 chapters (226 minutes) and stars Harold "Red" Grange, known as "The Galloping Ghost" for his spectacular runs at the University of Illinois, which he led to the 1923 national championship. In the serial, Grange tries to find the members of a gambling ring that's trying to fix college games and the cliffhangers have him falling from an airplane without a parachute, driving over a cliff, and steering his car toward a head-on collision with a train. Wilfred Lucas is the sportscaster whose voice opens and closes the series. He is never seen at the games, however, as he calls the action sitting before a mike with a plain studio background, with shots of the action interspersed. In Chapter 12 of *The Galloping Ghost*, not surprisingly, the gambling ring is broken up and the hero returns to campus to don his old uniform and lead the team to victory by rushing for the winning touchdown.

Of historical interest in these early films is the types of microphones used by the announcers, as well as their styles of delivery and dress. The outfits usually include suits or sports coats and ties, and sometimes overcoats and fedoras, and the delivery styles are somewhat more flamboyant than today's audiences are accustomed to hearing. Sports films often lack realism in that the play-by-play description is not continuous as in real life. Naturally, for dramatic effect and to maintain viewers' interest, plays such as a halfback carrying the football for little or no gain, and repetitious foul balls in baseball, are seldom seen unless directly relevant to the plot. In many films, radio descriptions are heard only sporadically when the announcer is seen, but not over shots of the action, and this is particularly true of boxing movies.

The verisimilitude of announcing scenes varies greatly. In many instances the announcer sits at a microphone in front of a blank wall and the dialogue is intercut with scenes of the action (the approach taken in *The Galloping Ghost*). In more ambitious productions, a press box or announce booth is constructed for a somewhat realistic atmosphere in which the announcer appears to be at the game. In some cases, announcers are actually seen at the stadium, field, or boxing ring and these, of course, are the most believable.

In most films in which announcers are used to add an element of excitement, they are never identified on screen, nor are the stations' call letters. In some later films it is unclear whether they are announcing for radio or television, since TV cameras or monitors, used by real announcers to follow the action as the viewers see it, are not in evidence. Play-by-play broadcasts of events that would likely not be given coverage in the real world are sometimes heard, such as at amateur matches or entry-level contests that would hardly warrant such broadcasts. These scenes are usually designed to add excitement or build tension or sometimes to add a humorous note but, upon reflection, ring less than true because in reality the sporting events would not have justified the broadcasts. Of course, commercials are never heard in sports movies as they would be in actual broadcasts, and announcers never refer to taking a commercial time out. As will be seen from the following descriptions, several actors specialized in portraying play-by-play announcers and covered various types of athletic contests.

Boxing

Pugilism was popular internationally in radio's early years. In Canada, radio-equipped railway cars carried the 1927 Jack Dempsey-Gene Tunney heavyweight championship bout, and it was a big incentive to travelers when deciding which rail line to choose.[18] Later, *Friday Night Fights*, sponsored by the Gillette Company, was used to sell men's shaving products across North America; it became a weekend staple on radio and later on television until 1960.[19] Boxing was also the first sport in which Hollywood showed an interest in using blow-by-blow for a dramatic purpose such as to advance a storyline.

Boxing lends itself to cinematic depictions as well as or better than most sports since the action is virtually continuous and quite dramatic, often unrealistically so in movies. Ring action can be captured by extreme and often graphic close-ups of punches landing, heads snapping back from the impact, and sweat and blood flying off faces, bodies, and gloves. Unencumbered by uniforms or headgear, boxers' faces can display a range of emotions, especially in those fights in which the protagonist is the underdog. Tight shots of the boxers' bloody visages add realism and visual impact while close-ups of screaming fans, often punching the air, contribute to the drama or in some cases lend a comedic touch. The aural element also helps create ambience and builds tension. The sounds of leather hitting bodies, the boxers grunting, and the crowd's roar building to a crescendo at the climactic punch or knockout significantly enhance the drama of boxing films.

Boxing also offers interesting storylines: shady gamblers or promoters fixing the outcomes (a staple of many movies), an underdog protagonist battling the odds of a stacked deck or fighting to escape a deprived childhood or to fulfill dreams. In its most primal sense, a boxing movie is the story of good versus evil which usually ends in triumph for the protagonist. However, other outcomes are possible. These may include despair after defeat, as in *The Set-Up* (1949), or even death, as in *Champion* (1949). Occasionally, the protagonist realizes that the prize of winning is not worth the price (*The Ring*, 1952). Boxing movies frequently deal in stereotypes: at least one promoter will be crooked, bribes are frequently offered for the throwing of fights, the underdog protagonist is often supported by a woman — girlfriend, wife, mother — who sometimes pleads with him to "quit the game," winners of fights will seldom retire happily to enjoy the riches they have earned in the ring, and so on.

Many boxing movies of the 1930s and '40s did not include radio broadcasts, since the plots often pertained to preliminary or non–championship bouts that in reality would not have been aired. More recent films have included televised matches and several have cast real-life TV sportscasters for authenticity. Some fight films, such as *Requiem for a Heavyweight* (1962), *Rocky* (1976), and *Million Dollar Baby* (2004), have earned both critical and popular accolades.

A fight movie was among the first features to depict a sports broadcast. In *The Big Chance* (1933), "Knockout" Frankie Morgan (John Darrow) is an up-and-coming welterweight managed by crooked gambler Flash McQuaid (Matthew Betz). As the film begins, Frankie knocks out his opponent and McQuaid reveals that his plan is for Frankie to win his next several bouts in order to qualify for the championship match — which he will then throw in return for a big financial payoff from gambling wins. The plan goes well until

Frankie falls in love with Mary (Merna Kennedy), a girl who lives in the town where he trains for the big fight, and he decides not to go along with the crooked scheme. With Mary and her kid brother Arthur (Mickey Rooney) listening to the fight description at home, Frankie wins the championship with a knockout. Announcer Sam Balter, the uncredited actor, leaps into the ring with his large carbon microphone, the type most commonly used at that time:

> Hey, champ, champ. Say a few words over the air, will you, old boy? Ladies and gentlemen, the next voice that you will hear will be that of the new welterweight champion, "Knockout" Frankie Morgan!

Palooka (1934) was based on the comic strip character Joe Palooka, a rube boxer played here by Stuart Erwin; Jimmy Durante is manager Knobby Walsh. Palooka's first fight is against champion Al McSwatt (William Cagney, Jimmy's brother) and features a blow-by-blow description, a home listening scene with Palooka's family, and a post-fight ring interview with the winner, who says hello to his mother and girlfriend: "Oh, and ma, it's kinda cold here in the city. Will ya look in the bureau and see if I've got an extra pair of those long, woolen under-drawers? Well, bye, mom." The film's climactic bout is a rematch with McSwatt for the middleweight championship, which Palooka loses. It is interesting for showing the creation of the ticker by which news and sports information was sent to newspapers and radio stations.

The 1936 Republic Pictures release *Laughing Irish Eyes* began with announcer Eddie Bell (Ray Walker) doing a ringside broadcast of a poor fight which is roundly booed by the fans. The president of the Irish-American Athletic Club bets his partners that within six months he can find an Irish boxer to contend for the championship. He travels to Ireland where he discovers a handsome blacksmith (singer-bandleader Phil Regan), the possessor of a wonderful singing voice who also claims to be an amateur boxer. Needless to say, he comes to New York and, despite his lack of experience, eventually wins the championship.

In *Born to Fight* (1936), boxer "Bomber" Brown (Kane Richmond) becomes involved in a barroom brawl with gambler "Smoothy" Morgan (Jack La Rue) and hits the road under an assumed name to avoid assault charges. In Chicago he meets promising lightweight "Baby Face" Madison (Frankie Darro), whom he begins tutoring in ring techniques. Madison works his way up the ranks and is offered a title fight in Madison Square Garden, which leads to an interesting dilemma for Brown, who still faces assault and battery charges should his true identity become known. Morgan makes Madison an offer: throw the fight and the assault charges against Brown will be dropped. Blow-by-blow descriptions of the movie's opening and closing fights are included, with Donald Kerr as the announcer, although as usual only sporadically during the ring action. The championship fight is also unusual in that various sportswriters are seen furiously typing their stories as the action continues, and Madison gives a post-fight radio ring interview.

Harold Lloyd starred in another 1936 boxing movie, *The Milky Way*. The comic actor is meek milkman Burleigh Sullivan, who accidentally becomes a professional boxer. Defending his sister in a street brawl, he knocks out the middleweight boxing champ who is standing nearby. The champ's promoter takes Sullivan on as a protégé and the movie's finale is a bout for the middleweight championship. Numerous blow-by-blow descriptions of Sullivan's bouts are included throughout the film.

Kid Galahad (1937) featured a knockout (pun intended) cast of Edward G. Robinson, Humphrey Bogart, and Bette Davis. Two boxing promoters, Nicky Donati (Robinson) and Turkey Morgan (Bogart), have long been at odds. Morgan currently manages heavyweight champion Chuck McGraw (William Haade). At a party, a bellhop (Wayne Morris) Kayoes McGraw with one punch after McGraw pushes Donati's girlfriend Fluff (Davis). Realizing the bellhop may be his next title contender, Donati convinces him to turn pro, as Kid Galahad. To train, they move to Donati's farm, where live his mother and sister Marie (Jane Bryan). Naturally, Galahad and Marie fall in love, much to Donati's displeasure. Fluff has fallen in love with Galahad but, realizing that he loves Marie, leaves Donati to resume her singing career. In a warm-up publicity bout, Galahad beats McGraw's brother Sam (Bob Evans) in a fight that features a blow-by-blow broadcast as well as a "listening at home" scene with Marie and her mother. The final boxing scene is the championship bout between Galahad and McGraw, which also has a ringside announcer calling the action. (The 1962 Elvis Presley movie of the same title bore no resemblance to the original in terms of either plot or acting.)

In *Hollywood Stadium Mystery* (1938), announcer Nick Nichols (Jimmy Wallington) reports on a murder inside a boxing ring after the lights mysteriously go out and one of the fighters is found dead. Nichols subsequently and improbably provides live coverage of the police investigation by reporting from various locations before being unmasked as the killer himself.

They Made Me a Criminal (1939) starred John Garfield as Johnnie Bradfield, a New York fighter who wins the championship. After the big fight, a reporter leaps into the ring with a microphone and a humorous scene follows:

> REPORTER: Hey, Johnnie, come on, boy. Come on, you gotta say a few words to the public.
>
> JOHNNIE: Oh, I don't know what to say [*Points to microphone*]. That thing scares me.

REPORTER: Aw, come on, go ahead, say somethin.'
JOHNNIE: Are ya listenin,' Mom? I won, Mom, and there isn't a mark on me,
not a mark. I'll be home soon, sweetheart. Don't wait up for me.
REPORTER: Hey, listen, this isn't a private telephone line. Ya gotta say something
to the public.

After the fight, Johnnie passes out drunk at a party. His manager accidentally kills a reporter and leaves, after arranging evidence to make it appear that Johnnie is guilty. Fearing for his life, Johnnie flees to Arizona with a detective in hot pursuit and ends up in a home for boys, among whom are Leo Gorcey and the rest of the Dead End Kids. Trying to eke out a living, he enters a contest which pays $500 a round against a boxer who takes on all comers. Implausibly, the sideshow event is broadcast on radio with Sam Hayes as the announcer.

Victor McLaglen was former champion "Gunner" Grey in *Ex-Champ* (1939). Working as a doorman, he discovers a potential welterweight champ whom he begins to train and who falls in love with his daughter Joan (Nan Grey). His snobbish son Jeffrey (Donald Briggs) leaves the family's modest home to marry a woman he believes is a rich heiress, but who actually is as broke as he. When Jeffrey faces prison for embezzling clients' funds, Grey's protégé saves the day by winning the championship, which is broadcast on the radio. The film also includes a depiction of a Western Union ticker.

James Cagney entered the ring in *City for Conquest* (1940) as truck driver Danny Kenny, who is trying to fight his way out of the New York slums. With the support of his girlfriend Peggy (Ann Sheridan), he proves to be a winner but Peggy has other plans. An aspiring dancer, she yearns to see her name in lights and joins Murray Burns (Anthony Quinn) to form a dance team that meets with some success. Danny's career comes to an end when an opponent blinds him, and Danny is knocked out as a distraught Peggy listens on the radio. His career over, the virtually blind ex-fighter opens a newsstand and then is visited by Peggy, who has given up her dancing career to return to the man she loves.

The Leather Pushers (1940) included a woman in a position of power, something rarely seen in movies at that time. Pat Danbury (Astrid Allwyn) is a newspaper sports columnist, but the fact that she's a woman is concealed by her non-gendered name. A slick promoter signs up local fighter "Kid" Roberts (Richard Arlen), then raffles him off as a publicity gimmick at a boxing match. Danbury wins the raffle, and the remainder of the film depicts her efforts to arrange a championship bout for her fighter. Several matches are covered by radio. Character actor Andy Devine provides comic relief as Roberts' trainer.

In *Knockout* (1941), Arthur Kennedy was Johnny Rocket, a fighter who plans to get married after his next fight and quit the ring. Promoter Harry Trego (Anthony Quinn) buys Rocket's contract, unaware of his retirement plans. He becomes upset when Rocket announces he's quitting and arranges for the ex-fighter to lose his job as a trainer. Unable to find other employment, Rocket returns to the ring but when he becomes involved with attractive newspaper reporter Gloria Van Ness (Virginia Field), his wife Angela (Olympe Bradne) leaves him. Achieving success in the ring, Rocket fires Trego, who then drugs him so that he loses a bout that would have set him up for a championship match. Angela listens at home to a blow-by-blow account of the fight, as Rocket is knocked out. In addition to the radio broadcast, ringside newspaper reporters are seen dictating their copy into telephones.

The setting for *Sunday Punch* (1942) was a Brooklyn boarding house that bans women because several boxers live there. Humorous complications arise when the niece of the boarding house owner arrives and two of the boxers (Dan Dailey and William Lundigan) fall in love with her. Of course, they meet in the ring, as Tom Hanlon calls the action. *The Kid from Brooklyn* (1946) was a remake of the 1936 Harold Lloyd film *The Milky Way*, with Danny Kaye as Burleigh Sullivan, the meek milkman who accidentally becomes a boxer due to a lucky punch in a street confrontation and Jerome Cowan as the fight announcer.

Arthur Kennedy was back in the ring in 1949's *Champion*. Kirk Douglas garnered an Academy Award nomination for Best Actor for his performance in the film. *Champion* took the Oscar for Best Film Editing and was also nominated for Best Actor in a Supporting Role (Kennedy), Best Black and White Cinematography, Best Music Scoring (Dimitri Tiomkin), and Best Screenplay (Carl Foreman). *Champion*, based on a Ring Lardner short story, tells the story of Midge Kelly (Douglas) who, like his brother Connie (Kennedy), is a down-on-his-luck drifter seeking work. After an amateur brawl, Kelly is approached by boxing manager Tommy Haley (Paul Stewart), who suggests he may have a career in the ring. Following Midge's flirtation with a waitress that results in a shotgun wedding, the brothers head for Los Angeles where Midge hooks up with Haley and begins his boxing career. Several wins bring him to the attention of the media. *Champion* includes a rarity: a woman commenting on sports. A short scene features an uncredited actress portraying an announcer who gives the female perspective on Kelly:

> I met Midge Kelly this morning and I must admit that all of my preconceived ideas about prizefighters have been shattered for good and all. He's modest and even a little shy, and very handsome in a rugged, masculine way. And girls, he's unattached and fancy free.

The description of Kelly actually proves to be chimeric, and *Champion* is a study of how the corruptive power of fame and fortune can destroy relationships. In his insatiable drive for the championship and the glory it will bring, Kelly abandons the women with whom he has been involved. His quest for power also ruptures his relationship with his brother.

Mickey Rooney played the title character *Killer McCoy* (1947): New York newspaper vendor Tommy McCoy, who takes a fight on a dare and wins by a knockout. With his alcoholic father, he travels about the country trying to eke out a living while boxing on the side. Continuing to win, he comes to the attention of gambler Jim Caighn (Brian Donlevy), who buys his contract. Tommy falls in love with Caighn's daughter Sheila (Ann Blyth). The plot includes not only this romantic entanglement but also a knockout that leads to the death of an opponent (hence McCoy's nickname), and Tommy's kidnapping by rival gamblers to ensure that he loses a big match. Several blow-by-blow descriptions are included, along with home listening scenes.

In *Ringside* (1949), Joe O'Hara (Tom Brown) was a boxer blinded in the ring by "Tiger" Johnson (John Cason). Joe's brother Mike (Don Barry), a former boxer turned concert pianist, promises revenge, goes into training as King Cobra, and meets Johnson in a title match. The blinded Joe listens at home to the blow-by-blow description by the unnamed announcer (Lyle Talbot), unaware that his brother is in the ring. Midway through the bout, a gambler slips the announcer the news that King Cobra is really Joe's brother, and Joe rushes with his nurse to the arena. Mike knocks out Johnson and all ends on a happy note.

The Ring (1952) was unusual for its sympathetic portrayal of Hispanic Americans and the prejudice they faced in the U.S. at that time. Lalo Rios is Tommy Cantanios, a young man living with his family in East Los Angeles. His father Vidal (Martin Garralaga) has been laid off and explains to the family why they must return their new furniture:

> VIDAL: I thought everything was fine. But today they told me I am too old. I wasn't keeping up my end of the job. Just because I had a little headache and had to rest for awhile.
> ROSA: Oh, it's all right. You'll get another job.
> VIDAL: Where? Where will I get a job? When an Anglo becomes old, he's promoted to a boss. But when a Mexican becomes old, he is laid off.

In a subsequent scene, Tommy and his friends are refused service in a restaurant because of their ethnicity and only the intervention of a friendly white police officer defuses the situation. Against his father's wishes, Tommy takes up boxing under the name Tommy Kansas and soon becomes a local hero. His big chance comes when a last-minute illness leaves promoter Harry Jackson (Jack Elam) searching for a replacement for the main event on a boxing card in which Tommy is to appear in a preliminary bout. Unbeknownst to Tommy, his opponent Art Aragon (a real-life lightweight) has agreed to carry him for several rounds and then take the bout on a decision but, not knowing of this arrangement, Tommy goes all out to win. The fight is broadcast with Sam Balter as the announcer. Tommy is knocked out when Aragon realizes he's being double-crossed. In the end, Tommy recognizes that his future is not in boxing, and his girlfriend Lucy (Rita Moreno) stands by him. In the final scene, Tommy burns his boxing gear after seeing his younger brother emulate him and declare that he also intends to become a fighter.

Champ for a Day (1953) was the story of young heavyweight George Wilson (Alex Nicol) who is stranded in a small town when his manager fails to show up as scheduled for a promotional bout. He becomes involved with a mysterious blonde who's staying at his motel and who also has a connection with the missing manager. Of course, crooked gamblers and promoters play prominent roles as George eventually steps into the ring for a supposedly fixed climactic bout. Reid Kilpatrick is the ringside announcer for some of Wilson's fights; his on-screen shots are brief and his commentary is minimal.

The Joe Louis-Max Schmeling story was brought to the small screen in *Ring of Passion* (1978). The American Louis and the German Schmeling met twice and both fights had political and racial overtones. This TV movie starred Bernie Casey as Louis and Stephen Macht as Schmeling, and was noteworthy for its blow-by-blow descriptions in English with Dan Avey as the announcer and in German with Clement St. George at the microphone. The depiction of the first Louis-Schmeling bout (June 19, 1936) included home listening scenes of Louis' family and also Schmeling's wife Amy (Britt Ekland) in Germany. Schmeling knocked out Louis to give the American fighter his first loss and Germany was jubilant; Adolf Hitler saw the victory as evidence of Aryan superiority.

After the loss to Schmeling, Louis fought James Braddock and won the world heavyweight championship. *Ring of Passion* includes a radio description of the match, as well as a home listening scene with Louis' family. The movie's depiction of the second Louis-Schmeling fight (won by Louis with a knockout on June 22, 1938) is particularly interesting because the home listening scenes include Hitler (Barry Dennen) at a party to which Amy Schmeling has been invited. A Nazi party official sits beside the German announcer in Yankee Stadium and pulls a plug to disconnect the microphone when Schmeling hits the canvas. When the German broadcast ends abruptly, a nonplussed Hitler paces about the room trying to comprehend what must be happening in New York.

Marciano (1979) starred Tony Lo Bianco as the undefeated heavyweight champ in one of two biopics about Rocky Marciano. Although the film focuses on his relationship with his wife Barbara (Belinda Montgomery), many of his important bouts are seen with veteran ring announcer Don Dunphy providing the descriptions. Dunphy was probably the most famous radio fight announcer of all time, broadcasting many of the important matches of the 1940s and '50s, including most of Marciano's bouts.

Another 1979 effort was *The Prize Fighter*, starring Don Knotts and Tim Conway. Billed as "a knockout comedy," it had a predictable plot. A former boxer named Bags (Conway) and his manager Shake (Knotts) are approached by a gambler who arranges for Bags to resume fighting against opponents who deliberately throw the bouts. Bags advances to the championship match in which the gambler bets heavily against him. Naturally, Bags wins and the gambler is hauled off to jail. An additional comedic boost is provided by Fred Saxon as the ringside announcer who sees through Bags' efforts and adds numerous deprecating comments.

Raging Bull (1980), the story of middleweight boxer Jake LaMotta, starred Robert De Niro in an Oscar-winning performance. Directed by Martin Scorsese, it also won an Academy Award for Best Film Editing for the fight scenes, and was nominated in six other categories. Don Dunphy is heard and briefly seen with a description of one of the fights.

Treat Williams made his first television film appearance as Jack Dempsey in *Dempsey*. The 1983 movie depicted the milestones of the heavyweight champ's life, including marriages to Maxine Cates (Sally Kellerman) and Estelle Taylor (Victoria Tennant). Championship fights against Gene Tunney (Jimmy Nickerson) feature Walker Edmiston as the ringside announcer, and the film includes a home listening scene when Dempsey's distraught family hears him go down to defeat.

Rocky Marciano (1999), the second of two biopics, starred Jon Favreau, with Penelope Ann Miller as Marciano's wife and George C. Scott as his father. Both the 1979 and 1999 films included home listening scenes in which Rocky's parents follow the action in their living rooms. In 2010, *Undefeated: The Rocky Marciano Story* was the first authorized version of Marciano's career, with Rocky's brother Lou serving as adviser.

Radio blow-by-blow accounts again helped create the ambience for another take on the Joe Louis-Max Schmeling saga in the 2002 TV movie *Joe and Max*. As in *Ring of Passion*, Schmeling is presented as a propaganda tool of Hitler's regime rather than the Nazi sympathizer which the American media portrayed him as at the time. In the second of their two bouts, announcers from around the world are seen at ringside.

The Italian production *Carnera: The Walking Mountain* (2008) was the story of Primo Carnera, the first and only Italian heavyweight champion. It starred Andrea Laia as the giant who won the championship in 1933 by beating Jack Sharkey and then lost it to Max Baer the following year in an eleventh-round knockout. Radio accounts of several matches, including the Sharkey and Baer fights, have actor Christopher Troxler as the announcer. However, his delivery style and the sound quality are unrealistic, seeming more like that of a public address announcer. There are several home listening scenes, including Carnera's mother with a jubilant crowd outside a bar in his home town when he wins the championship, and his wife Pina (Anna Valle) at home when he loses to Baer.

Baseball

Baseball has been a popular film subject and the storylines of these movies are filled with dramatic moments such as game-winning home runs or other spectacular plays. Due to the nature of the game and the athletes who play it, baseball lends itself to humor moreso than boxing so that comedies, while rare in boxing movies, are common in baseball films. Radio play-by-play descriptions have been used in baseball movies as in boxing films — to create drama and add ambience — and home listening scenes are also frequently seen. As with boxing, biographical baseball films have been popular and the lives of numerous diamond greats have been portrayed. Biopics with radio descriptions include the stories of Lou Gehrig, Babe Ruth, Jackie Robinson, Grover Cleveland Alexander, "Satchel" Paige, and "Dizzy" Dean.

One of the earliest baseball movies was *Elmer, the Great* (1933), a comedy starring Joe E. Brown as Elmer Kane, a small-town hitting phenomenon who has no desire to play professional baseball, despite the pleas of a scout for the Chicago Cubs. After his girlfriend tells him she doesn't love him any more so that he'll accept the Cubs' offer, Elmer leaves Indiana for the big city, where he promptly becomes a slugging star. A problem arises when he goes to a casino and, unaware he's gambling for real, loses $5,000. The casino owner offers to cancel the debt if Elmer agrees to throw a big game. He's later suspended when the deal becomes known to the Cubs' owner but all works out well in the end and Elmer hits the winning home run against the New York Yankees. Fred Santley portrays the announcer for the World Series games.

Brown's second baseball movie in two years was *Alibi Ike* (1935), in which he plays Cubs pitching star Frank X. Farrell, who's habitually late for just about everything in his life, hence his nickname. The plot involves gamblers who threaten Ike and then kidnap him to ensure that the Cubs lose the big game. Play-by-play announcers are portrayed by actors Sam Hayes and Selmer Jackson.

It Happened in Flatbush (1942) was the story of Frank "Butterfingers" Maguire (Lloyd Nolan), who, after having been out of the game for several years, is hired to manage the Brooklyn baseball team (never identified as the Dodgers). The octogenarian owner dies shortly after signing Maguire, however, and her heirs know nothing about baseball. The plot includes Maguire's struggles to build a contending team while romancing the attractive Kathryn Baker (Carole Landis), one of the new owners. Hal Berger is the announcer for the National League championship game with St. Louis (never identified as the Cardinals), which, of course, Brooklyn wins. This movie is unusual in that the radio station is identified as WHN by a microphone flag. In most sports movies of that era, the radio stations and play-by-play announcers are not identified, and the actors portraying the announcers are usually uncredited.

One of the most celebrated sports movie of all time was 1942's *The Pride of the Yankees*, which was nominated for 11 Academy Awards, including Best Picture. Gary Cooper was nominated for Best Actor as Lou Gehrig, the New York Yankee "Iron Man" who played in 2,130 consecutive games from 1925 to 1939. Teresa Wright was nominated for Best Actress for her performance as Gehrig's wife Eleanor, and the film won the Oscar for Best Film Editing. Gehrig's career is told chronologically from his boyhood days playing stickball in the back lots of New York through the diagnosis of amyotrophic lateral sclerosis (ALS), the disease that killed him and that now bears his name. Included is the famous "luckiest man alive" speech he delivered to a Yankee Stadium crowd at the end of his career. Bill Stern is the play-by-play announcer and Babe Ruth plays himself.

Images of another New York icon came to the screen in 1948 when William Bendix portrayed the Babe in a saccharine interpretation of the slugger's career, which has been called a "perfectly dreadful bio."[20] *The Babe Ruth Story* included scenes from his childhood orphanage days while focusing on his playing career and glossing over his well-known drinking and carousing excesses. Many of his most famous games are depicted, with Mel Allen, the Yankees' long-time play-by-play voice, and Harry Wismer, another New York sportscaster, calling the action. Both are seen in the booth.

No telling of the Ruthian story would be complete without the famous "called shot" and "Little Johnny" stories and *The Babe Ruth Story* and *The Pride of the Yankees* do not disappoint. Ruth purportedly pointed to the Wrigley Field bleachers in Game Three of the 1932 World Series and, according to legend, proceeded to blast what has been called by some the longest home run ever hit in Wrigley to the designated spot. This feat is in doubt, however. Ruth himself never confirmed it and, although some film of the moment exists, it's unclear as to exactly what Ruth was doing at the plate when he made his supposed gesture. As Hollywood has never refrained from embellishing a storyline, both *The Babe Ruth Story* and *The Pride of the Yankees* present the called shot as fact.

The Babe Ruth Story combined the called shot with the "Little Johnny" Sylvester story, which actually occurred some six years before. A man asked the Yankees office if someone could help boost the spirits of his son, who was seriously ill with a blood disease. Prior to Game Four of the 1926 World Series against St. Louis, the Babe supposedly visited Johnny in the hospital and promised to hit a home run for him in the next game. He followed through on his promise and later the lad was given the home run ball and eventually made a recovery. Several years later, retired banker Johnny Sylvester produced a ball with the Babe's signature, although what actually happened on that fabled day is still unclear.[21]

In *The Babe Ruth Story*, the slugger gets a call from Johnny's doctor and drives to the boy's home in Gary, Indiana. Johnny (Gregory Marshall) lies with eyes closed, apparently lifeless, as the slugger sits by his side with melancholy music in the background.

> Johnny. Johnny, look at me. Look at me, Johnny [*Johnny opens his eyes*]. Atta boy. Now listen. I'm gonna make a deal with you, Johnny. You listen to that World Series game in Chicago over the radio this afternoon. Will you do that for me? [*Johnny nods*]. Good. And I'll sock a home run in the center field bleachers for you. That's a promise, Johnny. When you hear that over the radio, it'll be all yours. It'll have your name on it. Is it a deal? [*Johnny nods*].

At the plate, Ruth defiantly gesticulates three times to center field and deliberately takes two called strikes, then drives a pitch into the stands as the announcer screams:

> He did it! It's a home run! In the centerfield bleachers! Right where he pointed! [*Johnny laughs*]. Ladies and gentlemen, that was the most dramatic gesture ever seen on a baseball diamond! The Chicago fans are cheering their heads off for the man who just a moment ago they scorned and ridiculed!

The Pride of the Yankees added a twist to the sickly kid legend, having Lou Gehrig visit the hospital along with the Babe (here, the real thing) to visit little "Billy" (Gene Collins). Unlike the wan youth of *The Babe Ruth Story*, Billy is enthused about meeting the legend and bounces excitedly in his hospital bed. The Babe autographs a ball and promises to hit a homer into center field and, as the horde of reporters leaves the room, Billy asks Gehrig to sign the ball as well. He tells Gehrig he likes to play baseball, to which the slugger replies, "You'll play again. Billy, you know, there isn't anything you can't do if you try hard enough." Billy then asks the Iron Horse to knock out two homers for him also and Gehrig agrees, if Billy will get up and walk on his own some day. Bill Stern is the announcer for the famous game:

> The Babe's gonna try for a home run, but it's not for the crowd, I'll tell ya something the crowd doesn't know anything about. This one's gonna be for a little boy in a St. Louis hospital. An I-O-U from the Sultan of Swat to a little crippled kid. Will he pay it?

Ruth hits his home run and numerous shots show Gehrig's family, other fans, and Billy, radio at his bedside, shouting "Whoopee!" Gehrig then steps into the batter's box.

> What a duel, what a duel this is! A batting duel between the two kings of clout, Ruth and Gehrig. Each one has knocked out a home run, but Gehrig has promised two home runs for that kid in the hospital. Can he do it?

In the ninth inning, with one homer driven out and with two called strikes, Gehrig blasts a pitch into the stands, as Billy grins widely in his bed.

> Whatta ya think of that one? Two home runs in one World Series game! He's really a man! From now on, they're gonna have to spell Gehrig's name in capital letters!

On his way into Yankee Stadium on July 4, 1939, to deliver his famous farewell speech, Gehrig is stopped by Billy (David Holt), now a young man:

> I been waitin' here all afternoon because I … I had to tell you something. I just got in town today and I had to tell ya. I did what ya said. I tried hard, and I made it. Look, I can … I can walk.

Another retelling of the slugger's story came in 1992's *The Babe*, with John Goodman as the Bambino. It included play-by-play calls of several of Ruth's most famous hits, and also combined the called shot with the Little Johnny home runs. In this telling, Johnny (Stephan Caffrey), a pale and listless youth, apparently hovers near death in his hospital bed while listening to the game on the radio. The Babe's blast flies out of the stadium and smashes through a store window beside which several youngsters listen to the game on an old radio. After rounding the bases, Ruth fights his way through the frenzied crowd to the play-by-play announcer (Wayne Messmer), who conveniently sits in a nearby seat rather than the press box. Lest the viewing audience miss the significance of the scene, the Babe grabs the microphone and yells, "That was for you, Johnny! Now get well!"

The Kid from Cleveland (1949) was unusual in that a sportscaster was the main character as well as the film's narrator. Mike Jackson (George Brent) is the announcer for the Cleveland Indians and is followed into the stadium one day by Johnny Barrows (Russ Tamblyn), a runaway who is also an Indians fan. Jackson takes him home upon learning that the boy has fled his home because his father has been beating him; Jackson attempts to resolve Johnny's domestic situation. The film is unique in that real Indians such as Bob Lemon, "Satchel" Paige, Mickey Vernon, and Larry Doby have speaking roles. The diamond action includes archival footage of real games with Jackson's voice added.

The 1949 comedy *It Happens Every Spring* starred Ray Milland as bespectacled professor Vernon Simpson, who invents a liquid that causes baseballs to be repelled by wood. He takes a leave of absence from the university to talk his way into becoming a pitcher for the St. Louis Cardinals under the pseudonym King Kelly. He takes the baseball world by storm because no one can hit his pitches as the ball swerves around the bats. But he breaks his hand making a spectacular catch in the final game of the World Series and his meteoric baseball career comes to an end. Tom Hanlon and Sam Hayes are the announcers for various matches.

Broadcast descriptions of many historic games were included in *The Jackie Robinson Story* (1950), a biopic starring the Brooklyn Dodger great himself and Ruby Dee as his wife Rae. The film follows his collegiate career through his signing with the Dodgers' Montreal farm team to the breaking of baseball's color barrier with the Dodgers in 1947. It illustrates the racial abuse he suffered as well as the fortitude he displayed in not striking back at his attackers. Minor Watson plays Branch Rickey, the president of the Brooklyn Dodgers and the man responsible for signing Robinson to break baseball's color barrier.

William Bendix appeared in another baseball movie in 1950, but not as a player. In *Kill the Umpire* he is Bill Johnson, a baseball fanatic who hates umpires. Although he's continually being fired for leaving work to watch the games, to save his marriage he agrees to get a steady job by attending an umpire school (run by veteran character actor William Frawley). Johnson eventually becomes an ump for Texas minor league games where play-by-play broadcasts are done by Tom Hanlon in Western garb, including a cowboy hat.

In *Angels in the Outfield* (1951), Aloysius X. "Guffy" McGovern (Paul Douglas) was the irascible manager of the Pittsburgh Pirates, and his foul language and abrasive behavior endear him to no one, least of all his players. With his team mired deep in the standings, he is visited by an unseen angel (voiced by James Whitmore), who makes a deal with him: McGovern will clean up his act by controlling his language and behavior, in return for which the Pirates will begin winning. Things go smoothly until a young girl in the crowd sees the angels that are helping McGovern's players, and the story explodes onto the front pages. Complicating the situation is play-by-play announcer Fred Bayles (Keenan Wynn), who in an early scene is fired for uncomplimentary comments he made about the Pirates, and who undertakes a vendetta against McGovern in his weekly sportscasts. A 1994 film of the same title bore no resemblance to the original.

Two 1952 films featured diamond coverage. *The Winning Team* starred Ronald Reagan as Grover Cleveland Alexander and Doris Day as his wife Aimee. It depicts both the highs and lows of the Hall of Fame pitcher's life, including a threat of blindness and other physical ailments. Of particular interest to radio buffs is the re-enactment of Game One of the 1926 World Series between the New York Yankees and St. Louis Cardinals. Dayton Lummis is seen in numerous press box shots portraying the stentorian Graham McNamee, who died in 1942:

> Good afternoon, ladies and gentlemen. This is Graham McNamee bringing you the first transcontinental sports broadcast in history. It's the World Series coast to coast! Yankee Stadium is packed with the largest crowd to ever attend any baseball game. There are more than 61,000 fans here.

Numerous home listening scenes are included, both of Aimee and of fans crowded beside radios. When Aimee hears that Grover is being called in as a relief pitcher for the final scene, she rushes to the stadium and arrives in time for the strikeout of Yankees' second baseman Tony Lazzeri. Some baseball historians consider this one of the most dramatic moments in World Series history.

Another real-life story was translated to the screen in 1952 when *The Pride of St. Louis* chronicled the rise of Jerome "Dizzy" Dean from the backwoods of Arkansas to the pitching mound of the St. Louis Cardinals, with Dan Dailey as the hurler. His career ended by injury, Dean turns to announcing and the movie provides examples of the fractured English for which he became famous:

> And it looks like the left-handy hitters is a-goin' for 'em. Speakin' a left-handy hitters, they was only two kinds a hitters ever bothered me when I was in there, else I'd still be pitchin,' and that was left-handy hitters and right-handy hitters. Both of 'em can be mighty troublesome to a pitcher. And there they go off with the pitch, runnin' like hens a-leapin.' Looks like it's a hit and run, only Georgie McKinney, he only caught part of the ball and it was the wrong part. And there it goes ricketin' off the dugout fence for a foul and the runners are goin' back to their respectable bases. And so it's McKinney still at bat for the Brownies. Georgie always reminds me in that batter's box like I remind myself of me when I was pitchin'— very confidential at all times. Last time Georgie got on base, he mighta scored on Hefner's single if he'd a slood, but he didn't and he was out by a half er step. Well, what do you know, Georgie swang and slapped the breeze.

Guy Prosper's screenplay for *The Pride of St. Louis* was nominated for an

Academy Award. Dailey appeared in another baseball movie the following year when he played Larry Cooper in *The Kid from Left Field*. A former player, "Coop" now sells peanuts to the crowd but is fired after an argument with the concessions manager. His son Christie (Billy Chapin) decides to get his father's job back and runs into Marian Foley (Anne Bancroft), the secretary of the team's owner Fred F. Whacker (Ray Collins), who arranges for him to meet with Christie. The boy makes such an impression with his knowledge of the game, gleaned from his father, that Whacker gives him a job as a batboy. As he passes his father's advice along to the players, the team begins to win, and the nine-year-old is named as manager. Numerous play-by-play descriptions are included.

Roogie's Bump (1954) began with narration over street scenes of Brooklyn: "Hello, friends. I'm a sportscaster and I want to tell you about something strange that happened that I wouldn't have believed if I hadn't seen some of it with my own eyes." The voice is that of actor Tedd Lawrence, who is both the film's narrator and the sportscaster who calls the action on the field. The titular Roogie is Remington Rigsby (Robert Marriott), a boy who loves baseball. His schoolmates won't play with him, so his grandmother consoles him by giving him a baseball card featuring old-time star "Red" O'Malley, with which Roogie tries to bribe his way onto the team. Again rebuffed, Roogie meets O'Malley (William Harrigan) in the park and the oldtimer comforts him by patting him on the arm. Roogie soon notices a bump there and finds that he has developed amazing arm strength which he can use to fire a ball through a brick wall and topple statues. Roogie catches the attention of the Brooklyn Dodgers when he catches a fly ball and fires it back onto the field; he is soon a phenomenon and begins pitching for the Dodgers. The film has cameo appearances by Dodgers stars such as Roy Campanella and Carl Erskine. Eventually, O'Malley returns to tell Roogie he's an angel who exceeded his powers by giving the boy such supernatural strength, and he must take it away. Roogie then becomes the team's mascot and the Dodgers win the pennant without his help. Tedd Lawrence (not given an on-air name in the film) calls the play-by-play for the Dodgers' games.

A 1979 TV remake of *The Kid from Left Field* starred Robert Guillaume as Larry Cooper and Gary Coleman as his son Jackie Robinson "J.R." Cooper. This time the team is the San Diego Padres and Ed McMahon is the owner who gives J.R. the chance to manage the club. Jerry Coleman, former Yankees second baseman and Padres radio voice, calls the action for various games, including the Padres' World Series win.

Don't Look Back: The Story of Leroy "Satchel" Paige (1981), another TV movie, described the career of the legendary Negro League pitcher, with Louis

Gossett, Jr., in the title role. The play-by-play announcing is not particularly convincing, with Taylor Lacher as the unidentified sportscaster using a style that seems as much public address announcing as radio play calling.

Roy Scheider was Detroit Tigers slugger Billy Young in *Tiger Town* (1983). The Walt Disney film, made for home video, tells the story of Alex (Justin Henry), an avid baseball fan whose father Buddy (Ron McLarty) is out of work. Despite his problems, Buddy tells Alex that anything is possible if you only believe strongly enough. When Buddy dies, Alex sneaks out of school to go to the games and fervently wishes for Billy Young to break out of his slump. Naturally, each time Alex clenches his hands, closes his eyes, and wishes hard, Billy hits a home run. Soon his slump is broken and the Tigers go on to win the American League pennant. Real-life Tigers' broadcaster Ernie Harwell does the announcing and then-manager Sparky Anderson also appears, as himself.

The year 1989 brought the first movie in the *Major League* trilogy. The Cleveland Indians' new owner Rachel Phelps (Margaret Whitton) tries to field the worst possible team in order to draw the smallest possible crowds, thereby breaking her stadium lease and allowing her to relocate the franchise to a warmer climate. A ragtag group of wannabe and never-was players is assembled, including characters portrayed by, among others, Charlie Sheen, Tom Berenger, Corbin Bernsen, and Wesley Snipes. Describing the on-field action is the voluble Bob Uecker as Harry Doyle. Uecker was the real-life announcer for the Milwaukee Brewers and a 2001 inductee into the Baseball Hall of Fame. The players catch wind of the owner's nefarious plot and, naturally, begin playing inspired baseball and go on to win the division title, although losing to the Chicago White Sox in the American League Championship Series.

The *Major League* series continued in 1994 with *Major League II*, which included many of the actors from the original, as well as Bob Uecker reprising his Harry Doyle persona. *Major League: Back to the Minors* completed the series in 1998 without many of the name actors of the preceding films, but with Uecker behind the microphone to describe the on-field antics. His colorful commentary was a highlight of the *Major League* films for many moviegoers: "He struck him out swinging and the Hogster is bringing the heat. Throwin' gas. Tossin' aspirin. Blowin' smoke. Zinging BBs. Firing missiles. Zipping darts. Threading the needle."

Interestingly, *Mr. 3000* (2004), which featured Bernie Mac as a member of the Brewers, did not include Uecker, but rather prominent TV sportscaster Dick Enberg as the play-by-play voice, although it is unclear whether he's doing radio or television broadcasts, and his screen appearances are brief.

Summer Catch (2001) was both a love story and a baseball story. Each summer the country's best college players are asked to participate in the Cape Cod Baseball League. Ryan Dunne (Freddie Prinze, Jr.) is one of the few local boys ever to be invited but things go awry when he meets Tenley Parrish (Jessica Biel), a rich girl whose family vacations on Cape Cod every year and whose father adamantly opposes her involvement with the locals. Veteran broadcaster Curt Gowdy does the announcing for several games on WQRC radio from a flatbed trailer.

The HBO movie *61** (2001) chronicled the historic 1961 chase by Roger Maris to break Babe Ruth's home run record of 60 singles in a season. Directed by Billy Crystal, it starred Barry Pepper and Thomas Jane as Roger Maris and Mickey Mantle respectively. Christopher McDonald, playing the late Mel Allen, did the sportscasting. Joe Grifasi portrayed his announcing sidekick, ex-Yankee Phil Rizzuto, who was the play-by-play voice of the Yankees for several decades. Several scenes included their on-air banter in the booth.

Sugar, a 2008 HBO co–production, was the story of Miguel Santos (Algenis Perez Soto), a young man discovered by Kansas City Royals scouts in the Dominican Republic. He begins his pro career with the Quad City Swing in Bridgetown, Iowa, and the film depicts his struggles to adapt to a bewildering foreign environment while trying to prove himself on the mound. The play-by-play descriptions are realistic, the Quad City press box is cramped, and the broadcast equipment is typical of that used in such settings (both press box and equipment appear to be the facilities of the actual Quad Cities broadcast team). Included is a post-game interview by the play-by-play announcer, an event common in real life but unusual in a sports film. Santos is ultimately unable to handle the pressures and flees the team for New York City.

Football

Despite the sport's violence, football seems to lend itself to comedy as well as baseball does, at least in the eyes of Hollywood, and numerous football films have shown a lighter touch. The serial *The Galloping Ghost* brought football to movie screens in 1931 and the following year *The All-American* included numerous play-by-play scenes and a brief shot of a sideline reporter describing action at a college game. In this story, a star player (Richard Arlen) graduates and then returns to take the field as a member of an all-star team in order to play against his younger brother (John Darrow) with whom he has been arguing and who has replaced him on the college team. Several players of the day (including Ernie Nevers) are in the cast, and legendary coach Glenn "Pop" Warner also makes a brief non-speaking appearance. Andy Devine, a real-life football star at Ball State University before he found fame as a sidekick in numerous Western movies and TV shows, provides comic relief as one of the players.

Also in 1932, *The Sport Parade* opened with a play-by-play description of a Dartmouth-Harvard game with Robert Benchley as the bumbling announcer. He gets the scores and even the teams wrong and mangles subsequent game descriptions. The story is about the relationship between two senior Dartmouth players, Sandy Brown (Joel McCrea) and Johnny Baker (William Gargan). After graduation they end up working together as newspaper sports reporters but their relationship disintegrates when they fall in love with the same woman. After quitting his job, Brown turns to professional wrestling and the championship match again features Benchley stumbling through the bout's introduction.

College Coach (1933) was an interesting early look at the relationship between athletics and higher education. Pat O'Brien is James Gore, a football coach who will do almost anything to win, including allowing star players to cheat on exams. He is hired by Calvert College, which faces financial challenges and whose football team has a long losing record. The board of trustees, believing that a winning team will pack the stadium and generate enough money to salvage the school's academic programs, lures Gore away from another school. The film explores how Gore's drive for success on the field damages his relationship with his wife Claire (Ann Dvorak) and how his passion to win leads him to compromise all of his ethical principles. Sam Hayes is the announcer for numerous games.

In *Gift of Gab* (1934), Edmund Lowe is "Gift of Gab" Gabney, who calls the action for a college football game on WGAB. Fired when he argues with and then slugs the alumni president after the game, he publicly declares he will broadcast the next week's game despite being barred from the stadium. He attends the game as a spectator and surreptitiously sets up a microphone through an unexplained connection with the transmitting equipment and does the promised play-by-play. Graham McNamee, the famous early sportscaster, makes a cameo appearance in which he introduces Gabney from the announce booth and lets him continue broadcasting from the stands. Gabney then wraps up the show from the booth, but why McNamee, who is referred to in the film as one of radio's stars, would let Gabney proceed with such a broadcast is both unclear and implausible.

Pigskin Parade (1936) was a musical comedy starring Jack Haley, Patsy Kelly, Stuart Erwin, and Judy Garland (her second screen appearance). Haley is Winston "Slug" Winters, a coach who heads west to Texas State University, a small school in the boondocks. He and his wife Bessie (Kelly) arrive to find their living quarters are in the dormitory and the team is virtually bereft of talent. Meanwhile, unbeknownst to them, Yale University's Board of Regents decides it's too risky for its team to play Michigan the week before the big Harvard game, so they choose instead a team they think will be an easier opponent — the University of Texas. Bumbling assistants, however, mistakenly call Texas State (enrollment 700) in Plainville.

While the game is being arranged, Bessie Winters injures her husband's star player while showing him how to block. Desperate, "Slug" and Bessie go on a talent hunt and discover a hayseed (Erwin) who can toss a melon with deadly accuracy and whose sister (Garland) urges him to take the offer of a free education by attending Texas State. The team arrives for the big game against Yale wearing woolly chaps and cowboy hats, and wins the game on the strength of their hayseed quarterback's long passes. The match features play-by-play accounts with Sam Hayes as the uncredited announcer. Stuart Erwin was nominated for an Oscar for Best Actor in a Supporting Role for his performance as the bumpkin quarterback. He had a long career in film and television and later had his own TV show which ran for five years in the early 1950s. Jack Haley starred again with Judy Garland as the Tin Man in *The Wizard of Oz.*

Over the Goal (1937) was interesting not for its plot but rather for the announcing. A college football star risks injury by playing in a big game, and is kidnapped by supporters of the opposing team to keep him off the field. Sam Hayes is one of the few announcers to identify himself during the broadcast, using his real name. His descriptions are also heard over the action, rather than being intercut with shots of the field, as is usually the case, so that the movie achieves a higher level of realism than most such play-by-play scenes.

A woman was the star player in the 1938 comedy *Hold That Co-ed.* Rusty Stevens (George Murphy, future California governor) is a former All-American quarterback who arrives to coach tiny State College, which is verging on bankruptcy and lacks basic equipment and even footballs. Stevens leads a group of students to the capital to protest to Governor Gabby Harrigan (John Barrymore), who is persuaded by a near-riot in his office that the key to success in the next election is to turn State College into a football powerhouse so he can speak to the crowds of fans at their games. He orders a new stadium seating a hundred thousand to be built within three weeks and quickly arranges for the team to play Louisiana, Yale, and Princeton. Co-ed Lizzie Olsen (Joan Davis) turns out to be a better player than many of the men assembled for practice, with a particular knack for kicking long field goals.

Her final-play kick ties the game against Louisiana (Douglas Evans is the announcer). After victories against Yale and several other teams, State College meets cross-town rival Clayton State in a grudge match. Sam Hayes is the announcer in a humorous setting when a windstorm descends on the field. Wind whips through the press box and forces him to clutch his papers and fedora as he calls the action.

The Cowboy Quarterback (1939) was a remake of 1933's *Elmer, the Great*, with the action playing out on the football field rather than the baseball diamond. A scout for the Chicago Packers signs small-town star running back Harry Lynn (Bert Wheeler) to play professionally. Lynn visits a gambling joint and, unaware he's playing for real money, runs up a $5,000 debt. He's then blackmailed into throwing the big game against the California Ramblers so the gamblers can cash in by betting on the Ramblers. The Packers' owner yanks Lynn from the game after being apprised of the situation, but again all ends happily and Lynn comes back in to score the winning touchdown. Reid Kilpatrick is the announcer for the crucial game.

Rise and Shine (1941) was based on James Thurber's *My Life and Hard Times*. College star Boley Bolenciecwcz (Jack Oakie) meets every stereotype of dumb football players, including a propensity for sleeping anywhere. The president of Clayton College is given an ultimatum by the board of trustees: win every game or be fired. This means keeping Boley awake and on the field. An inane plot includes numerous songs by dozens of cheerleaders in tribute to Bolenciecwcz ("He's the man who never quits, on the bench he never sits!"), a kidnapping by gangsters, one of whom (Milton Berle) whinnies whenever he gets excited, and a championship game in which Boley falls asleep on the field. Included is a play-by-play broadcast and a rare sideline report from the field.

Broadcasts of both football and hockey games were included in *I'll Tell the World* (1945). Gabriel "Gabby" Patton (Lee Tracy) is watching a football game when the KPQ play-by-play announcer wanders into the stands to get reactions from the fans. Patton grabs the mike and launches into an impromptu and non-stop description of the action. The station's owner and daughter are so impressed that they hire Patton, who later broadcasts a hockey game and another football game. The film's storyline includes Patton's attempts to land his girlfriend a singing gig at the station, including a halftime performance with the band during another broadcast.

In the 1949 comedy *Father Was a Fullback*, Fred MacMurray was college coach George Cooper, who's trying to deal with both the pressure from an alumni association unhappy with the team's performance and the behavior of two precocious daughters. Complications arise when Cooper tries to boost his eldest daughter's sagging self-esteem by hiring a gas station attendant to ask her for a date under a fake name. Meanwhile, a local high school star decides to attend Notre Dame, and Cooper's state university team continues to lose. Many of the games are broadcast, with the ubiquitous Tom Hanlon as the announcer, and Cooper's various problems are resolved before the movie's final fade to black.

Tony Curtis starred in *The All American* (1953) as a star quarterback who switches colleges and has a hard time being accepted at his new school until he tries out for the team and begins to lead them to victories. Bill Baldwin is the announcer for several games.

Some years passed before another football movie included either radio scenes or play-by-play announcing. In the aforementioned *Possums* (1998), Will Clark (Mac Davis), a hardware store owner in a small Oklahoma town, doubles as the radio announcer for the Nowata Possums high school football team. The movie opens with a young Will emulating the announcer he will become, moving toy football players about and using a kitchen utensil as a microphone. Flashing forward to the present, Clark strives to help maintain the sense of community that the team generates by broadcasting fictitious games after it's disbanded due to its lengthy losing record and lack of fan support. Despite scorn and ridicule from both the fans and former players, Clark continues broadcasting and slowly builds a following. The real high school champions eventually agree to play the make-believe team. *Possums* provides a captivating look at the importance of high school football in small-town America.

Friday Night Lights (2004) was another tale of a high school football team and the passion for the sport that is the focus of life in many small towns, particularly in the South and Southwest. Based on the book of the same title by H.G. Bissinger, it's the story of the Permian Panthers of Odessa, Texas, and the hunger of its citizens for the team to win the state championship. Billy Bob Thornton is Coach Gary Gaines and Connie Britton is his wife Sharon, who also struggles to cope with the daily pressures of winning. Filmed in a docudrama style, *Friday Night Lights* uses radio to illustrate the importance of football to the town. Over the opening credits, a Mojo Radio talk show is heard and the topic is, of course, the high school team. Play-by-play descriptions of various games are heard in the movie and the announcers are briefly seen in a few scenes. Throughout, the talk show illustrates the fans' feelings about both the coach and the team's performance, especially after losses. Gaines listens to the show in his car as callers excoriate him and the fact that the star running back was injured on a meaningless play. In 2005, the movie spawned a popular NBC-TV series with the same title.

We Are Marshall (2006) was the saga of Marshall University's football team. On November 14, 1970, a plane crash killed virtually all of the Thundering Herd and its coaches, as well as many fans. The movie depicts the crash's devastating impact on the community of Huntington, West Virginia, and the efforts by both the university and the town to rebuild the team and numerous game broadcasts are included.

The Ernie Davis story was told in *The Express* (2008), with Rob Brown as the Syracuse University running back, the first African American player to win the Heisman Trophy as the nation's top collegiate football player. The film illustrates the racism faced by black athletes in the late 1950s and early '60s on many campuses, and includes radio descriptions of numerous games. Davis was drafted by the Cleveland Browns but died of leukemia before playing a single NFL game. *Leatherheads* (2008) was a comedy about the formative years of the NFL, when crowds were sparse and teams struggled to survive. Directed by and starring George Clooney, it includes a play-by-play account of a game between Chicago and Duluth, Minnesota, which fielded an NFL team in the early 1920s. Patt Noday is the Chicago radio announcer.

Basketball

A few films included play-by-play descriptions of basketball games, although most of the classic basketball movies did not. *Here Come the Co-eds* (1945) was an Abbott and Costello farce in which bumblers help save a women's college from bankruptcy by staging a basketball game with a rival school. The announcing is done by Bill Stern, the famous voice and host of *The Colgate Sports Newsreel*. He sits at a microphone before a plain background as he comments on the action, and these shots are intercut with scenes from the basketball court.

The Harlem Globetrotters (1951) was essentially a paean to the famous team. The sketchy plot entails a talented college player making the team but needing to learn many lessons about life and respecting others. The film is comprised mainly of scenes in which the Globetrotters display their court wizardry against numerous opponents, including the Boston Celtics. The real Globetrotters play themselves and Thomas Gomez is coach Abe Saperstein. Radio play-by-play of all the games once again includes Sam Balter and Tom Hanlon. The movie also includes sportscasts in which the achievements of the team are discussed by the announcer. This is rare in sports movies, as radio commentary is usually limited to play-by-play descriptions, and sportscasts or interviews are seldom seen. The film is also noteworthy for an appearance by Dorothy Dandridge as Ann Carpenter, the girlfriend and then wife of the college phenom Billy Townsend (Billy Brown).

The 1982 slasher flick *Girls Nite Out*, described more fully in Chapter Two, begins with a basketball game involving the hometown Dewitt University team. Charlie Kaiser, the DJ who airs the scavenger hunt clues and takes calls from the bear-suited killer, does the play-by-play. Al McGuire, former Marquette University men's coach, Hall of Fame inductee, and broadcaster, appears in a cameo role as Coach Kimble, whose Dewitt team is victorious in the film's opening scene.

Glory Road (2006) told the story of the 1965–66 national championship season of the Texas Western Miners. New coach Don Haskins (Josh Lucas), knowing he can't win with the talent he has inherited, undertakes a national recruiting drive to find the best players he can persuade to come to the small rural university and ends up fielding the country's first all-black starting lineup. The movie depicts the racial taunting and culture shock the players, many of whom are urban youths, must overcome to eventually form a cohesive unit that beats Kentucky's legendary coach Adolph Rupp (Jon Voight) in the championship game. Play-by-play descriptions are used throughout the film to inform viewers of the significance of each move on the court. The Texas Western win changed college basketball forever, because Rupp, seeing that he could not continue to win championships with all-white teams, began to recruit talented black players and the college game was finally integrated on a national scale. In 1967, Texas Western became known as the University of Texas at El Paso.

Hockey

Hockey was never much of an audience-grabbing sport in America outside of the upper Midwest and the Northeast until recent years, but it has been the subject of a handful of radio movies. In *Hell's Kitchen* (1939), a judge gives racketeer Buck Caesar (Stanley Fields) a suspended sentence if he can remain out of trouble for a year. He goes to work for a boys' home and finds it's being used for nefarious purposes by its operator, Hiram Krispan (Grant Mitchell), who is taking money donated to the school to line his own pockets. The youngsters include Leo Gorcey and the other Dead End Kids. Caesar decides to use his strong-arm tactics to clean up the school and forms a hockey team that plays an orphanage squad sponsored by a rival racketeer. The game is broadcast on radio with Reid Kilpatrick doing the play-by-play. Ronald Reagan has a minor role as Caesar's lawyer Jim Donahue.

The aforementioned hockey game of *I'll Tell the World* (1945) included a brief play-by-play description on KPQ by "Gabby" Patton. At home, the station owner's daughter Marge (June Preisser) listens to Patton's broadcast and mimes the rink action by running around the living room with a long-handled fireplace ash pan for a stick. Patton wanders into the stands with a microphone to get comments from the fans before introducing his girlfriend, who sings with an orchestra that materializes on the ice.

Also in 1945, MGM released *It's a Pleasure* to cash in on the popularity of three-time Norwegian Olympic figure skating champion Sonja Henie. The film opens with a broadcast of a hockey game. A fight breaks out and star player Don Martin (Michael O'Shea) slugs a referee and is banned from the game for life. The between-periods entertainment is provided by an ice-skating revue, the star of which is Chris Linden (Henie). Secretly in love with Martin, she gets him a job performing with the revue. The plot includes numerous romantic entanglements and several scenes in which Henie displays her skating prowess. The off-screen announcer for the opening hockey scene is again Tom Hanlon.

Hanlon was heard once more in *White Lighting* (1953), in which a gambling syndicate bribes players to throw games. When team owner Jack Monohan (Steve Brodie) hires his childhood friend Mike Connors (Stanley Clements) as a player, the Red Devils start winning. Connors later agrees to take bribes but during the championship match an encounter with a young fan causes him to change his mind and he inspires the team to win the big game. Besides Hanlon's game descriptions, the film features Lee Van Cleef as a member of the gambling syndicate. Van Cleef would find later fame as a movie bad man and Western star.

One of the most highly acclaimed sports movies of all time, both by critics and the ticket-buying public, was *Slap Shot*, George Roy Hill's zany 1977 look at the world of professional hockey. Paul Newman was Reggie Dunlop, the playing coach of a minor-league team on the verge of financial extinction. The film contains several memorable scenes with Andrew Duncan as sportscaster Jim Carr, including this from Carr's interview show:

> DUNLOP: I have a personal announcement, though. I'm placing a personal bounty on the head of Tim McCracken. He's the coach and chief punk on that Syracuse team.
> CARR: A bounty?
> DUNLOP: Yeah. A hundred dollars of my own money for the first of my men that really nails that creep. Uh, that's eight o'clock at the War Memorial, Syracuse and the all-new Charlestown Chiefs.

Besides Newman's portrayal, the highlights of the film were the shenanigans of the Hanson Brothers (real-life players Jeff Carlson, Steve Carlson, and David Hanson), a trio of roughnecks who leave a trail of carnage on the ice.

Two productions attempted to replicate the film's box office popularity. *Slap Shot 2: Breaking the Ice* (2002) featured Jake Edwards, Fred Keating, and Ted Friend as announcers and *Slap Shot 3: The Junior League* (2008) included a father-son announcing team (Eric Keenleyside as Dickie Dunn, Jr., and Brett Kelly as Dicky Dunn III). Neither of the latter films displayed the wit or insight of the original, although both starred the Hanson Brothers reprising their destructive antics.

Other Sports

Besides baseball, boxing, football, and hockey, play-by-play broadcasts of various other types of sports events have been seen on film. Two wrestling matches were described in *The Sport Parade* (1932), one by actor Robert Benchley as an uncredited announcer. Benchley was also briefly seen covering a six-day bicycle race in the same film, despite a problem with staying awake in a scene designed for comic relief.

Most auto racing movies have used the public address track announcers to provide descriptions of the races and also add excitement, although some films have included radio broadcasts. Howard Hawks directed *The Crowd Roars* (1932) with James Cagney as race driver Joe Greer and Ann Dvorak as his girlfriend. Greer tries to dissuade his younger brother Eddie (Eric Linden) from also becoming a driver. The brothers clash on the track, then become partners, but break up due to Eddie's immature behavior. Joe is haunted by the racing death of his friend Spud Connors (Frank McHugh), for which Joe is blamed. The film's tear-jerking climax comes at the Indy 500 when Eddie is injured and Joe comes out of the stands to overcome his personal demons to win the race. Although many of the race descriptions are done by track announcers, including Sam Hayes, the climactic race is described on radio by John Conte.

The Crowd Roars was remade in 1939 as *Indianapolis Speedway*, directed by Lloyd Bacon, with Pat O'Brien as Joe Greer and John Payne as Eddie. Frank McHugh reprised his role as Spud Connors, with Wendell Niles, Sam Hayes, and John Conte as the announcers for various races. Both movies were produced by Warner Brothers.

In *To Please a Lady* (1950), Clark Gable was driver Mike Brannan, who becomes involved with newspaper reporter Regina Forbes (Barbara Stanwyck). The film's climactic race is again the Indy 500, for which the announcer is the famous sportscaster Ted Husing, but the depiction of the race broadcast is unclear. While Husing seems to be the track announcer and his voice is heard through the grandstand loudspeakers, he also sits beside a WMGM radio microphone (the movie was produced by MGM). This movie is also interesting for its inclusion of television broadcasts of some of Brannan's races, becoming one of the first films to depict TV coverage of a sporting event.

Of the many horse racing movies produced over the years, only a handful have included radio commentary, as track announcers usually fill the play-by-play role to add excitement. *From Hell to Heaven* (1932) was a comedy in which the lives of various residents of a hotel are affected by the results of a horse race they have all bet on. One of the residents is Charlie Bayne (Jack Oakie), a fast-talking singer and songwriter who thinks he's ready for the big time (but can't get anyone in New York to listen to him). His radio opportunity comes when he's given the chance to announce for the big horse race. The station manager warns him against singing on the air, but when the race is over he says, "Maestro, do your stuff," waves his hand and an off-screen orchestra begins playing as he croons into the mike.

Henry Fonda took a turn behind the microphone in one of his earliest film appearances. In *Spendthrift* (1936), Fonda was Townsend Middleton, a profligate playboy who discovers that his inheritance has dwindled to nothing. In order to keep his creditors from taking his prize possession, the racing horse Black Mamba, he gives the filly to her trainer, "Boots" O'Connell (Pat Paterson), who in turn sells the horse to her Uncle Morton (George Barbier). With no inheritance money to support himself, Middleton turns to sports announcing and convinces a railroad owner to sponsor his broadcasts by ad libbing an audition about honesty in sports. In a home listening scene, "Boots" and Uncle Morton hear Middleton wrap up the Army-Navy football game and promote his next broadcast, "the big handicap." Of course, Black Mamba wins the race. Middleton seems to be as much track announcer as radio broadcaster; following the race he works his way through the crowd with his microphone, interviews Uncle Morton and then proposes to "Boots" on the air.

The Story of Seabiscuit (1949) included broadcasts of some of the great horse's matches, but with none of the flair of the broadcasts given by the William H. Macy character in many years later. *Seabiscuit* (2003) featured a memorable performance by Macy as announcer Tick Tock McGlaughlin, who adds some extra entertainment with various sound effects devices.

The 1944 classic *National Velvet* told the story of 12-year-old Velvet Brown (Elizabeth Taylor) and her love for a horse that eventually leads her to enter and win England's Grand National Steeplechase. Radio coverage of the race is provided by a team of announcers who are uncredited but presumably with the BBC, although not explicitly identified as such: "A girl, ladies and gentlemen! A bit of a girl, clutching the neck of a bandy-legged outsider, streaks across the line to win the greatest race in turfdom! A girl wins the

Grand National!" Also starring Mickey Rooney, *National Velvet* won two Academy Awards, for Best Supporting Actress (Anne Revere as Velvet's mother) and Best Editing. In 2003 it was entered into the National Film Registry by the National Film Preservation Board.

Another type of racing was the subject of *Freshman Love* (1936). The Tri-State Regatta boat race is the big event on the campuses of Billings College and Chase College and the Billings coach uses the school president's beautiful blonde daughter to entice top rowing athletes. Almost certainly the only radio broadcasts of regatta races ever seen on film are done by Dick Purcell, although shots of the actor in the broadcast booth are intercut with racing scenes and his voice is not heard describing the action as seen on the screen.

While perhaps not classified as an athletic event, a match of a different type was described in *All American Chump* (1936). This time it's bridge and perennial screen hick Stuart Erwin is Elmer Lamb, a meek bank clerk who turns out to be a whiz at the card game. He eventually becomes involved with gangsters and plays in a week-long 50 rubber match that is broadcast on radio. Harry Lash is the announcer.

Sports Talk Radio

In 1964, Bill Mazer began hosting the country's first sports talk phone-in show on WNBC-AM New York. The Enterprise Radio Network, America's first all-sports network, started in 1987 but folded within a year. WFAN-AM New York (replacing WHN) became the country's first local all-sports talk station in 1987 and ESPN Radio, which would become the dominant voice in sports talk radio, started in 1992.[22] Listeners today have access to sports talk radio from terrestrial stations affiliated with networks such as ESPN Radio or Fox Sports Radio, and from Sirius XM satellite radio. The success of the sports talk genre has been a phenomenon in radio's recent history.

Besides play-by-play announcers and color commentators, sports radio personalities generally fit into one of three categories: talk show hosts who are usually expected to be opinionated in order to generate reactions from listeners, reporters who report from the scene of the action, and anchors who read sportscasts or sports updates, usually without editorial comment. Some of the air personalities have playing experience at either the professional or collegiate level, although many do not. Sports talk shows often employ multiple hosts who frequently disagree in order to provoke listeners and also to help create a "guy talk" ambience to encourage listener participation. A few movies have included talk show scenes.

In *Eddie* (1986), Whoopi Goldberg was limo driver and New York Knicks fanatic Edwina "Eddie" Franklin. She calls a talk show hosted by real-life ESPN personality Chris Berman while unknowingly chauffeuring "Wild Bill" Burgess (Frank Langella), the Knicks' new owner. Through a series of unbelievable plot twists, Eddie becomes the team's coach and, predictably, chaos ensues. Long-time basketball announcer Marv Albert calls the action for various games on radio from courtside.

Ten years later, *The Fan* starred Robert De Niro as psychotic baseball fan Gil Renard and Wesley Snipes as Bobby Rayburn, a slugger who has rejoined the San Francisco Giants. Ellen Barkin is tough-talking Jewel Stern, co-host of KNBR's *Jewel & Bernie* talk show, with Kurt Fuller as Bernie. Renard's obsession with the Giants and with Rayburn in particular spirals out of control and Stern finds herself on the field during the violent climax. Barkin is convincing as Stern and dominates her somewhat meek partner Bernie when taking calls.

Naughty or Nice was a 2004 Hallmark television movie starring George Lopez as Chicago sports talk personality Hank "The Bleacher Bum" Ramiro, whose trademark slogan is "Get outta a here, ya bums." Known to his fans as "The Captain of Cruel" and "The Master of Mean," his schtick is insulting callers with rejoinders such as "Come back when you can form a sentence." Although a good man at heart, his sarcastic on-air comments embarrass his wife and daughter. His life is changed by an encounter with Michael (James Kirk), a teenager suffering from cancer. Ramiro makes a deal with him to be nice to everyone and turns his show into a feel-good forum. However, while Michael's health improves and Chicago's teams begin to win, Ramiro's ratings drop. Faced with losing his job due to a format change, he reverts to bad-mouthing his callers but then finds they want to keep the positive talk going. He also discovers that Michael is actually an angel who died a few weeks before. Ramiro reconnects with his family and, being a Hallmark movie, all ends happily.

Another contemporary film with radio sports other than play-by-play having a significant role was *The Upside of Anger* (2005). Baseball star turned sportscaster Denny Davies (Kevin Costner) becomes involved with a neighbor struggling to cope with the unexpected disappearance of her husband, and he befriends her four daughters. The radio scenes were shot at WRIF-FM Detroit and the film's director, Mike Binder, does a fine job as Costner's sleazy producer, who hires and then sleeps with one of the girls.

Big Fan (2009) had Paul Aufiero (Patton Oswalt) as a parking lot attendant who lives with his mother and whose life revolves around the New York Giants football team. He makes daily calls to New York talk show host Chris "Mad Dog" Russo and engages in an on-air duel with "Phil from Philadelphia," an avid Eagles booster. Aufiero's life is changed by a violent barroom encounter with a Giants player in which he receives a savage beating. He then faces the decision whether to press charges against the star player, which would almost certainly result in a suspension and thus damage the team's playoff hopes, or take no action, enhance the Giants' chances for success, but leave the player unpunished. "Mad Dog" Russo was also heard for ninety seconds over the opening credits of *Bad Lieutenant* (1992), arguing with a caller about the chances of the New York Mets winning the World Series, but was not seen on screen.

Oakland all-night sports talk show host Johnny Rizzo (Matt Bush) faces a dilemma: In *Nice Guy Johnny* (2010), he loves his job but has promised his fiancée that by the age of 25 he'll find a career with a more promising financial future. Complications arise when he flies to New York for a job interview arranged by his uncle Terry (director Edward Burns), a womanizing bartender who gets him involved with another woman.

Besides Ellen Barkin in *The Fan*, my research did not uncover any films that portrayed women as radio sports reporters or talk show hosts. Those with women as TV sports reporters or anchors are numerous but are not included in the filmography. Many African Americans have in recent years worked in television as sportscasters, reporters, and play-by-play announcers or color commentators, and many are heard on radio as talk show hosts or doing play-by-play or color commentary of various sports. While some men and women of color have appeared in movies as TV sportscasters or reporters, the next African American actor to portray a radio sports reporter or talk show host apparently will be the first.

Five

"Station G-O-D": Religion, Radio, and Film

As described in Chapter Four, the roots of both sports and religious radio can be traced to the dawn of broadcasting in America. Sports and religion were both important programming staples in radio's earliest years, and continue to be so today. Financial considerations have been important to both sports and religious broadcasting — radio sports through the generation of advertising revenue and religious radio by providing religious broadcasters with an opportunity to greatly expand both their audiences and the resulting monetary rewards of increased financial donations from those listeners.

Sports and religious broadcasting each require a type of specialized announcing, and the announcing styles developed in radio's early years have continued to the present in both sports broadcasting and religious radio. While the preceding pages discussed sports radio on film, including the depictions of play-by-play announcers and talk show hosts, this chapter examines the film-religion nexus and how religious radio has been portrayed in movies.

Religion and Radio

Religious organizations were among the first radio station owners to be issued broadcast licenses by the Department of Communications, the forerunner to the FCC.[1] In the early 1920s, "the possibilities of broadcasting had only begun to dawn on American religious leaders. So few stations competed for use of the airwaves that broadcasts could be heard for thousands of miles."[2] This would soon change, however, as the radio band rapidly filled with programs of every description. By 1930 more than 600 American radio stations were on the air[3] and churches and other religious organizations found that many listeners embraced the emerging medium:

> Churches were quick to realize the power of radio to reach new audiences, and stations found religious programs an economical way to fulfill their public service

obligation. Just a few weeks after receiving the nation's first broadcast license, KDKA aired live services from Calvary Episcopal Church in Pittsburgh and the broadcast soon became a regular part of the station's program schedule.[4]

Other religious radio pioneers included Paul Rader, heard on numerous Chicago stations beginning in 1922, Dr. R.R. Brown on WAOW in Omaha starting in 1923, and Donald Gray Barnhouse, heard nationally on CBS from 1928 to 1932.[5] By 1925, religious organizations, including churches, owned or controlled more than ten percent of American broadcasting stations.[6] Through the 1930s, most stations aired some kind of religious broadcasts. Women in particular seemed appreciative of such programming due to the geographical isolation of many in rural America and the attendant difficulties in getting to church on Sunday. Programs such as *The Catholic Hour* on NBC and *The Old Fashioned Revival Hour* on the Mutual Broadcasting System were popular nationally[7] and in many homes the radio served as a kind of altar at which the family could gather to worship and pray.[8]

As with sports, a number of fascinating religious air personalities made use of the airwaves in the early years. These included Charles Fuller, founder of *The Old Fashioned Revival Hour* on KNX Los Angeles,[9] Father Charles Coughlin, an anti–Semitic priest heard on WJR Detroit from the mid–1920s to the late '30s,[10] "Fighting Bob" Shuler on KGEF Los Angeles,[11] and "Sister" Aimee Semple McPherson, whose personality filmmakers have found particularly interesting and whose career is discussed later in this chapter. Preachers such as Oral Roberts and Billy Graham, both of whom would find greater fame through their television ministries, first reached the masses and, like their sports exemplars, honed their deliveries on radio. Graham's oratorical power is illustrated in *Billy: The Early Years of Billy Graham* (2008), also discussed later in this chapter. Many of these early religious radio programs were fundamentalist or evangelical in nature:

> Radio and fundamentalism were a good match for each other. The messages of fundamentalists were simple, straightforward and represented a broadly conceived amalgam of conservative, nativist American cultural values. Radio gave these evangelists a reach they had never had before — into thousands of American homes.[12]

Although today they are often critical of the secular media, fundamentalists soon learned how to use the various media forms to their own ends, to popularize their own culture, and to become "expert marketers of religion," from gospel music to book publishing to electronic media.[13] With the arrival of television, the power of the electronic church grew exponentially to reach worldwide audiences. Television made stars of evangelists such as Jerry Falwell, Oral Roberts, Pat Robertson, Jimmy Swaggart, and Jim and Tammy Bakker, all of whom held fundamentalist or conservative religious views.[14] A few, such as Falwell and Robertson, openly expressed conservative political opinions, and Robertson even undertook a high-profile but fugacious bid for the Republican presidential nomination in 1988. Despite their flamboyance and the headlines their political and social pronouncements garnered, however, none of these latter-day religious figures have attracted the attention of filmmakers.

Hollywood and Religion

Film and religion share common roots since some of the first films ever seen, at the turn of the twentieth century, were produced by religious organizations such as the Salvation Army. Early movies included Biblical titles such as *Ben Hur* (1907) and *Quo Vadis* (1912), but as the film industry began to mature, themes of a decidedly secular nature emerged as cowboys, gangsters, and other characters appeared on screen. A public backlash against the perceived personal and professional excesses of the filmmaking community resulted in quasi-censorship vehicles such as the 1930 Production Code (the Hays Code), which to a certain extent regulated film content, the Catholic Church's Legion of Decency in 1933, and a voluntary movie rating system developed by the Motion Picture Association of America in 1966 that continues to this day.[15]

One of the most outspoken movie critics for the past several years has been Michael Medved, a conservative talk show host who sees Hollywood as being detached from the sensibilities of the "real world." He perceives incompatible views of both culture and freedom of expression between filmmakers and the rest of American society.[16] This has resulted, according to Medved, in the abandonment of a once-reverential attitude toward religion evident in the movies of earlier periods. He sees this attitude shift as an assault on organized religion:

> On no other issue do the perspectives of the show business elite and those of the public at large differ more dramatically. Time and again, the producers who shape our movies, television, and popular music have gone out of their way to affront the religious sensibilities of ordinary Americans.[17]

Medved specifically deplores many film depictions of religious figures as "comic book clergy" and cites examples of the "bashing" of both born-again evangelicals and Catholics.[18] Although a detailed analysis of the relationship between religion and film is beyond the purview of the present discussion, and many might disagree with Medved's assessment that much contemporary film content represents a "sickness of the soul,"[19] a review of religious radio movie themes does indicate that filmmakers generally have not been kind in their portrayals of religious figures.

Religious Radio on Film

Given the plethora of interesting and downright eccentric personalities that populated religious radio's formative years, one might surmise that Hollywood would have extensively mined the field, but such is not the case. Relatively few movies have dealt with religious radio in any fashion. Not so with televangelists, who have proven to be more attractive to Hollywood than radio's religious figures. Most of the films depicting televangelists have portrayed them in a less than flattering light (*Pray TV*, 1980; *Fall from Grace*, 1990; *Paradise*, 2004, and many others). Religious leaders such as rabbis, priests, and imams have been conspicuous by their absence from radio films, as have any discussions of faith or religious issues on talk shows. Religious practitioners who have appeared in movies have almost exclusively been fundamentalist preachers or con artists. Despite the number of Christian radio stations on the air today and the evident popularity of Christian music in all its forms, from gospel to rock and rap, no radio movies have included DJs or talk show hosts at religious stations.

The first film with a religious theme was also the first to depict a woman as an air personality and it was in fact a reasonably positive portrayal. The actress was Barbara Stanwyck and the film was the 1931 Columbia Pictures release *The Miracle Woman*. Directed by Frank Capra, it was inspired by, although not based on, the career of Aimee Semple McPherson, one of the more intriguing personalities in an industry not noted for a lack of offbeat characters.

Aimee Kennedy was born in Canada, married evangelist Robert Semple and, later, magazine salesman Harold McPherson. In 1921, on a San Francisco station, she became the first woman to preach a radio sermon. "A gratifying number of calls flooded the switchboard when she finished, proving that her invisible audience had indeed been large and far-ranging."[20] On July 28, 1922, she conducted her second broadcast sermon, talking of divine healing and praying for the sick. This use of radio put her at "the cutting edge of the communications revolution that was rapidly transforming the world."[21]

McPherson was nothing if not flamboyant. She founded the Angelus Temple in Los Angeles, and "got ideas for titles, props, staging, and music from the entertainment world around her."[22] The first woman granted a broadcasting license by the FCC, McPherson hired engineers from other Los Angeles stations to construct a facility at the Angelus Temple. KFSG (Kall Four-Square Gospel) went on the air February 6, 1924, and radio "soon made her voice one of the most familiar in the United States."[23]

In *The Miracle Woman*, Stanwyck is Florence Fallon, the daughter of a

minister whose death she blames on his congregation. She renames herself
Sister Fallon after being persuaded by a promoter to become a faith healer,
and reaches the masses through KXMY:

> And I bring you the promise and pledge that God's in His heaven and all's right
> with the world. Oh, my dear ones, I can't see you but I can feel you all around
> me. Thousands and thousands of you, tuning in on station G-O-D, God, on a
> wavelength that carries His blessed word to the furthermost reaches of the uni-
> verse. Just as the little microphone before me carries my voice to your ears, so am I
> just a human microphone which the Lord broadcasts to you on a universal wave-
> length that penetrates the hearts and souls of those who are ready for His program.

Fallon promotes the Temple of Happiness Church in which she performs fake
miracle cures. Her relationship with a blind man whom she is unable to help
and with whom she falls in love eventually leads her to recant her ministry.
Realizing the inherently delusive nature of her preaching, under suspicion of
embezzlement, and with her church being consumed by flames, Fallon flees.
In the movie's final scene she marches with a Salvation Army band while
singing "The Battle Hymn of the Republic" with a beatific smile of fulfillment.

The real Aimee Semple McPherson story has twice been explored on the
screen. A 1976 TV movie focused mainly on the most controversial aspect of
her life. In 1926, McPherson disappeared for six months before reappearing
to explain she had been kidnapped to Mexico; police believed she had actually
been engaged in a tryst with her radio station engineer, a married man. This
episode was the subject of the Hallmark Hall of Fame's *The Disappearance of
Aimee*, a courtroom drama with Faye Dunaway as McPherson and Bette Davis
as her mother. The film tells McPherson's story in flashbacks in scenes of faith
healing with the evangelist in flowing white robes, and also depicts the opening
of her radio station. Dunaway's performance conveys some of McPherson's
mesmerizing oratorical power but does not disclose whether she is sincere in
her beliefs or has the heart of a swindler. The IMDb website indicates that
Davis disliked Dunaway,[24] and tension is evident in scenes where Davis tries
to draw out the truth from her daughter about the mysterious absence.

Sister Aimee: The Aimee Semple McPherson Story (2006) included her
marriages to Semple and McPherson but touched only tangentially on her
radio career. Starring Mimi Michaels, the movie depicts her first broadcast
but overall replicates little of the fervor she inspired in her audiences. It seems
to have been a film with a limited budget; most of the scenes in which
McPherson preaches include only shots of the evangelist, and none show the
congregations that packed the church to hear her sermons. There are brief
shots of the church's exterior but the movie fails to portray either the power
that McPherson conveyed or the zeal and passion of her followers. It concludes

with archival photographs of the crowds attending her funeral, reported to be the largest in the history of Los Angeles.

Two years after *The Miracle Woman*, Stanwyck appeared in another film with religious overtones, although as a decidedly different type of character. In *Ladies They Talk About* (1933), she is Nan Taylor, a hard-bitten accomplice of bank robbers, and in the opening scene she acts as a decoy during a heist. Tabbed as a former criminal, her picture appears on the front page of the local newspaper. Meanwhile, "Fighting Dave" Slade (Preston Foster), a crusading radio preacher whose persona may have been modeled on the real-life "Fighting Bob" Shuler, broadcasts an anti-crime sermon on WDS radio and blasts the district attorney's office for being incompetent. He later meets Taylor in the D.A.'s office, recognizes her as a former classmate, and defends her on the radio. The D.A. offers to parole Taylor in Slade's custody, but she confesses to being the hold-up accomplice and is sent to prison. There, she runs afoul of convict "Sister" Susie (Dorothy Burgess), who has a crush on Slade, and the two have an altercation. Upon her eventual release, Taylor heads to Slade's church with a gun, intending to kill him during his *Old Fashioned Revival Hour* broadcast (where Susie is now a member of the choir). When he sees Taylor, Slade escorts her to his office, where she shoots him in the arm. Susie witnesses the scene through the keyhole but when the police arrive, Slade disclaims the shooting and, realizing he still loves Nan, hides his injured arm.

Radio was used for nefarious purposes in *Racketeers in Exile* (1937). William Waldo (George Bancroft) and his gang, on the run from the FBI, take refuge in Waldo's home town. After attending a church festival, they decide religion will make for a lucrative racket and start a radio show which soon begins raking in money from Waldo's claims that he's helping the poor. More loot comes from shakedowns of other racketeers in exchange for not exposing them on the air. In the end, Waldo recants, survives a shootout with police, and seems ready to live happily ever after with his childhood sweetheart, the church organist.

Several years passed before another religious film included radio references. *The Sickle or the Cross* (1949) combined religious and anti–Communist messages. Reverend John Burnside (Kent Taylor) is a missionary who is about to return to America from China to deliver anti–Communist lectures. Hearing of the plan, Chinese authorities imprison him and substitute Communist agent X-14, who has been trained to imitate the missionary's voice and speaking style. He is greeted warmly upon his arrival and eventually arranges to deliver a radio address in which he will explain that Communism is really a friend of the Church. Due to the kindness with which he has been treated in

America, however, X-14 breaks down during the broadcast, reveals his true identity, and denounces Communism.

In *The Next Voice You Hear…* (1950), God's voice begins coming from radios around the world, including that of aircraft factory worker Joe Smith (James Whitmore), his wife Mary (Nancy Davis, future first lady Nancy Reagan) and their son Johnny (Gary Gray), who are residents of Los Angeles. One evening as Smith sits down to listen to music on KWTA, a voice interrupts the program to say "This is God. I'll be with you for the next few days." Later reports from around the world indicate that listeners everywhere heard the same message, which is repeated the following evening, and the government begins an investigation into where the mysterious voice may be coming from.

On the fourth day, the voice commands listeners to perform acts of peace and kindness but on the seventh day, when everyone gathers for a special service to listen to the voice again, the radios are silent. The following year, Whitmore was heard in another film with religious overtones: *Angels in the Outfield*, described in Chapter Four, in which he voices the lines of the unseen angel who visits Pittsburgh Pirates manager "Guffy" McGovern.

Invasion of the Space Preachers (1991) was a marginally humorous B-movie in which aliens arrive to dominate the world by controlling people's minds through radio sermons. Naturally, they pick a backwoods setting populated by various stereotypical rednecks but their plans are thwarted by a beautiful blonde space princess and two vacationing city geeks. The special effects are crude, as are the sets, and the acting is of the caliber usually associated with such productions.

At the other extreme, Robert Duvall turned in a mesmerizing performance as Euliss "Sonny" Dewey in *The Apostle* (1997). Starting as a tent preacher with the Holy Ghost Revival, Dewey builds his own congregation. He has, however, a propensity for violence and when he finds that his wife has been sleeping with another man, a Little League baseball diamond confrontation leaves the man dead on the ground. One step ahead of the law, Dewey finds himself in a small Louisiana town where he takes a job as a mechanic and his Biblical ways soon earn him the appellation "The Apostle." The power of preaching is still with him and he approaches the somewhat hesitant manager of KBBR for an opportunity to air a new show:

> MANAGER: So what kind of preacher are you, anyway?
> APOSTLE: Oh, well, I can preach on the Holy Trinity, Old and New Testament, Hell, resurrection, you name it, I can do it. I can preach on the Devil backwards and forwards. Now if you got anything you want to hear, but no tongues.

The Apostle's first morning sermon rains fire and brimstone:

I'm preachin' like I'm goin' to war this mornin.' I'm a genuine Holy Ghost, Jesus-filled preachin' machine here this mornin.' I tell ya, I'm a Jesus-filled preachin' machine here this mornin.' Now if God be for us, who can be against us? He's God here in this radio station, He's God in Georgia, He's God in Tennessee, He's God in the pulpit, He's God in the front door, He's God in the 7–11.

The Apostle starts the One Way Road to Heaven Church and soon builds a following, but the power of radio is his undoing when his broadcast is picked up back in Texas. The police arrive at his church in mid-sermon and, with the sounds of the congregation's "I'll Fly Away" in his ears, he is driven away in handcuffs. The script for *The Apostle* was written by Duvall in the 1980s. He directed the film, which also features Farrah Fawcett as Dewey's wife Jessie. Duvall's riveting performance garnered him an Academy Award nomination for Best Actor in a Leading Role.

An immaculate conception seemed about to take place in *False Prophets* (2006), a film with mystical overtones. Maggie Tate (Lori Heuring) is a young woman who can't believe she's pregnant because several years before she was raped and had her ovaries removed, and her boyfriend is sterile. A fundamentalist religious group, believing a virgin birth is imminent, convinces Maggie to give up the child for adoption rather than have an abortion. Although she agrees, she becomes suspicious of the Christians' intentions; their leader turns violent when Maggie tries to back out of the deal. She flees with her boyfriend and when their car breaks down on a Georgia back road she takes refuge in a gas station run by Isaiah (Tucker Smallwood) and his son Manny (Antonio David Lyons). Manny was left on Isaiah's doorstep as an infant many years before and his character has mystical religious qualities which become evident in the philosophical thoughts he shares with Maggie about life and faith. Isaiah's gas station also houses a radio station from which he airs political and religious views that are, for rural Georgia, more than a little unconventional:

What you do when you go home, behind your closed bedroom doors, ain't nobody's business but your own. That's what I say. If God created man, He created all of mankind, not just the card-carryin' Bible thumpers. He created straight people, He created gay people, He created people don't even give a damn about knockin' hoops in the midnight hour. And what's wrong with that? Live and let live, that's what I say. You hear what I'm sayin'? Wake up! Huh. Wake up and smell the coffee. You need to wake up and start thinkin' for yourselves. That you never heard of false prophets.

Tracked down by the fundamentalists, Maggie flees with Manny, who is shot and mortally wounded in a meadow where Maggie gives birth to an apparently stillborn girl. Manny's powers save the child when Maggie expresses her desire for the infant to live. In a flash of light, Manny dies and the film concludes with Maggie driving away with her baby girl.

Facing the Giants (2006) was similar to *Friday Night Lights* in that it focused on high school football, but the films are significantly dissimilar. *Facing the Giants* was made on a shoestring budget by the Albany, Georgia, Sherwood Baptist Church, whose members assisted in its production. The director, producer, screenwriter, and most of the actors were church members. The movie tells the story of the Shiloh Eagles, whose coach, Grant Taylor (Alex Kendrick), has not had a winning season in six years with the team. *Facing the Giants* expresses a fundamentalist religious viewpoint, the script by Alex and Stephen Kendrick is laced with Biblical references, and much of the dialogue is expostulatory, as the following scenes illustrate. David Childers (Bailey Cave), a soccer kicker, tries out for the team as a placekicker, but is inept. An assistant coach approaches him on the field:

> COACH: Now see, you kickin' wide left or wide right, but that ain't what's gonna get you home. The ball has got to go through the middle.
> DAVID: I know, coach.
> COACH: No, no, you don't. Now what does Scripture say about this?
> DAVID: Um...
> COACH: Scripture says "Wide is the gate and broad is the way that leads to destruction. And many there'll be that find it." Not for us. That's wide left and wide right. "But narrow is the gate and straight is the way that leads to life. And few there'll be that find it." Anybody can kick it wide left or wide right. My momma can kick it wide left and wide right. But that ain't what's gonna get you home. It don't have to look pretty. It don't have to look smooth. It can look like a dyin' duck. But the ball has got to go through the middle. Now, David, you gonna have to choose the narrow way. 'Cause that's the only path where you'll get your reward. Now send this ball through these here pearly posts.

Thus inspired, David immediately begins booting the ball squarely through the goal posts. In the finale, the Eagles trail the Richmond Giants 23–21 in the dying seconds of the state championship game. With no time for another play, David is faced with making a 51-yard field goal, far beyond anything he has ever attempted:

> DAVID: Coach, it's too far!
> COACH: Listen to me. Do you think God can help you make this kick? Do you believe it, David?
> DAVID: Yeah, if He wants to.
> COACH. So do I, but you have gotta give me your best and leave the rest up to Him. Will you do that for me?
> [*David's paralyzed father rises from his wheelchair on the sidelines*].
> COACH: David, whether you make this field goal or not, we're gonna praise Him. But don't you walk off this field having done any less than your best
> [*David's father stands and raises his arms in victory*].
> DAVID: God, help me make this kick.
> COACH: Kick it now! Kick it now!
> [*David kicks*].
> RADIO ANNOUNCER: Kick is up, it's on its way. It's long enough! It's high

enough! Does it have the distance? It does. It's good! It's good! It's good! The Eagles have won! The Eagles have won the state championship. I can't believe what I've just seen! I cannot believe what I've just seen! A miracle has occurred here tonight!

God's role in selecting winners and losers of athletic contests is beyond the scope of this discussion, but Shirl J. Hoffman has delved into the issue in some depth, asking "whether or not prayer, interjected into the world of play, can ever escape the illusory, make-believe nature of sports themselves."[25] *Facing the Giants* received a PG (Parental Guidance) rating from the Motion Picture Association of America, apparently because of its overt religious theme and also for the depictions of on-field violence during the games.

Changeling (2008) was directed by Clint Eastwood and based on a true story. Christine Collins (Angelina Jolie) searches for her son Walter, who vanished without a trace in Los Angeles in 1928. Five months later, police announce they've found the child, but Collins doubts it's her real son. She pressures the police to keep looking, but her insistent demands lead to her being hospitalized as delusional and an unfit parent. Enter radio preacher Reverend Gustav Brieglieb (John Malkovich), who quickly takes up her case and turns his broadcasts on KGP into diatribes against police corruption. In an oratorical delivery reminiscent of "Fighting" Dave Slade in *Ladies They Talk About*, Brieglieb preaches:

> On the radio and in the newspapers, we are told that the Los Angeles Police Department is doing its very best to reunite mother and child and I'm sure that that is true. But, given its status as the most violent, corrupt, and incompetent police department this side of the Rocky Mountains, I am not sure it's saying a great deal [*Congregation applauds*].

Changeling was nominated for three Academy Awards, including Best Actress for Jolie. Also in 2008, a biographical portrait of a radio evangelist was painted in *Billy: The Early Years of Billy Graham*. The story of Graham's remarkable career focuses, as the title indicates, on the period during which his oratorical powers were being formed. It explores Graham's relationship with fundamentalist preacher Charles Templeton, whose crisis of faith caused him to leave the evangelical movement and who later became a respected television journalist and commentator in his native Canada. Directed by Robbie Benson, the movie starred Armie Hammer as Graham with Kristoffer Polaha as the young Templeton. Martin Landau is the aged and dying Templeton who explains their relationship in flashbacks. The beginning of Graham's radio career is depicted, and at a tent rival meeting he issues his famous call to sinners:

> Now, I'm going to ask you to get out of your seat, wherever you are, and stand in front of these platforms and say, by coming, "I know that I am a sinner. I want to

receive God into my heart. I want my sins forgiven. I want to know that I am going to Heaven, and I want a new life, and I want it to begin right here, and I want it to begin right now." And you know what? It can. I don't care if you are a movie star or the biggest drunk walking the streets of Los Angeles. God is waiting for you right now. Come down. Come down and give your life to Christ. Come down.

Perhaps due to his magnetic personality or, more probably, the vast worldwide audiences his radio and television broadcasts commanded, Graham has been one of the few religious media personalities of modern times to have his life portrayed on film. The 1990 TV movie *Fall from Grace* chronicled the fall of televangelists Jim and Tammy Faye Bakker (played by Kevin Spacey and Bernadette Peters). Graham's contemporaries, such as Oral Roberts, Jerry Falwell, and Pat Robertson, have also used radio effectively but none has proven of interest to mainstream filmmakers, possibly because of the nature of their messages, which veer considerably more to the right than those of Graham. Another factor is undoubtedly financial considerations as to whether the subject matter is too limiting to return a box office profit for a theatrical release or sufficiently high television ratings to justify a small screen production. It is also possible that Hollywood's lack of interest in contemporary religious topics and leaders supports Michael Medved's view that many if not most in the film community do not hold favorable views of religion per se and therefore are not interested in producing films dealing with such subject matter.

Six

"Play 'Misty' for Me":
Psychos on the Air

Radio movies changed considerably beginning in 1951. Gone were the fast-talking agents trying to turn unknowns such as waiters and electricians into radio singing stars. Radio detectives had likewise vanished, and movie cowboys had ridden off into the sunset. Movie radio stations, the scenes of so many murders in earlier decades, were quiescent during the 1950s and '60s. *No Trace* in 1950 would be the last film for several years to feature a radio station murder.

While DJs had begun to attract Hollywood's attention in 1948's *I Surrender Dear*, the plot of 1951's *Disc Jockey* was based on the influence of the DJ in creating a star. Also in 1951, *A Millionaire for Christy* was the last movie in which a secretary tried to break into radio but, reflective of the changing nature of radio films—and radio itself—she set out to seduce a millionaire announcer rather than try to become a star on her own show, or as a singer. The last radio crooner appeared in *Hit Parade of 1951*; *Queen for a Day* (1951) was the final movie based on a popular radio show. Screen images of radio personalities changed dramatically in 1971, however, when a new and interesting personality was introduced.

In that year, *Play Misty for Me* starred Clint Eastwood as an announcer who becomes the target of an obsessive listener. Thus came to the screen the psychopathic audience member, referred to in this book as the "psycho listener." Psychopathy is a clinical construct describing those operating outside of societal norms:

> They engage in a socially deviant (not necessarily criminal) lifestyle that includes irresponsible and impulsive behavior, and a tendency to ignore or violate social conventions and rules. These are individuals whose ... general lack of behavioral inhibitions make it easy to victimize the vulnerable and to use intimidation and violence as tools to achieve power and control over others. They are capable of

"reactive" forms of aggression and, more ominously, aggression and violence that are predatory, premeditated, instrumental, or "cold blooded" in nature.[1]

This irresponsible and impulsive behavior can take many forms including, at its most extreme, murder. A less violent, but perhaps no less frightening, form of psychopathy that has been depicted in radio films is stalking, to which media personalities seem especially susceptible:

> These victims are most often encountered through radio, television and film but may also include politicians, royalty, sports champions and other prominent public figures. Their stalkers are drawn from the socially incompetent, morbidly infatuated, erotomanic, and the resentful…. Some harbour delusional beliefs that they have an intimate relationship with their victim.[2]

While hard data are scarce, evidence suggests that in the electronic media, female newscasters or TV actresses are most likely to be stalking victims, perhaps because they "can be easily incorporated into the relationship fantasy of a stalker."[3] While cases of celebrity stalking often make headlines, the incidence of such cases resulting in homicidal violence seems relatively rare.[4] In radio films, stalking usually results in acts of violence against DJs or talk show hosts.

The premise of *The Fan* (1996) was based on celebrity stalking although in this case the object (Wesley Snipes) of the stalker (Robert De Niro) is a sports star rather than a media personality. Other radio movie stalking examples are found in *Don't Answer the Phone!* (1980; a Vietnam vet kills women and stalks a talk show host); *When the Dark Man Calls* (1995; a talk show host is stalked by her husband's killer); *Acts of Contrition*, aka *Original Sins* (1995; a caller admits to a murder on the air and then stalks the talk show host); *Shattered Illusions* (1998; a psycho stalks a talk show host and her mentally challenged sister); *The Night Caller* (1998; a shy store clerk stalks a talk show host); *Attraction* (2000; a DJ stalks his ex-girlfriend and then her friend); *Cherish* (2002; a DJ stalks a listener); and *Sinful Desires* (2002; a listener stalks the host of a sex talk show).

Those who stalk public figures such as media personalities have been categorized in two ways. "Hunters" are a small percentage of psychopaths but represent the greatest danger because "they truly act on their intent to use lethal violence to avenge some perceived injustice."[5] Another group is "howlers" or individuals who "like to threaten and frighten with words, or to express some unrequited emotional attachment, but they never follow through with any actions."[6] They are usually more interested in commanding attention or perhaps generating fear, but most of the psycho listeners in radio films are hunters since they often pose a threat to the air personalities. These threats, in fact, constitute the storylines of many psycho listener films, which often end in a deadly confrontation between the psycho and the DJ or talk show host.

Radio film psychos generally fall into one of two groups: those who threaten the DJ or talk show host in some way, such as with death, and those who use the talk show host or his/her program for some purpose, such as taunting police or providing them with clues about their crimes. Psychotic personalities have not been limited to members of the listening audience, however. Another interesting film persona is the DJ or talk show host with a personality disorder that sometimes manifests itself in some kind of aberrant behavior. The first American production in which this type of character appeared was *Choose Me* (1984), with Genevieve Bujold as "Dr. Love," a talk show counselor with psychological problems.

Most of the air personalities who exhibit personality disorders in movies are talk show hosts and most of these are women. Despite their air of authoritativeness as they dispense advice, they frequently reveal character flaws or display emotional weaknesses that cause distress for themselves or others, including listeners. With some exceptions —*A Cry for Help* (1975); *The Gladiator* (1986); *Open House* (1987); *Talk Radio* (1988); *Militia* (2000); *Statistics* (2006); *Blue Chip Mint* (2007)— movie talk shows usually focus on listeners' personal tribulations or on relationship issues. Current events or politics, which dominate the conversations in real talk radio, are seldom discussed in the talk shows seen on movie screens.

The Psychology of Talk Radio

"Talks" and informational programming have been heard since the earliest days of radio. Listeners' problems also titillated audiences long before the modern psychiatrists and psychologists of the airwaves became popular. In 1937, John J. Anthony helped listeners resolve personal issues on *The Goodwill Hour*. An excerpt from the show was used under the opening credits of *The Couch Trip*, a 1988 comedy in which escaped mental patient Dan Aykroyd assumed the identity of a Los Angeles psychiatrist to become a hit radio talk show host:

> ANNOUNCER: Is the sweetheart you married the husband you expected him to be? Has the war created new problems for you in your marriage? To answer these and other personal problems: John J. Anthony, founder of the famed Marital Relations Institute in a brand new program of daily sessions of kindly and helpful advice. Mr. Anthony, are you ready for your first case?
> ANTHONY: Quite ready, George.
> ANNOUNCER: The first case is that of Miss C. A.
> ANTHONY: All right, let's go. Your problem, please? Come in.

John J. Anthony was actually Lester Kroll, a high school dropout turned radio announcer who spent time in jail, claimed to have three university degrees, and to have studied under Sigmund Freud.[7] He did not air the calls live, but rather paraphrased the listeners' comments.[8] His modern counterparts, although with genuine academic credentials, are advice givers such as Dr. Laura Schlesinger, Dr. Joy Brown, Dr. Ellen Kenner, and many more whose shows are either syndicated nationally or produced locally in larger cities. Such program hosts are the most common types seen in films and are overwhelmingly female, both in real life and on film. Aside from Anthony's pioneering advice efforts, shows that enabled listeners to air their views publicly were not widely heard until the mid–1950s when improved telephone line quality made them more practical.[9] Two Los Angeles stations led the way: KABC with an all-talk format in 1966, followed shortly thereafter by KLAC with a 24-hour call-in format.[10]

If, as discussed in Chapter Two, movies are to a degree a reflection of the times in which they are produced, then Hollywood's depictions of the radio world in recent years would be somewhat unsettling. First, it would appear that much of America, or at least that segment that listens to and calls talk radio shows, has relationship issues. Many of these seem to be of a sexual nature, and those calling talk shows about their personal situations often appear to have additional psychological or sociological problems, not the least of which is a frequent propensity to engage in some kind of violent behavior. Listeners displaying a variety of deviant personality traits have been common in the radio films of the past four decades.

There are several reasons why radio might attract listeners with psychological problems and thus offer film scriptwriters and directors characters upon which to build a story. First, such people may feel a connection with DJs or talk show hosts because part of the announcer's job is to be personable, as a suicidal caller to a radio psychologist in *Open House* (1987) makes clear: "But who are you? I mean, you go on the radio and you yak it up, and you get paid, a lot, to pretend like you're everybody's best buddy."

Exceptions to the jovial air personalities are the shock jocks and talk show hosts who specialize in caustic comments to call-in listeners. These types are depicted in *A Cry for Help* (1975; Robert Culp abuses his listeners until he needs their help to find a suicidal caller); *Talk Radio* (1988; Eric Bogosian's acerbic on-air persona gets him killed); and *Joe Dirt* (2001; Dennis Miller ridicules a janitor who's trying to find his birth parents). However, show hosts of all stripes invite listener interaction by "opening up the phone lines" through which listeners can "become part of the program." Music stations frequently have a "request line" for listeners to ask for their favorite song, sometimes by speaking directly to a DJ. Request lines were more common in the 1960s and '70s before the advent of programming software and satellite program distribution. Nevertheless, some stations continue to use them as a promotional tool even if all the music is pre-programmed and stored in a computer.

The nature of the announcer-listener relationship may also be partially explained by a phenomenon known as parasocial interaction, a concept defined by Donald Horton and R. Richard Wohl in 1956 as the "seeming face-to-face relationship between spectator and performer."[11] Parasocial interaction was one unintended result of the emergence of mass media:

> One of the striking characteristics of the new mass media — radio, television, and the movies — is that they give the illusion of face-to-face relationship with the performer.... The most remote and illustrious men are met *as if they* were in the circle of one's peers.[12]

Parasocial interaction today is epitomized by social networking sites such as Facebook and Twitter where entertainment and sports celebrities may have thousands of "friends" they have never met, about whom they know nothing, but with whom they converse daily. In talk radio, participants engage in a discussion as if they were together in an informal setting although they may actually be separated by hundreds or thousands of miles. Since many talk show hosts and some disc jockeys encourage this familiar relationship, it would not be surprising if listeners with psychological problems might perceive the radio personalities as friendly and receptive sounding boards to which those problems might be confided. Examples of this type of misconception are seen in *Play Misty for Me* and also *The Night Caller* (1998), in which a shy convenience store clerk becomes enamored of a radio psychologist and eventually inserts herself into the doctor's life.

Another reason talk shows have been popular in recent years is that they provide an outlet for the otherwise voiceless to express their views. One talk show producer opined:

> Callers to talk shows are seeking companionship and entertainment more than information. They are lonely, stuck at home, or stuck in traffic. Many feel disenfranchised from society and they desire an opportunity to be heard; they are convinced they have something to say.[13]

Much talk radio since the early 1990s has been political in nature, and right-wing or conservative hosts dominate, the most popular being Rush Limbaugh. Although dozens of hosts such as Limbaugh, Sean Hannity, Bill O'Reilly, and their countless local imitators are heard on hundreds of stations and attract millions of listeners, they often portray themselves as being a minority alternative to the "mainstream media." This phrase was popularized by Limbaugh in referring to media outlets such as the *New York Times, Wash-*

ington Post, and the major television networks, which are perceived by many conservatives as controlling the public discourse with news coverage and editorial comments politically slanted to the left.

Since radio is the most personal of the mass media, it "creates a sense of community and privacy simultaneously, so listeners can share their thoughts with others in a safe community of anonymity."[14] Thus is formed a bond not only between announcer and listener, but among listeners themselves, and this sense of community is particularly fostered by right-wing talk show hosts. Limbaugh coined the term "dittoheads" in referring to the followers who agree with his views and who often express on the air their pride at being so described. Whether of a political or a personal nature, a call to a talk show is thus a contribution to the group or association of like-minded listeners. This sense of community was reinforced in earlier years when announcers referred to "everyone out there in radioland," or to "members of the listening audience." As explicated by Marshall McLuhan, radio's very nature is "its power to turn the psyche and society into a single echo chamber."[15] Today it is exceptionally easy to hear one's voice resonate in this echo chamber: Simply pick up the telephone at the behest of the talk show host. Talk radio in all its permutations, including sports talk, is one of the most popular formats on the dial today, even having its own trade magazine.[16]

In addition to a sense of community, some individuals may be attracted to radio personalities because of the celebrity factor. Most talk show listeners could probably never imagine themselves as actors or singing stars, but they can become celebrities in a fashion by calling a DJ or talk show. In fact, talk shows often limit the number of calls that any individual may make within a specified time such as a week or month, to restrict those who would air their views daily regardless of the topic under discussion. At the most basic level, some listeners may consider themselves as becoming, however tangentially, a part of show business. They are engaged in a media production and are, in a way, performers through their on-air participation. Thus, like the unknowns who strove for radio fame in so many films of the 1930s and '40s, anonymous callers achieve stardom of a sort through their participation in a talk show broadcast. The voices of frequent callers become familiar to program hosts and listeners alike. This is especially true of sports talk shows, as seen in *Big Fan*, when the avid New York Giants fan Paul Aufiero engages in an ongoing air battle with "Phil from Philadelphia" on a New York talk show (and eventually tracks him down for a physical confrontation).

The DJ or talk show host of course usually has no desire for a relationship with a listener, especially one exhibiting any sort of psychological problem or fixation. However, when they attempt to dissuade the listener, the results can be deadly if the caller feels that the perceived relationship has been betrayed. This is depicted in *Play Misty for Me* when DJ Dave Garver confronts his stalker, Evelyn Draper:

> GARVER: I just don't know what to say to you.
> DRAPER: I'm sorry I mistrusted you, I should have known you'd never do anything to spoil it.
> GARVER: To spoil what?
> DRAPER: What we have between us.
> GARVER: We don't have a goddamn thing between us! Now how many ways am I gonna have to say this to you?
> DRAPER: I don't care how many ways you say it! It's not true!

Draper's fixation with Garver is such that she attempts to kill both herself and him rather than accept his rejection. The "hunter" personality's fixation also forms the basis for *Attraction*, in which the stalker is a talk show host who cannot be dissuaded from pursuing his ex-girlfriend, with violent results, and *Cherish*, in which a DJ unobtrusively takes pictures of a young woman and then stalks her, which leads to a final confrontation.

The psycho listener film is virtually an American phenomenon. This may reflect American society's propensity to spawn such personalities, or perhaps the fascination of American filmmakers with such aberrant behavior. It may also be a product of the American broadcasting system in which talk shows and DJs historically have played a much larger role than in, for example, European countries where for many years broadcasting was more closely regulated than was the American system. While numerous air personalities have been seen in international films, noticeably absent have been the psycho listeners or emotionally troubled DJs so prevalent in American movies in recent decades.

Many of the titles discussed in the following pages were made for television or cable television, some of the latter bordering on pornography with superfluous nudity or sexual scenes unrelated to the plot. The storylines of many psycho listener films are quite predictable, although with occasional plot twists or surprise endings. Complex character development could not be considered a strong suit of most, especially the made-for-TV movies.

The films often lack verisimilitude when threatening phone calls are put on the air live. In reality, almost all talk shows use a system which delays calls by five to ten seconds before being aired so the audience will not hear them in real time. This allows an operator or technician to cut off a call before comments are broadcast, and prevents obscene language or defamatory statements from being aired. On movie talk shows, however, calls are seldom delayed and threatening calls are often heard by listeners. When the threatening calls are heard, the engineer sometimes apologizes to the host for not reacting fast enough to cut it off. Police sometimes trace threatening calls to track down the perpetrator of a crime, occasionally finding and arresting the perpetrator on the air, in the midst of the call (*Sinful Desires*; *Laser Moon*).

Movie talk show hosts are sometimes unable to cut off threatening callers and plead with them to "please hang up" or otherwise get off the air. In reality, callers do not control when they speak on the air and it is easy for the host, producer, or a technician to terminate a threatening or obscene call. Threatening callers in films frequently use electronic devices to disguise their voices by altering the pitch or otherwise making them unrecognizable. This is an especially useful tool when the callers are women (*City in Panic*; *Acts of Contrition*) but is rarely if ever used in real life. When a movie caller uses a voice-altering device, it usually indicates a surprise ending when the caller turns out to be not the obvious suspect.

The women who call movie talk shows are usually beautiful, even those with substantial emotional issues. Overweight or anorexic women do not call talk shows or DJs, and the women who call often do so while wearing provocative clothing or none at all. Likewise, overweight or physically unattractive men may be psycho listeners but not talk show hosts or DJs. In fact, issues such as obesity or anorexia, which are real concerns in the real world, do not exist in the world of movie talk shows.

Movie talk show hosts often visit bars after work, where they can meet interesting or dangerous people with whom they can become involved. DJs and talk show hosts in movies do not have children and never read books, newspapers, or magazines to stay informed; neither do they watch television or listen to news on the radio. Stable personal relationships are also rare, and if a show host or DJ has a spouse or significant other there will usually be some friction or problem between them. Hosts of talk shows about relationships or personal problems frequently come from dysfunctional families themselves or have a background of violence, abuse, or some other trauma. Female hosts sometimes sleep with the detectives investigating psycho callers (*Bare Deception*; *Requiem for Murder*; *Don't Answer the Phone!*).

As with the DJ and sports films discussed earlier, the verisimilitude of the sets varies widely. Some of the control rooms and studios are quite realistic while others are crude approximations of a radio station. In a few cases (*The Gladiator*; *Militia*), little attempt is made to depict a studio, so that the viewer sees only the host and a microphone, perhaps with some blinking lights or a tape machine in the background. Control room or studio equipment is sometimes seen but with the backgrounds in darkness, obviating the need for a set. This is more frequently the case with made-for-television movies.

Many of the talk show films begin with a panoramic shot of a city skyline, often from an helicopter, usually at night, with the host heard in a voiceover stating his or her name, the name of the show, and the station's call letters (and sometimes the city), to quickly orient the viewer. Many movie talk shows take place late at night or overnight, presumably to add an element of danger or terror when the threatening calls begin. In some instances, talk show hosts are accosted or otherwise face danger when they leave the station at night (*Sinful Desires*; *Requiem for Murder*; *Betrayed*; *Talk Radio*). Although real talk shows, especially late at night or overnight, require few people to produce, in movies numerous people are often seen in the studios or control rooms, including the program director or even station manager, as well as call screeners, equipment operators, or engineers. Unlike real radio, hosts of movie talk shows often decide when commercial breaks will be taken, and commercials are rarely heard in the background during these breaks. Many air personalities of both sexes are seemingly addicted to nicotine because they smoke frequently, even when on the air.

Regardless of the quality of the sets or acting and despite the abundance of threats and even murders, with few exceptions (*Talk Radio*; *Betrayed*) the air personalities that are threatened usually survive. No matter the type of psycho involved and his/her *modus operandi*, the film's protagonist will most likely live to talk on the airwaves again after the psycho has been caught or killed (often the latter). The following discussion looks at the various types of psycho listeners who inhabit radio films, and some of the air personalities who have also exhibited psychological problems.

Psycho Listeners

Motion picture disc jockeys or talk show hosts in recent years have frequently been targeted by listeners with serious personality disorders. As has been mentioned, the first of these was Clint Eastwood in *Play Misty for Me*, which was also his first directorial effort. Eastwood is Dave Garver, a laid-back air personality on KRML in Carmel, California (Eastwood's home town, which he once served as mayor). He plays jazz and reads poetry on his late-night show and begins to receive requests from a female listener for Errol Garner's "Misty":

> GARVER: KRML, Dave Garver speaking.
> CALLER: Hello.
> GARVER: Hi, what'll it be?
> CALLER: Play "Misty" for me.
> GARVER: "Misty" huh? We have that right on the play rack. Thanks for calling.
> MONTE: I see you got your little "Misty" chick callin' ya again.

The caller is Evelyn Draper (Jessica Walter), who eventually arranges a "chance" meeting with Garver in a bar. They soon have a brief sexual encounter but Draper doesn't want the relationship to end and begins to insinuate herself into Garver's life. She shows up uninvited and buys his groceries, and when Garver abruptly ends the relationship she attempts suicide. Draper then turns her attention to his girlfriend Tobie (Donna Mills) by becoming her roommate, then threatening to kill her. The film's climax comes with a knife attack on Garver which ends when he punches her in the face to send her over a balcony to her death on the rocks below.

The next psycho listener appeared several years later in *Don't Answer the Phone!* (1980), which marked the first film portrayal of a radio psychologist. Vietnam war veteran Kirk Smith (Nicholas Worth) is a serial killer who calls Dr. Lindsay Gale (Flo Gerrish) and commits one of many strangulation murders while on the air with her. Smith later attacks Gale in her home but the police detective (who Gale earlier slept with) arrives in time to save her life.

City in Panic was a 1986 Canadian production in which talk show host Dave Miller (David Adamson) helps police find the person who's been killing homosexuals. This was one of the first radio movies to mention homosexuality. Someone has been killing homosexuals in a variety of gruesome ways and the psycho is dubbed "M" because of his propensity for carving the initial into his victim's bodies. Police request Miller's help by asking the killer to call his show and he complies: "Somewhere in our city, there's a killer. And I ask that person, who's been called 'M,' to phone this program. If you're out there listening, 'M,' call. I'm ready to talk."

Of course, "M" takes the bait and calls, in a voice disguised electronically. In a later interview with Miller, a psychologist blames society, including the media, for shaping the killer's psychotic personality. Miller disagrees, saying that the killer and no one else is to blame, and this spurs another call from the psycho:

> "M": I'll warn you just once. Stop this.
> MILLER: Stop what?
> "M": Turning the city against me.
> MILLER: The city is already against you.
> "M": They'll understand. They'll find out why and they'll be sorry.
> MILLER: If you'd listen, they don't want to hear you, they don't want to understand you.
> "M": If you don't stop this, I'll stop you.

Miller is later enticed by "M" into a meeting and the killer is revealed to be a woman whose husband has AIDS and passed it along to her and their child, hence her hatred of all homosexuals.

Several female real estate agents turn up dead in *Open House* (1987). The killer calls Dr. David Kelly (Joseph Bottoms), a radio psychologist and host of *Hot Spots* on KDRX Los Angeles. Kelly engages Harry, the confessed killer, in a conversation:

> HARRY: I think they deserved it.
> KELLY: Come again?
> HARRY: You heard me, I think they got what they probably deserved.
> KELLY: How the hell do you figure that? What do you base that on?
> HARRY: Pretty expensive homes they died in. What gave them the right?
> KELLY: To what, Harry?
> HARRY: To a house. To live like that, to spend that money. A lot of people out there wish they just had somethin' to eat.

Harry turns out to be a homeless man who hates realtors because one sold the vacant house he was living in. Police tap the station's phone lines in an attempt to track the killer and the film ends with a confrontation between Kelly and Harry, who holds Kelly's girlfriend (Adrienne Barbeau) hostage in their home.

Jeanne Quester (Catherine Deneuve) is an emergency room psychiatrist by day and a radio psychologist by night in *Frequent Death*, aka *Frequence meurtre*, aka *Murder Rate* (1988; France). It was based on Stuart Kaminsky's book *When the Dark Man Calls* and therefore mirrors the 1995 American TV movie of that title. Quester's parents were slain fifteen years earlier and now the killer has been released from a mental institution. When she begins to receive threatening calls on the air with the voice electronically disguised, her police commissioner brother is called in. Then the suspect is himself found dead and the search for the real culprit culminates in a confrontation between Quester and the psycho before the police arrive.

Violence on Los Angeles highways set the stage for *Freeway* (1988) in which Richard Belzer is KIEV talk show host Dr. David Lazarus. He receives calls from a Bible-quoting psycho who then begins shooting drivers while on the air and listeners hear the murders because the calls are not delayed. The protaganist of the movie is actually "Sunny" Harper (Darlanne Fluegel), a nurse whose husband was killed in a freeway shooting and who's unhappy with the pace of police efforts to find the freeway killer. She becomes involved with Frank Quinn (James Russo), an ex-cop turned bounty hunter, and they do some sleuthing to deduce that the likeliest suspect is former priest Eddie Heller (Billy Drago). With Lazarus' help, they're able to pinpoint the freeway location where and when the next killing will take place and Heller dies in a shootout with Harper and Quinn.

Norman Bates, the most famous film psycho of all time, returned to the screen in the 1990 TV movie *Psycho IV: The Beginning*. Anthony Perkins reprised his role in this last production in the *Psycho* series, calling a radio talk show in which the topic of the evening is "What makes boys kill their mothers?" CCH Pounder is Fran Ambrose, the host of *The Fran Ambrose Show* on KTK, who arranges for a panel of experts to discuss matricide. Following the infamous Bates Motel murders, Norman was treated at a psychiatric hospital and released. In flashbacks, he explains to Ambrose what led him to kill four people, including his mother Norma (Olivia Hussey). Vignettes depict his mother's sexual repression and how her domineering personality led young Norman (Henry Thomas) to poison her and her boyfriend. Norman says that he now has a wife, a nurse at the hospital, but tells the audience he plans to kill her as well:

> AMBROSE: Norman. Norman, why? You said she deserved to die. How? What did she do that she should pay for it with her life?
> NORMAN: She let herself get pregnant!

Norman rationalizes that the Bates line must have no progeny who could also grow up to be killers. The ending is unconvincing because when his wife (Donna Mitchell) comes home from work to help celebrate his birthday, he takes her to the Bates Motel where he pulls out a knife, and she flees in terror. When he captures her, however, she convinces him not to kill her because she loves him and Norman sets the motel ablaze to exorcise his demons.

Zane Wolf (Harrison Le Duke) is a WLI talk show host in *Laser Moon* (1992). His ratings are slipping and his marriage is falling apart because his wife is having an affair. To make matters worse, a listener seems to be developing a fixation with him because she calls him every night from her bathtub to invite him over. One night Wolf's topic is "fantasies" and a listener says he's committed a murder. It seems someone has been killing beautiful women with a laser weapon every full moon. Former porn star Traci Lords is a rookie detective, one of the officers assigned to the case ("I have a four-year degree in police science"). When the police ask Wolf to discuss the crimes on his show to trace the killer should he call again, he arranges an expert panel.

Wolf asks question of Dr. Kostikov, a forensics expert:

> DR. KOSTIKOV: Well, the laser penetrates the cranium and damages the cortical matter. Death is almost instantaneous.
> WOLF: Painful death?
> DR. KOSTIKOV: I don't know. How would I?
> DR. VON KILLIAN: I'd like to comment on this if I may.
> WOLF: Well, be my guest. Since you are my guest.

The movie concludes with one of the more unbelievable psycho movie scenes. The killer calls in, within seconds the police trace the call, race to his apartment, burst in, and arrest him. The arrest is aired live, of course, because he's still on the air with Wolf.

In *Acts of Contrition*, aka *Original Sins*, a 1995 TV movie, priest Jonathan

Frayne (Mark Harmon) hosts the late-night talk show *True Confessions* on WPOV Boston. On his first show he admits to killing a friend by locking him in a refrigerator when they were children and then invites listeners to share their secrets. Callers admit to numerous crimes and when one admits to a murder, police become interested and want Frayne to help track the killer by tracing the calls. Then the killer begins making threatening calls to Frayne at home and on the air, with his voice disguised electronically.

The 1995 TV movie *When the Dark Man Calls* was based on the Stuart Kaminsky novel, as was the 1988 French production *Frequent Death*. This time, WRAP talk show host Julianne Kaiser (Joan Van Ark) is stalked by the man who killed her husband 25 years before. Kaiser's testimony put the killer behind bars but now he's served his sentence and he's back with threatening calls to Kaiser's show. The radio audience is able to hear these threats, of course, since there is no delay system in use. Later, when the ex-con himself turns up dead, the film turns into a whodunit with numerous possibilities as to who the real psychopath may be.

Vanessa Scott (Carol Hoyt) hosts a sex talk show in *Midnight Confessions* (1995) with Mitch (David Millbern) as her operator. As the film opens, the police are investigating a series of prostitute murders. Much of the movie is comprised of superfluous scenes depicting the sexual fantasies of Vanessa's listeners, most of whom are beautiful women who wear little clothing. One evening Mitch says he has to take a break and while he's gone Vanessa gets a call from "Rick," who says "I love you, Vanessa" and describes her activities that day. Shots of the empty control room as Vanessa talks to Rick reveal the caller's true identity, although Vanessa fails to pick up on it. When Mitch is late for work one day, Vanessa gets another call from Rick. Mitch also visits his brother Johnny in prison, where they discuss their mother's murder; when Johnny urges Mitch to kill Vanessa, it is apparent that Mitch has a split personality. Naturally, Mitch turns out to be the prostitute killer but the unknowing Vanessa invites him home where they make love. Vanessa then decides to take a shower which is interrupted when Mitch/Rick/Johnny opens the shower door. Despite the film's vapid plot and B-movie acting, the ending is mildly interesting because it concludes with Mitch in prison but leaves unclear whether he actually killed Vanessa, since the final credits roll and she is not heard on the air again, as is the usual case in these films.

Death follows Lynn Richards (Colette O'Connell) in *Shattered Illusions* (1998) when she's hired to host a talk show on KBST Los Angeles. Richards spent time in a mental institution after attempting suicide and has nightmares about the accident that caused her mother's death and left her sister mentally impaired. Her father, who caused the fatal accident, has been released from prison after 12 years and wants back into his daughters' lives. Then Richards starts getting phone calls from "Adam" (Leland Crooke), a listener who seems to know intimate details of her life. Richards' obstreperous neighbor and a rip-off mechanic, both of whom she complained about on the air, are gruesomely murdered. Next to meet their fates are her father and a neighbor's dog that Richards also griped about on her show (and whose remains arrive in a box at the station). After her father's murder, Richards refuses to take Adam's calls, which pushes him over the edge and incites him to kidnap Richards' sister. This film is different from most psycho movies in that the face of the killer is seen early in the proceedings and any tension arises from his motivation and how the threat to Richards will be resolved.

Tracy Nelson is the shy and lonely convenience store clerk Beth Needham in *The Night Caller* (1998), but she summons up the nerve to call a radio psychologist she admires, Dr. Lindsey Roland (Shanna Reed) at KBEX San Diego. Unaware that Needham has a fixation on her, Roland advises her to "think of someone you'd like to have as a friend," which triggers a further fixation on Needham's part. It is later revealed that Needham killed her father at the age of seven and was institutionalized for some time. When her domineering and bedridden mother ridicules her idolization of Roland, Needham lets her die when her oxygen tank runs out. Needham begins stalking Roland, gets a job at her telephone answering service, then as her babysitter. The answering service job lets her take control of Roland's life by manipulating her appointments, and she kills anyone whom she believes is threatening her perceived relationship with the psychologist. Needham thus displays the classic "hunter" psychopathic personality.

Molly Ringwald is WZIN classical music announcer Anne Winslow in *Requiem for Murder*, a 1999 Canadian film set in Philadelphia. She begins receiving red roses coinciding with murders in which the victims drank poisoned wine. All were listening to Winslow's program when they were killed and the crimes become known in the media as the "Mozart murders" because of the music being played at the times of their deaths. Police suspect a serial killer with a fixation on the DJ and possible suspects include a co-announcer with a drinking problem and an admitted attraction to her, a professor of music she interviewed and who makes sexual advances, and her operator, a young man with an attitude. The culprit, however, turns out to be the stage manager at Fisher Hall where Winslow is about to announce a concert. The manager (Charles Powell) admits to Winslow that he's the killer and only wants to protect her. He dies by accidentally hanging himself in the rigging above the stage as he's chased by the detectives who arrive at the concert in the nick of time. The ending is unsatisfactory because little motivation is given for the murders, there's no reason for the killer to suddenly confess, and the confession violates one of the rules of mystery movie scriptwriting by introducing at the end a killer who has not previously been seen. This cheats the audience, which has been guessing which of the suspects might be the person responsible. Both a DJ and a news anchor are threatened by a caller in *Dead Air* (1999). Jack Auphil (John Marlo) is the shock jock and Amanda Quaker (Margot Hope) is the news anchor. In a throwback to the 1930s and '40s radio murder films, station personnel start dying and as they do the station's ratings go up. Then a caller threatens both Auphil and Quaker but police suspect Auphil himself and he has to prove his innocence.

The Midnight Hour, aka *Tell Me No Lies* (2000), also discussed in Chapter Three, began with the murder of a co-ed. Her sister Alex (Amber Smith) decides to find the killer and gets a job at the school's radio station. Why she believes this would aid her investigation is not clear but, in the type of coincidence found mostly in B-movies, the job leads her to the killer. David (Byron Bay), the program director, was the dead girl's boyfriend; upon meeting Alex, he immediately gives her her own talk show. This allows the killer to surface because the second call she takes is from "Henry," who threatens her by saying, "I'm gonna kill you just like I killed her." On her second night, Henry is the first caller and he tells her that he killed her sister. With no delay system used, listeners hear the confession. On her third night, Alex decides not to take any more calls, but David says perhaps Henry will call and police can identify him. Sure enough, Henry is the second caller and explicitly describes her sister's death, which the audience again hears. The following evening when a power blackout knocks the station off the air, Alex and David find the engineer dead in the basement. They flee to David's mother's house where they end up naked in a hot tub. The film ends when David's brother Brad shows up and takes David and Alex hostage. He explains that he always hated David and wants to take everything that David has had, including Alex and her sister. Once the killer's motivation has been explained, the hostages break free and Alex kills Brad by hitting him on the head with a baseball bat fortuitously lying nearby.

Radyo was a 2001 Philippines film with Mila (Rufa Mae Quinto) as a DJ who takes listeners' song requests but who makes a big mistake by ridiculing the musical tastes of a caller named Ruben (Jeffrey Quizon). He requested a song in hopes of impressing one of the office girls he works with, but not only does Mila denigrate his song choice on the air, the office girl will have nothing to do with him either. Twice humiliated, Ruben decides to vent his anger by killing as many women as he can, including Mila, but inexplicably calls her show with clues about his next murders.

The Canadian TV movie *You Belong to Me* (2001) was based on a Mary Higgins Clark novel of the same title. Dr. Susan Chancellor (Lesley-Anne Down), a psychologist who hosts a talk show on WQUR New York discusses the three-year-old case of a missing heiress financier who disappeared while on a cruise. This prompts a call from Karen, who says she was given a ring inscribed "You Belong to Me" by a stranger who tried to lure her off a cruise ship in Algiers. The missing heiress' mother reveals that her daughter also had been given such a ring. Karen is hit by a car and put into a coma as she goes to Chancellor's office to bring her the ring, as is another woman who called to say her boyfriend gave her an inscribed ring. The jeweler who made the rings is also found dead. The key to the case is the words to the song "You Belong to Me" because each location mentioned in the lyrics, Algiers, the pyramids along the Nile, etc., is the scene of an abduction attempt or murder.

American Nightmare (2002) put a slasher spin on the psycho listener theme. A DJ named Caligari (real-life Dallas air personality Chris Ryan) hosts an all-night show on a Texas pirate station. One Halloween he invites his listeners to share their nightmares by asking, "What makes you scared?" Several college students decide to call in with their fears, unaware that a psycho is also listening. One by one the callers begin dying in gruesome ways corresponding to the fears they expressed on the air, and then the psycho calls Caligari to send taunting dedications to the dead and threats to the remaining students. This movie is unusual on three counts: The psycho is a woman, her identity is known from the beginning, and she is not captured or killed at the movie's end.

In *Sinful Desires* (2002), Angelica Weston (Jacy Andrews) goes by the on-air name Gia when she hosts the Los Angeles sexual advice show *Nightwatch*. The plot consists mostly of sexual scenes depicting callers' stories, and lacks a logical storyline. One day Gia receives pictures of herself taken inside of her home, and also threatening phone calls with the voice disguised electronically. Someone creates a website and posts explicit videos of her having sex. Then Nick (Alex Ferro), a good-looking stranger, approaches her in the station parking lot and within days they are having sex in her living room, with the drapes conveniently open so more explicit pictures can be taken. For some unexplained reason Gia later goes to the station manager's house but finds him dead on the floor and her most recent explicit photographs on a table. Next she receives an anonymous threatening call from "Jake," whose voice is electronically disguised. Jake, however, was the name of a bar owner that Gia had been having sex with and who died of a drug overdose in the bar. The caller turns out to be a jealous waitress in Jake's bar, who had also been sleeping with him. Police inexplicably arrive at the bar to arrest her during the call, and it's all broadcast to Gia's audience. As the film ends, Nick visits Gia in the control room where they engage in some sexual activity for the amusement or gratification of the listeners ("I'm gonna share with all of you my own sexual fantasy, live on the air...").

A slightly more coherent script was provided for a Canadian made-for-TV movie, again set in Philadelphia. In *A Lover's Revenge* (2005), Alexandra Paul is Dr. Liz Manners, who dispenses relationship advice on WLOR. Over the opening credits, a female caller says her husband James (William R. Moses) is controlling her life. Unfortunately for her, James arrives home during the call. Terrified, the woman flees and is struck and killed by a passing car. In the type of elaborate plan seen only on film, James takes revenge on Manners by paying a woman to seduce her husband Rob (Gary Hudson) to break up their marriage. He later kills Rob and makes it appear that Manners is the culprit. Manners eventually solves the case by listening to several months' worth of tapes of her show and deducing who James is and why he wants her dead. The film concludes, as do many of the psycho listener movies, with the killer chasing the talk show host and the police arriving just in time to save her life.

Psycho Air Personalities

In some films, the air personalities, usually psychologists, have more personal or emotional problems than the listeners. Interestingly, the first of these was the Polish film *Cma*, aka *The Moth* (1980), which told the story of a talk show host who develops a severe psychological disorder. Jan (Roman Wilhelmi) hosts a show in which he invites callers to share their problems with the audience, but his own troubles are mounting. Station management is not happy with the program, his wife is an alcoholic, his mistress does not appreciate him either, and he begins to suffer from a nervous breakdown. ("I feel like an ashtray where everyone can dump all their problems and move on and I'm left with that dirt.") As the pressures mount, Jan is less and less able to cope and he eventually ends up in a mental institution.

As previously mentioned, *Choose Me* (1984), the first American film to feature an air personality with psychological problems, starred Genevieve Bujold as KCMY radio psychologist Dr. Nancy Love. Eve (Lesley Ann Warren), a bar owner, calls Dr. Love to discuss her inability to maintain relationships with men. In the type of coincidence often seen in movies, Eve takes Love as a roommate, not knowing her identity since Love inquired about the arrangement under an assumed name. Love also has numerous psychological problems, for which her show apparently serves as a kind of therapy, and her unstable nature is revealed in a phone conversation with her own psychologist, Dr. Ernest Greene:

> LOVE: I'm beginning to, uh, understand myself better, now. Entering a more knowing phase. And I know that I remain my own worst enemy. And I also know that I am my own savior, because freedom means responsibility, Ernest.
> GREENE: Nancy, you're not making any sense.
> LOVE: And believe me, I also know how easily desire can be converted to deed. Even when I close my eyes, I have to be careful of what I dream and how ... I ...
> GREENE: All right, Nancy, now it's happening again. I want to see you first thing in the morning. I don't care what your schedule is.

Enter Mickey (Keith Carradine), a homocidal drifter just released from a mental institution who takes advantage of the insecurities of both Eve and Love. The movie is both a story of relationships and a study of a psychologist who's unable to help herself while diagnosing the problems of others.

Dr. Clair Archer (Lisa Pescia) also has problems in *Body Chemistry 2: Voice of a Stranger* (1992). She's a sex show therapist who's been hired to boost the ratings of KSAV in a town near Los Angeles. Arriving in town about the same time is Dan Pearson (Gregory Harrison), an ex-cop booted from the LAPD for his violent behavior, who now runs his father's garage. His girlfriend Brenda (Robin Riker) happens to be the call screener for Dr. Archer's show. The psychologist herself has a propensity for sexual violence that she reveals to her listeners: "Remember, pain defines pleasure. If you are always happy, you'll never know it. Without pain, you're not truly alive."

Dan calls her show as "John" to ask for Archer's advice in ameliorating his proclivities for violence. After the show, Dan arrives to pick up Brenda and meets Archer, who later visits his garage to say she recognized his voice. She advises him to go into therapy and they soon have a rough and steamy sexual encounter. Then KSAV station manager Big Chuck (real-life TV personality Morton Downey, Jr.) reveals to Archer that he has a porno tape she made some years before and blackmails her into signing a syndication contract with him. To break the contract by blackmailing him, she later secretly videotapes a bondage scene with Big Chuck in the control room during which he dies of an apparent heart attack. The film ends with Dan being shot by police as he threatens to kill Archer; he's had enough of her domineering personality but she won't end the relationship. The film's final image is of a billboard promoting Archer's show on Los Angeles station KCLA.

This was the second of four titles in the *Body Chemistry* series. In the 1990 original, Clair Archer (Lisa Pescia) was a Los Angeles sexologist; in *Body Chemistry 3: Point of Seduction* (1994) a producer wants to turn Archer's story into a TV show (Shari Shattuck plays Archer); and in *Body Chemistry 4: Full*

Exposure (1995) Archer (former Playboy Playmate Shannon Tweed) has become a TV producer who must defend herself against a murder charge in the death of a co-producer.

The title of the TV movie *Sexual Response* (1992) is also the name of a show hosted by Dr. Eve Robinson (Shannon Tweed) on KRSX. Robinson's husband Philip (Vernon Wells) is an extremely jealous man. One day after work, Robinson goes to a bar where she dances with a good-looking motorcycle rider. Shortly thereafter, she gets a call on her show from "Edge" (Emile Levisetti), who says he's in love with her without mentioning her name; Robinson recognizes his voice as that of the motorcyclist. Edge, a sculptor, picks up Robinson on his bike and takes her to his loft studio where they have the first of several sexual encounters. Philip intuits that his wife is seeing another man and the situation isn't helped when Edge leaves a life-sized nude statue of Robinson in their driveway. The film ends in a violent confrontation between the two men in which Edge reveals that Philip is his father.

Los Angeles radio sex therapist Dr. Amanda Grace (Kate Vernon) has a sex addiction problem herself in *Dangerous Touch* (1994). This is made evident to the audience in the opening scene in which she has an early-morning sexual encounter with a man in a hallway. Grace dispenses advice on her show *Ask Amanda* and when an engaging young man asks for her autograph at a book signing they soon discover a common fondness for rough sex. The man is Mick Burroughs (Lou Diamond Phillips), an ex-con on the run from the mob after stealing their money. Burroughs entices Grace into a lesbian bondage session and then blackmails her with a surreptitious video recording to get information about one of her clients, the mob boss. Grace won't go along with the blackmail attempt and the tape is made public, which turns her into an even bigger media star. The film's climax is a shootout between Grace, Burroughs, and the mob.

Dead Air (1994) was a TV movie with Gregory Hines as DJ Jim Shepard at KHR All-Hit Radio. His off-air name is Mark Jannek and he's haunted by the death of his former girlfriend. Shepard begins receiving threatening phone calls from a woman while he's on the air, apparently a stalker because she knows personal details about his life. When a woman he meets in a bar is murdered, he becomes a suspect. Complications arise when Shepard's dead girlfriend's sister arrives on the scene, followed by the murder of the radio station's secretary. This would have been considered a psycho listener film except for the surprise ending which reveals that Shepard has a split personality, alternating between Jim and Mark. Mark made the threatening phone calls to Jim by recording them and altering the pitch to make it seem as though the stalker was a female listener.

Likewise, *Power 98* (1996) is seemingly a psycho listener film but its ending puts it in the psycho air personality category. Karlin Pickett (Eric Roberts) is a talk show host on KOZY Power 98 in Los Angeles. The station switched from classical music and Pickett was hired for the afternoon drive time program with the promise of a lucrative new contract if his show gets at least a 25 share (25 percent of the listening audience). Pickett convinces the manager to let intern Jon Price (Jason Gedrick) co-host and they dream up increasingly explicit sexual topics for the show. The ratings skyrocket when a caller claims to have killed a woman, but Pickett reveals to Price that the call was faked and made by his friend Eddie to boost the ratings. However, police confirm the woman's death and then Eddie calls again to confess to another murder, a woman Jon met in a bar. The film's climax comes in an abandoned warehouse when Jon confronts Pickett, who admits he's Eddie and made the calls to himself. He demonstrates his equipment, including a tape machine, timer, and electronic device to disguise his voice. Jon then reveals he's been wearing a police wire and Pickett's confession has been aired on KOZY. The following police shootout (in which Pickett is killed by plunging to his death from the building) is also broadcast. Although the plot is plausible only to a movie script writer, it raises an interesting ethical question about the lengths to which an air personality might go in a quest for higher ratings and the resultant financial rewards.

The 2000 TV movie *Bare Deception* is another film that might have been considered a psycho listener film but for the ending. It raises ethical issues similar to *Power 98*: Julia Collins hosts *Talk Love* on KTLK Los Angeles. The ratings are abysmal and her producer Christian Moss (Daniel Anderson), who's also her live-in boyfriend, says the show needs something sensational to attract listeners. Collins tries a matchmaking idea and the first woman to call in describes herself as a beautiful blonde. "David" calls to make a match but it's really Christian using his car phone. After Christian and the blonde meet and have sex, he leaves and she is smothered to death by an anonymous intruder. When a second caller also turns up dead after being matched with Christian under another assumed name, police come to the station to compare tapes of the male callers in hopes of identifying the voice. Someone has been tipping off the other media about a possible connection between *Talk Love* and the murders, and TV reporters gather outside the KTLK building. Christian is arrested and Julia later hears that her show is rated number one in Los Angeles. However, at the movie's end a TV reporter tells a detective that the tipster was a woman, which rules out Christian, and a subsequent scene reveals the killer to be Julia, trying to increase her ratings.

The title of *Mad Song* (2003) was taken from a William Blake poem of the same name. The film is the surrealistic and disjointed story of KRCK Los Angeles talk show therapist Dr. Tessa Crystal (Kandeyce Jorden), whose life begins to fall apart when her father dies. She tells a caller, "The past will find you, Katherine. It's simply not possible to lock out," which serves both as a warning and a prediction for her own life, and for the film itself. Crystal's story is told in flashbacks; she's haunted both by her mother's preternatural singing voice and also by her mother's emotional and sexual problems that traumatized Crystal as a child. As she tries to adjust to her father's death, an acquaintance from the past asks for her help — a Goth singer he manages is having psychological problems. The singer, Dawn (Colette O'Connell), displays signs of a split personality as well as other emotional issues and this additional stress begins to push Crystal over the edge. By the film's end, it is not possible for either her or the audience to differentiate the real from the fantasies of her past.

Matthew Altman (Matthew Settle) is a writer who stalks his ex-girlfriend Liz (Gretchen Mol) in *Attraction* (2000). Matthew also hosts a talk show in which he dispenses relationship advice but he himself has deep psychological problems that manifest themselves in intense jealousy. He then meets and has sex with Liz's friend Corey (Samantha Mathis) and transfers his obsession to her. Liz's friend Garrett (Tom Everett Scott) tries to protect Liz by stalking Matthew, and the film becomes a four-way psychological thriller. Despite the unsavory nature of the characters, this is one of the more interesting psycho films in that the characters and the relationships between them are more complex than those usually found in such movies.

In *Cherish* (2002), Zoe Adler (Robin Tunney) plays an insecure young woman who enjoys listening to oldies station KXCH Cherish Radio. One evening she meets a man who also loves oldies music. While driving home drunk with him, she strikes and kills a police officer, and her unidentified passenger disappears with her cell phone. Awaiting trial, Zoe is put into an electronic bracelet program in a secure house and begins receiving threatening calls from her lost cell phone. In an implausible plot twist, she is able to escape from her electronic bracelet and track down the mystery man who turns out to be a DJ at KXCH. He had been stalking Zoe and his room is filled with numerous pictures of her. A rooftop chase ensues as he tries to kill her but police arrive in time, having tracked her by the GPS ankle bracelet.

Undoubtedly the most psychopathic air personality seen on film was JoBeth Williams as Dr. Lillian Rose in *Deranged*, aka *The Rose Technique* (2002). A radio psychiatrist on KWSP in Eureka, California, she dreams of becoming a television personality. She promotes her "Rose technique" (Root, Own, Separate, Eliminate) to help her patients and callers overcome their anxieties. She has personality problems, however, which are evidenced by the tantrum she throws when her radio show is cancelled and by the mannequin to whom she expresses her anxieties at home. Her radio show axed, Rose heads to Los Angeles to pursue a television career and in the meantime takes a part-time college teaching job. She enjoys rose gardening but her shears are soon put to good use for other purposes. When a loan application is turned down by an obnoxious loan officer, she attacks him after work and cuts off his ears. A student who uses a drug to date rape another student in her class loses his fingers. A skeptical journalism student who investigates her murky background (discovering a name change and other interesting information) is attacked with a baseball bat and has his leg broken.

Rose is an unparalleled manipulator who uses another student to help her produce a video in her attempt to land a cable TV hosting job. Although the story has numerous improbable plot twists, *Deranged* is an interesting study of one person's obsession with media fame and the lengths to which she will go to remove any obstacles to achieving it.

Jodie Foster was late-night talk show host Erica Bain on WNKW New York in *The Brave One* (2007). Her psychological problems arise from a mugging and do not involve listeners. When Bain and her fiancé are viciously attacked by a street gang, and her fiancé killed, she buys a gun to seek revenge. The film has echoes of *Death Wish*, a 1974 revenge movie with Charles Bronson but, unlike the Bronson character, Bain does not relish her role as vigilante. Having sought out the men who attacked her, she finds that she can't stop killing and takes to the streets night after night. Bain, however, hates the vigilante she has become and the life she has lost: "And you look at the person you once were walking down that street and you wonder, will you? Will you ever be her again?" And later she answers her own question: "There is no going back to that other person, that other place. This thing, this stranger, she is all you are now."

The film is as much a portrait of the urban American landscape as it is a study of the troubled Bain's addiction to vengeance. She narrates her feelings through much of the film; Terrence Howard is the detective trying to track down the serial killer she has become.

One radio film psycho air personality stands out from the others: the aforementioned Dan Aykroyd in *The Couch Trip*, the only psycho comedy. Aykroyd is John W. Burns, Jr., a con man trying to convince the authorities he's deranged to avoid prison time. He escapes from the mental institution where he's been sent for a psychiatric evaluation and through an unbelievable chain of events assumes the identity of Los Angeles psychiatrist George Maitlin (Charles Grodin). Burns is then offered a job hosting a radio talk show under his assumed name and becomes a sensation with his blunt and often foul-mouthed advice to listeners. The plot entails Maitlin's attempts to get his identity back and Burns' efforts to stay one step ahead of the law.

Several films have had storylines in which talk show hosts face problems of various types, but who cannot be classified as psychopathic personalities. As they struggle with the usual vicissitudes of life, they keep a grip on reality and try to work through their problems as real people might. These include *The Truth About Cats and Dogs* (1996; the host of a show for pet lovers has problems with her personal life); *A Valentine Carol* (2007; a talk show host with a domineering personality learns what it means to be human when the ghost of her former mentor takes her to visit boyfriends past); *Amy's O*, aka *Amy's Orgasm* (2001; a shock jock forces a feminist author to re-examine her feelings and her theories); *The Republic of Love* (2003; a talk show host looks for true love); and *Radio Cape Cod* (2008; a talk show host copes with the loss of her husband). Many more of the titles in the filmography depict air personalities trying to resolve personal problems, to which the thumbnail descriptions will attest.

While psycho listeners or air personalities are rare in foreign films, many international movies have included storylines in which DJs or talk show hosts face relationship issues or personal problems. A few of these were *Escuela de seduccion* (2004, Spain; a feminist talk show host begins a relationship with a sexist caller); *salaam namaste* (2005, India; a DJ begins a relationship with a chef); *Piter FM* (2006, Russia; a talk show host becomes involved with another man on the eve of her marriage); *Radio Love* (2008, Spain; a talk show host tries to cope with the reality of aging); *Radio: Love on Air* (2009, India; a DJ's personal life is thrown into turmoil by his divorce); *Hello My Love* (2009, South Korea; a DJ struggles with her emotions when she discovers her boyfriend is gay); and *Hikidashi no Naka no Love Letter*, aka *Listen to My Heart* (2009, Japan; a DJ copes with her father's death). While these films may lack the drama, violence, and intensity of American psycho listener movies, they obviously present a more realistic picture of both the real and radio worlds.

Likewise, the psycho listener films discussed in this chapter no more reflect the actual world of talk radio than, say, the radio detective or cowboy films discussed in Chapter Two were historical documents of those eras. While I have argued that since radio films are a product of the times in which they were produced and therefore reflect those societies to a degree, films should be considered neither as literal cultural photographs of America at any given time nor completely accurate pictures of radio broadcasting, as I have indicated throughout the book.

Filmography

The filmography includes only feature-length live-action films and movies made for television. All are U.S. productions unless noted. Many have not been released on either DVD or VHS, although some are available online, and some foreign films do not have English subtitles. Asterisks indicate the movies I viewed when researching this book.

The Radio Detective (1926, Universal Pictures). Silent. Directors: William James Craft, William A. Crinley. Producer: Henry MacRae. Cast: Jack Dougherty, Margaret Quimby. Thieves rob dancers listening to radio broadcast.

*Say It with Songs (1929, Warner Bros.). 95 min. Director: Lloyd Bacon. Producer: Darryl F. Zanuck. Cast: Al Jolson, Davey Lee, Marian Nixon. Radio singer kills man who had been making advances to his wife, goes to jail, tries to resurrect career.

*Weary River (1929, First National Pictures). 86 min. Director: Frank Lloyd. Producer: Richard A. Rowland. Cast: Richard Barthelmess, Betty Compson. Convict wins early release by singing with prison band on radio.

Remote Control (1930, MGM). 65 min. Directors: Nick Grinde, Malcom St. Clair, Edward Sedgwick. Producer: Edward Sedgwick. Cast: William Haines, Mary Doran. Announcer discovers colleague has mob involvement.

The Concentratin' Kid (1930, Hoot Gibson Productions). 57 min. Director: Arthur Rosson. Producer: Carl Laemmle, Jr. Cast: Hoot Gibson, Kathryn Crawford. Cowboy bets he can marry radio singer he has never seen.

*The Miracle Woman (1931, Columbia Pictures). 90 min. Director: Frank Capra. Producer: Harry Cohn. Cast: Barbara Stanwyck, David Manners. Con artist uses radio to start career as evangelist.

Scareheads (1931, Richard Talmadge Productions). 67 min. Director: Noel Smith (as Noel Mason). Producer: Richard Talmadge. Lead actor: Richard Talmadge. Confession secretly broadcast clears convicted killer.

*The Spider (1931, Fox Film Corp.). 59 min. Directors: Kenneth MacKenna, William Cameron Menzies. Producer: William Sistrom. Cast: Edmund Lowe, Lois Moran. Radio clairvoyant tries to solve murder.

*The Secret Witness, aka *Terror by Night* (1931, Columbia Pictures). 66 min. Director: Thornton Freeland. Producer: J.G. Bachmann. Cast: William Collier, Jr., Una Merkel, ZaSu Pitts. Hidden pistol is triggered by radio broadcast to commit murder remotely.

*Caught Plastered (1931, RKO Radio Pictures). 68 min. Director: William A. Seiter. Producer: William LeBaron. Cast: Bert Wheeler, Robert Woolsey. Ex-vaudevillians use radio to save diner from foreclosure.

War Correspondent (1932, Columbia Pictures). 76 min. Director: Paul Sloane. Producer: Harry Cohn. Cast: Ralph Graves, Jack Holt, Lila Lee. Radio reporter becomes involved with Chinese prostitute.

*The Big Broadcast (1932, Paramount Publix Corp.). 80 min. Director: Frank Tuttle. Producer: Benjamin Glazer. Cast: Bing Crosby, Stuart Erwin, Sharon Lynne. Marital problems affect singer's on-air performance.

*Are You Listening? (1932, MGM). 73 min. Director: Harry Beaumont. Cast: William Haines, Madge Evans. Announcer leads on-air hunt for wife's killer.

*The All-American (1932, Universal Pictures). 79 min. Director: Russell Mack. Producer: Carl Laemmle, Jr. Cast: Richard Arlen, John Darrow, Andy Devine. Play-by-play description of college football game pitting brother against brother.

*The Sport Parade (1932, RKO Radio Pictures). 64 min. Director: Dudley Murphy. Producer: David O. Selznick. Cast: Joel McCrea, William Gargan, Marian Marsh. Play-by-play broadcasts of college football games, six-day bicycle race, and wrestling matches.

*The Crowd Roars (1932, Warner Bros.). 85 min. Director: Howard Hawks. Cast: James Cagney, Eric Linden, Ann Dvorak. Radio coverage of Indy 500 in which driver substitutes for injured brother.

*Professional Sweetheart (1933, RKO Radio Pictures). 70 min. Director: William A. Seiter. Producer: Merian C. Cooper. Cast: Ginger Rogers, Norman Foster, ZaSu Pitts. Radio singer rebels against her all-American image.

*From Hell to Heaven (1933, Paramount Pictures). 67 min. Director: Erle C. Kenton. Cast: Carole Lombard, Jack Oakie, Adrienne Ames, David Manners. Broadcast of horse race that affects many lives.

*My Woman (1933, Columbia Pictures). 76 min. Director: Victor Schertzinger. Producer: Felix Young. Cast: Helen Twelvetrees, Victor Jory. Singer gets husband network radio job but success goes to his head.

*The Phantom Broadcast (1933, W.T. Lackey Productions). 72 min. Director: Phil Rosen. Producer: Trem Carr. Cast: Ralph Forbes, Vivienne Osborne. Murder of radio singer whose real voice is hunchbacked piano player.

*International House (1933, Paramount Pictures). 72 min. Director: Edward Sutherland. Producer: Emanuel Cohen. Cast: Peggy Hopkins Joyce, W. C. Fields, George Burns, Gracie Allen. Chinese scientist's device to add television pictures to radio doesn't work exactly as planned.

*Torch Singer (1933, Paramount Pictures). 71 min. Directors: Alexander Hall, George Somnes. Producer: Albert Lewis. Cast: Claudette Colbert, Ricardo Cortez, David Manners. Night club singer uses children's radio show to find long-lost daughter.

*Myrt and Marge (1933, Bryan Foy Productions). 62 min. Director: Al Boasbert. Producers: Bryan Foy, Eddie Foy, Jr. Cast: Myrtle Vail, Donna Damarel. Song-and-dance troupe's struggles to make it to Broadway turn out to be radio play.

Mr. Broadway (1933, Broadway-Hollywood Productions). 63 min. Director-Producer: Johnnie Walker. Cast: Ed Sullivan, Jack Dempsey, Ruth Etting. Newspaper columnist Ed Sullivan visits club where Ted Husing is broadcasting show and regales patrons with interesting stories.

*The Big Chance (1933, Morris Shiller Productions). 62 min. Director: Albert Herman. Producer: Morris Shiller. Cast: John Darrow, Merna Kennedy. Broadcast of fight that boxer refuses to throw.

*Elmer, the Great (1933, First National Pictures). 72 min. Director: Mervyn LeRoy. Cast: Joe E. Brown, Patricia Ellis. Play-by-play broadcasts of hick becoming Chicago Cubs star.

*College Coach (1933, Warner Bros.). 76 min. Director: William A. Wellman. Cast: Pat O'Brien, Dick Powell, Ann Dvorak. Play-by-play accounts of football games that coach will do anything to win.

Ladies They Talk About (1933, Warner Bros.). 69 min. Directors: Howard Bretherton, William Keighley. Producer: Raymond Griffith. Cast: Barbara Stanwyck, Preston Foster. Radio evangelist falls in love with bank robbers' accomplice.

Housewife (1934, Warner Bros.). 69 min. Director: Alfred E. Green. Producer: Jack L. Warner. Cast: George Brent, Bette Davis, Ann Dvorak. Housewife helps husband start ad agency.

The Loudspeaker (1934, W. T. Lackey Productions). 67 min. Director: Joseph Santley. Producer: William T. Lackey. Cast: Ray Walker, Julie Bishop, Charley Grapewin. Wannabe radio star becomes host of network program and lets success go to his head.

Death at Broadcasting House (1934, Phoenix, Britain). 75 min. Director: Reginald Denham. Producer: Hugh Perceval. Cast: Jack Hawkins, Ian Hunter, Austin Trevor. Actor is murdered during live broadcast.

A Successful Failure (1934, Monogram Pictures). 67 min. Director: Arthur Lubin. Producer: George Yohalem. Cast: William Collier, Sr., Lucile Gleason. Fired newspaper reporter finds success as host of children's radio show.

Shoot the Works (1934, Paramount Pictures). 64 min. Director: Wesley Ruggles. Producers: Albert Lewis, Adolph Zukor. Cast: Jack Oakie, Ben Bernie, Dorothy Dell. Sideshow barker lands radio job.

Take the Stand (1934, Liberty Pictures). 78 min. Director: Phil Rosen. Producer: M. H. Hoffman. Cast: Jack La Rue, Thelma Todd. Hated radio gossip columnist is killed.

Fifteen Wives (1934, Invincible Pictures). 65 min. Director: Frank R. Strayer. Producer: Maury M. Cohen. Cast: Conway Tearle, Natalie Moorhead, Raymond Hatton. Man known as "The Electric Voice" broadcasts sound waves at specific frequency to break container of deadly acid and kill listener.

Palooka (1934, Edward Small Productions). 86 min. Director: Benjamin Stoloff. Producer: Edward Small. Cast: Stuart Erwin, Jimmy Durante, Lupe Velez. Radio broadcast of fight in film based on comic strip character.

The Woman Condemned (1934, Progressive Pictures). 66 min. Director: Dorothy Davenport. Producer: Willis Kent. Cast: Claudia Dell, Lola Lane, Richard Hemingway. Reporter tries to solve murder of radio star.

Melody in Spring (1934, Paramount Pictures). 75 min. Director: Norman McLeod. Producer: Douglas MacLean. Cast: Lanny Ross, Charles Ruggles, Mary Boland. Singer gets radio job with help of sponsor's daughter.

King Kelly of the U.S.A. (1934, Monogram Pictures). 66 min. Director: Leonard Fields. Producer: George C. Bertholon. Cast: Guy Robertson, Edgar Kennedy. Entertainers stranded in Europe raise money by using radio to sell mops to housewives.

Gift of Gab (1934, Universal Pictures). 70 min. Director: Karl Freund. Producer: Carl Laemmle, Jr. Cast: Edmund Lowe, Gloria Stuart, Ruth Etting. Radio reporter fired over fake broadcast redeems himself by doing live broadcast while parachuting.

Strictly Dynamite (1934, Universal Pictures). 71 min. Director: Elliott Nugent. Producer: Pandro S. Berman. Cast: Jimmy Durante, Lupe Velez, Norman Foster. Radio gag writer's life falls apart when he runs out of jokes.

One Hour Late (1934, Paramount Pictures). 74 min. Director: Ralph Murphy. Producer: Albert Lewis. Cast: Joe Morrison, Helen Twelvetrees, Conrad Nagel. File clerk tries to make it as radio singer.

Twenty Million Sweethearts (1934, First National Pictures). 89 min. Director: Ray Enright. Producer: Samuel Bischoff. Cast: Pat O'Brien, Dick Powell, Ginger Rogers. Talent scout turns singing waiter into radio star.

Paradise Valley (1934, Imperial Productions). 51 min. Director-Producer: James P. Hogan. Cast: Sam Pierce, Jean Chatburn, Wheeler Oakman. Radio singer settles dispute between sheepherders and cattlemen by organizing them all into radio cowboy singing group.

__Many Happy Returns__ (1934, Paramount Pictures). 64 min. Director: Norman McLeod. Producer: William LeBaron. Cast: Gracie Allen, George Burns, George Barbier. Gracie Allen wreaks havoc with father's radio station, then heads to Hollywood.

__Broadway Gondolier__ (1935, Warner Bros.). 99 min. Director: Lloyd Bacon. Producer: Samuel Bischoff. Cast: Dick Powell, Joan Blondell, Adolphe Menjou. Taxi driver goes to Venice to develop radio singing career.

__Radio Parade of 1935__, aka *Radio Follies* (1935, Associated British Picture Corp., Britain). 96 min. Director: Arthur B. Woods. Producer: Walter C. Mycroft. Cast: Will Hay, Helen Chandler, Clifford Mollison. Radio producer saves job by staging variety show.

__Make a Million__ (1935, Monogram Pictures). 68 min. Director: Lewis D. Collins. Producer: Trem Carr. Cast: Charles Starrett, Pauline Brooks. Professor uses radio ads to prove his economic theories correct.

__Page Miss Glory__ (1935, Cosmopolitan Productions). 93 min. Director: Mervyn LeRoy. Producer: Marion Davies. Cast: Marion Davies, Pat O'Brien, Dick Powell. Con men turn chambermaid into media star.

__Thanks a Million__ (1935, 20th Century Pictures). 87 min. Director: Roy Del Ruth. Producer: Darryl F. Zanuck. Cast: Dick Powell, Ann Dvorak, Fred Allen. Radio entertainers become involved in political campaign.

__She Shall Have Music__ (1935, Twickenham Film Studios, Britain). 91 min. Director: Leslie S. Hiscott. Producer: Julius Hagen. Cast: Jack Hylton, June Clyde, Claude Dampier. Band does worldwide broadcast from ship, unaware of sabotage plans by rival shipowner.

__Every Night at Eight__ (1935, Walter Wanger Productions). 80 min. Director: Raoul Walsh. Producer: Walter Wanger. Cast: George Raft, Alice Faye, Patsy Kelly. Three young women fired from ad agency end up working at radio station.

__Millions in the Air__ (1935, Paramount Pictures). 71 min. Director: Ray McCarey. Producer: Harold Hurley. Cast: John Howard, Wendy Barrie. Eclectic group of hopefuls competes in radio talent contest.

__Radio Pirates__ (1935, Sound City, Britain). 89 min. Director: Ivar Campbell. Producer: Norman Loudon. Cast: Leslie French, Mary Lawson, Warren Jenkins. Youngsters start pirate station.

__Here Comes the Band__ (1935, MGM). 86 min. Director: Paul Sloane. Producer: Lucien Hubbard. Cast: Ted Lewis, Virginia Bruce, Harry Stockwell. Singer faces plagiarism charges after winning radio talent contest.

__The Old Homestead__ (1935, Liberty Pictures). 73 min. Director: William Nigh. Producer: M.H. Hoffman. Cast: Mary Carlisle, Lawrence Gray, Willard Robertson. Talent scout seeks rural talent for New York radio show.

__Stars Over Broadway__ (1935, Warner Bros.). 89 min. Director: William Keighley. Producer: Samuel Bischoff. Cast: Pat O'Brien, Jane Froman, James Melton. Hotel porter becomes opera singer, then radio crooner.

__Sweet Surrender__ (1935, Broadway Productions). 85 min. Director-Producer: Monte Brice. Cast: Frank Parker, Tamara, Helen Lynd. Fired radio singer heads for Europe on ship.

__The Big Broadcast of 1936__ (1935, Paramount Pictures). 97 min. Director: Norman Taurog. Producer: Benjamin Glazer. Cast: Jack Oakie, George Burns, Gracie Allen. Thin plot of mostly song, dance, and comedy.

__Sweet Music__ (1935, Warner Bros.). 100 min. Director: Alfred E. Green. Producer: Samuel Bischoff. Cast: Rudy Vallee, Ann Dvorak, Ned Sparks. Dancer finds it hard to get job as radio singer.

__Laughing Irish Eyes__ (1936, Republic Pictures). 70 min. Director: Joseph Santley. Producer: Colbert Clark. Cast: Phil Regan, Walter C. Kelly. Irish blacksmith becomes boxer, then radio singer.

All American Chump (1936, MGM). 64 min. Director: Edwin L. Marin. Producers: Lucien Hubbard, Michael Fessier. Cast: Stuart Erwin, Robert Armstrong, Betty Furness. Broadcast of championship bridge match.

*__The Singing Cowboy__ (1936, Republic Pictures). 56 min. Director: Mack V. Wright. Producer: Nat Levine. Cast: Gene Autry, Smiley Burnette, Lois Wilde. Plans to raise money for paralyzed girl go awry when broadcasting equipment is stolen.

*__The Big Show__ (1936, Republic Pictures). 53 min. Director: Mack V. Wright. Producer: Nat Levine. Cast: Gene Autry, Smiley Burnette, Kay Hughes. Complications arise when Gene Autry impersonates movie star by singing on radio show.

*__The Singing Kid__ (1936, First National Pictures). 85 min. Director: William Keighley. Producer: Robert Lord. Cast: Al Jolson, Sybil Jason, Beverly Roberts. Radio singer loses voice, goes to countryside to recuperate, falls in love.

*__Panic on the Air__, aka *You May Be Next* (1936, Columbia Pictures). 54 min. Director: D. Ross Lederman. Producer: Ralph Cohn. Cast: Lew Ayres, Florence Rice, Benny Baker. Robbers hijack remote broadcasting truck, use it to control station's airwaves.

*__Alibi For Murder__ (1936, Columbia Pictures). 61 min. Director: D. Ross Lederman. Producer: Ralph Cohn. Cast: William Gargan, Marguerite Churchill. Radio reporter investigates death of scientist.

*__House of a Thousand Candles__ (1936, Republic Pictures). 71 min. Director: Arthur Lubin. Producers: Dorothy Davenport, Nat Levine. Cast: Phillips Holmes, Mae Clarke, Irving Pichel. Spies send information to each other via radio broadcasts.

*__Here Comes Carter__ (1936, Warner Bros.). 58 min. Director: William Clemens. Producer: Bryan Foy. Cast: Ross Alexander, Glenda Farrell. Gangsters don't like radio gossip reporter digging up dirt on them.

Radio Bar (1936, AIA de la Plata, Argentina). 83 min. Director: Manuel Romero. Cast: Gloria Guzman, Olinda Bozan, Carmen Lamas. Tango singer seeks stardom in bar and on radio.

*__Poor Little Rich Girl__ (1936, Twentieth Century-Fox). 72 min. Director: Irving Cummings. Producers: Raymond Griffith, Darryl F. Zanuck. Cast: Shirley Temple, Alice Faye, Gloria Stuart. Little girl on way to school meets vaudevillians, becomes radio star.

*__Freshman Love__ (1936, Warner Bros.). 67 min. Director: William C. McGann. Producer: Brian Foy. Cast: Patricia Ellis, Warren Hull, Frank McHugh. Radio descriptions of college regatta races.

*__Sing, Baby, Sing__ (1936, Twentieth Century-Fox). 90 min. Director: Sidney Lanfield. Producer: Darryl F. Zanuck. Cast: Alice Faye, Adolphe Menjou. Fired nightclub singer perseveres to get radio job.

*__The Milky Way__ (1936, Paramount Pictures). 89 min. Director: Leo McCarey. Producer: E. Lloyd Sheldon. Cast: Harold Lloyd, Adolphe Menjou, Helen Mack. Radio description when meek milkman becomes prizefighter.

*__The Big Broadcast of 1937__ (1936, Paramount Pictures). 100 min. Director: Mitchell Leisen. Producer: Lewis E. Gensler. Cast: Jack Benny, Shirley Ross, Gracie Allen. Unknown singer stars in show sponsored by golf ball company.

*__Dancing Feet__ (1936, Republic Pictures). 70 min. Director: Joseph Santley. Producer: Colbert Clark. Cast: Edward J. Nugent, Joan Marsh. Disinherited dancer helps friend land job as radio dance instructor.

*__Spendthrift__ (1936, Walter Wanger Productions). 80 min. Director: Raoul Walsh. Producer: Adolph Zukor. Cast: Henry Fonda, Pat Paterson, Mary Brian. Wealthy playboy goes broke, starts sportscasting career.

*__Sitting on the Moon__ (1936, Republic Pictures). 53 min. Director: Ralph Staub. Producer: Nat Levine. Cast: Roger Pryor, Grace Bradley. Desperate songwriter turns former actress into radio star.

*__Two Against the World__ (1936, First National Pictures). 64 min. Director: William McGann. Producers: Hal B. Wallis, Jack L. Warner. Cast: Humphrey Bogart, Beverly Roberts. Radio play revives old murder case, leads to double suicide.

*__The Drag-net__ (1936, Burroughs-Tarzan Pictures). 61 min. Director: Vin Moore. Producer: W.N. Selig. Cast: Rod La Rocque, Marian Nixon. Radio reporter creates turmoil in D.A.'s office.

__Easy to Take__ (1936, Paramount Pictures). 67 min. Director: Glenn Tryon. Producer: Jack Cunningham. Cast: Marsha Hunt, John Howard. Host of children's show is appointed guardian of spoiled child.

*__Pigskin Parade__ (1936, Twentieth Century-Fox). 93 min. Director: David Butler. Producer: Darryl F. Zanuck. Cast: Stuart Erwin, Patsy Kelly, Jack Haley. Play-by-play broadcast of college football game.

__Love is on the Air__ (1937, Warner Bros.). 59 min. Director: Nick Grinde. Producers: Hal B. Wallis, Jack L. Warner. Cast: Ronald Reagan, June Travis, Eddie Acuff. Radio reporter investigates disappearance of businessman.

*__Larceny on the Air__ (1937, Republic Pictures). 67 min. Director: Irving Pichel. Producer: Nat Levine. Cast: Robert Livingston, Grace Bradley. Doctor uses radio broadcasts to expose dangerous patent medicines.

__Santa Fe Rides__ (1937, Reliable Pictures). 58 min. Director-Producer: Bernard B. Ray. Cast: Bob Custer, Eleanor Stewart. Cowboys want to audition for radio show to make money but other ranchers try to stop them.

__Behind the Headlines__ (1937, RKO Radio Pictures). 58 min. Director: Richard Rosson. Producer: Cliff Reid. Cast: Lee Tracy, Diana Gibson, Phillip Huston. Radio reporter rescues kidnapped newspaper reporter girlfriend.

*__Mr. Dodd Takes the Air__ (1937, First National Pictures). 58 min. Director: Alfred E. Green. Producer: Mervyn LeRoy. Cast: Kenny Baker, Frank McHugh, Alice Brady. Small town singer gets chance at radio show, then operation changes voice.

*__Murder Is News__ (1937, Kenneth J. Bishop Pictures). 55 min. Director: Leon Barsha. Producer: Kenneth J. Bishop. Cast: John Gallaudet, Iris Meredith, George McKay. Radio reporter becomes involved in murder of wealthy industrialist.

*__Kid Galahad__ (1937, Warner Bros.). 102 min. Director: Michael Curtiz. Producers: Jack L. Warner, Hal B. Wallis. Cast: Edward G. Robinson, Humphrey Bogart, Bette Davis. Broadcasts of boxing matches set up by rival promoters.

*__Sing While You're Able__ (1937, Conn Pictures). 66 min. Director: Marshall Neilan. Producer: Maurice Conn. Cast: Pinky Tomlin, Toby Wing. Toy manufacturers' car breaks down in Arkansas; they discover singing farmer to star in radio show.

*__Love and Hisses__ (1937, Twentieth Century-Fox). 82 min. Director: Sidney Lanfield. Producer: Darryl F. Zanuck. Cast: Walter Winchell, Ben Bernie, Simone Simon. Bandleader Ben Bernie feuds with radio gossip columnist Walter Winchell.

*__The Singing Marine__ (1937, Warner Bros.). 105 min. Director: Ray Enright. Producers: Hal B. Wallis, Jack L. Warner. Cast: Dick Powell, Doris Weston, Lee Dixon. Marine gets own radio show, then gets shipped to Shanghai.

*__Hit Parade__, aka __Hit Parade of 1937__ (1937, Republic Pictures). 83 min. Director: Gus Meins. Producer: Nat Levine. Cast: Frances Langford, Phil Regan, Max Terhune. Agent makes star out of unknown singer who turns out to be ex-convict.

*__All Over Town__ (1937, Republic Pictures). 63 min. Director: James Horne. Producer: Leonard Fields. Cast: Ole Olsen, Chic Johnson, Mary Howard. Radio comedians try to solve murder.

__Blonde Trouble__ (1937, Paramount Pictures). 67 min. Director: George Archainbaud. Producer: Paul Jones. Cast: Eleanore Whitney, Johnny Downs. Songwriter struggles for success, then singer makes one of his songs a hit.

__Behind the Mike__ (1937, Universal Pictures). 68 min. Director: Sidney Salkow. Producer:

Lou Brock. Cast: William Gargan, Judith Barrett, Don Wilson. New York radio producer loses job, moves to small town to start new station, foils embezzlers.

Big Town Girl (1937, Twentieth Century-Fox). 66 min. Director: Alfred L. Werker. Producer: Milton Feld. Cast: Claire Trevor, Donald Woods. Department store singer becomes radio star but has to keep identity secret because of husband's shady past.

The 13th Man (1937, Monogram Pictures). 70 min. Director: William Nigh. Producer: Lon Young. Cast: Weldon Heyburn, Inez Courtney. D.A. and a radio reporter are killed.

Wake Up and Live (1937, Twentieth Century-Fox). 91 min. Director: Sidney Lanfield. Producer: Darryl F. Zanuck. Cast: Walter Winchell, Ben Bernie, Alice Faye. Radio page battles mike fright to become singing star.

Meet the Boyfriend (1937, Republic Pictures). 63 min. Director: Ralph Staub. Producer: Colbert Clark. Cast: Robert Paige, Carol Hughes. Radio singer rescues girlfriend from kidnappers.

High Hat (1937, Imperial Productions). 70 min. Director-Producer: Clifford Sanforth. Cast: Frank Luther, Dorothy Dare, Lona Andre. Fired singer regains stardom when program changes format and she is re-hired.

Rhythm in the Clouds (1937, Republic Pictures). 62 min. Director: John H. Auer. Producer: Albert E. Levoy. Cast: Patricia Ellis, Warren Hull, William Newell. Unemployed songwriter cheats her way onto radio show by forging another writer's name on her song.

Git Along Little Dogies (1937, Republic Pictures). 54 min. Director: Joseph Kane. Producer: Armand Schaefer. Cast: Gene Autry, Smiley Burnette. Woman surreptitiously broadcasts Gene Autry singing to make it appear he supports oilmen against cattlemen.

Racketeers in Exile (1937, Columbia Pictures). 60 min. Director: Erle C. Kenton. Producer: Irving Briskin. Cast: George Bancroft, Evelyn Venable. Crooks develop phony religious radio show.

It Can't Last Forever (1937, Columbia Pictures). 68 min. Director: Hamilton MacFadden. Producer: Harry L. Decker. Cast: Ralph Bellamy, Betty Furness. Predictions of radio host "The Mastermind" are set up by con men.

Hitting a New High (1937, RKO Radio Pictures). 85 min. Director: Raoul Walsh. Producer: Jesse L. Lasky. Cast: Lily Pons, Jack Oakie, John Howard. Press agent turns opera singer into exotic "Bird Girl" to get her on radio.

Manhattan Shakedown (1937, Kenneth J. Bishop Productions). 56 min. Director: Leon Barsha. Producer: Kenneth Bishop. Cast: John Gallaudet, Rosalind Keith. Radio commentator accuses prominent psychiatrist of blackmail.

Over the Goal (1937, Warner Bros.). 83 min. Director: Noel M. Smith. Producer: Bryan Foy. Cast: William Hopper, June Travis. Play-by-play descriptions of college games.

The Big Broadcast of 1938 (1938, Paramount Pictures). 94 min. Director: Mitchell Leisen. Producer: Harlan Thompson. Cast: Bob Hope, W.C. Fields, Martha Raye, Dorothy Lamour. Radio broadcast is produced aboard ocean liner; best known for introducing Bob Hope's theme song "Thanks for the Memory."

Carefree (1938, RKO Radio Pictures). 83 min. Director: Mark Sandrich. Producer: Pandro S. Berman. Lead actors, Ginger Rogers, Fred Astaire, Ralph Bellamy. Radio singer falls in love with psychiatrist.

Rebecca of Sunnybrook Farm (1938, Twentieth Century-Fox). 80 min. Director: Allan Dwan. Producer: Darryl F. Zanuck. Cast: Shirley Temple, Randolph Scott, Jack Haley. Little girl lands radio singing job but aunt forbids involvement in show business.

Hollywood Stadium Mystery (1938, Republic Pictures). 66 min. Director: David Howard. Producer: Armand Schaefer. Cast: Neil Hamilton, Evelyn Venable, Jimmy Wallington. Sports reporter broadcasts murder investigation live.

Start Cheering (1938, Columbia Pictures). 78 min. Director: Albert S. Rogell. Producer: William Perlberg. Cast: Charles Starrett, Jimmy Durante, Joan Perry. Movie star goes to college to escape show business life, organizes radio concert to save Dean's job.

*__Thanks for Everything__ (1938, Twentieth Century-Fox). 70 min. Director: William A. Seiter. Producer: Harry Joe Brown. Cast: Adolphe Menjou, Jack Oakie, Jack Haley. Listener wins radio contest, unwittingly becomes pawn of advertising agency.

*__Garden of the Moon__ (1938, Warner Bros.). Director: Busby Berkeley. Producer: Louis F. Edelman. Cast: Pat O'Brien, Margaret Lindsay, John Payne. Club owner fights with bandleader about music played on radio show.

*__Danger on the Air__ (1938, Universal Pictures). 70 min. Director: Otis Garrett. Producer: Irving Starr. Cast: Nan Grey, Donald Woods, Jed Prouty. Station engineer tries to discover who murdered sponsor.

*__International Crime__ (1938, M & A Alexander Productions). 62 min. Director: Charles Lamont. Producers: Arthur Alexander, Max Alexander. Cast: Rod La Rocque, Astrid Allwyn, Thomas E. Jackson. Radio detective "The Shadow" becomes involved in robbery.

*__Men Are Such Fools__ (1938, Warner Bros.). 69 min. Director: Busby Berkeley. Producers: Hal B. Wallis, Jack L. Warner. Cast: Wayne Morris, Priscilla Lane, Humphrey Bogart. Secretary manipulates men to become radio star.

__The Higgins Family__ (1938, Republic Pictures). 54 min. Director: Gus Meins. Producer: Sol C. Siegel. Cast: James Gleason, Lucile Gleason, Russell Gleason. Housewife gets radio show.

*__The Old Barn Dance__ (1938, Republic Pictures). 54 min. Director: Joseph Kane. Producer: Sol C. Siegel. Cast: Gene Autry, Smiley Burnette, Joan Valerie. Gene Autry is duped into endorsing tractors on radio.

__Safety in Numbers__ (1938, Twentieth Century-Fox). 55 min. Director: Malcolm St. Clair. Producer: John Stone. Cast: Jed Prouty, Shirley Deane, Spring Byington. Listener gets own show, exposes pollution of town's water supply.

__Over the Wall__ (1938, Warner Bros.). 67 min. Director: Frank McDonald. Producers: Hal B. Wallis, Jack L. Warner. Cast: Dick Foran, June Travis, John Litel. Ex-boxer has promising future as radio singer until being framed for murder.

*__Five of a Kind__ (1938, Twentieth Century-Fox). 85 min. Director: Herbert I. Leeds. Producer: Sol M. Wurtzel. Cast: Cesar Romero, Claire Trevor, Dionne Quintuplets. Radio reporters compete to interview Dionne quintuplets.

*__Kentucky Moonshine__ (1938, Twentieth Century-Fox). 87 min. Director: David Butler. Producer: Darryl F. Zanuck. Cast: Harry Ritz, Jimmy Ritz, Al Ritz. Radio star goes to Kentucky to find new talent to boost ratings, takes fake moonshiners back to New York.

*__Hold That Co-ed__ (1938, Twentieth Century-Fox). 80 min. Director: George Marshall. Producer: David Hempstead. Cast: John Barrymore, George Murphy, Marjorie Weaver. Play-by-play broadcast of college football games in which woman is star player.

*__Cowboy from Brooklyn__ (1938, Cosmopolitan Productions). 77 min. Director: Lloyd Bacon. Producers: Hal B. Wallis, Jack L. Warner. Cast: Dick Powell, Pat O'Brien, Priscilla Lane. New York talent agent goes on vacation, finds cowboy singer.

*__Indianapolis Speedway__ (1939, Warner Bros.). 85 min. Director: Lloyd Bacon. Producers: Hal B. Wallis, Jack L. Warner. Cast: Ann Sheridan, Pat O'Brien, John Payne. Remake of 1932 film __The Crowd Roars__.

*__Ex-Champ__ (1939, Universal Pictures). 64 min. Director: Phil Rosen. Producer: Burt Kelly. Cast: Victor McLaglen, Tom Brown, Nan Grey. Blow-by-blow descriptions when former champ manages new fighter.

__Sued for Libel__ (1939, RKO Radio Pictures). 66 min. Director: Leslie Goodwins. Producer: Cliff Reid. Cast: Kent Taylor, Linda Hayes, Lilian Bond. Radio director fights libel charges in murder case.

*__Rovin' Tumbleweeds__ (1939, Republic Pictures). 62 min. Director: George Sherman. Producer: William Berke. Cast: Gene Autry, Smiley Burnette, Mary Carlisle. Gene Autry gets radio singing job to support ranchers, goes to Washington to fight for their rights.

*__They Made Me a Criminal__ (1939, Warner Bros.). 92 min. Director: Busby Berkeley.

Producer: Hal B. Wallis. Cast: John Garfield, Claude Rains. Blow-by-blow broadcast when boxer accused of murder tries to resurrect career.

The Girl from Mexico (1939, RKO Radio Pictures). 71 min. Director: Leslie Goodwins. Producer: Robert Sisk. Cast: Lupe Velez, Donald Woods, Leon Errol. New York talent scout goes to Mexico, brings back fiery-tempered girl.

Missing Daughters (1939, Columbia Pictures). 59 min. Director: Charles C. Coleman. Producer: Irving Briskin. Cast: Richard Arlen, Rochelle Hudson, Marian Marsh. Radio reporter infiltrates mob to solve murder and expose white slave ring.

Let's Be Famous (1939, Associated Talking Pictures, Britain). 83 min. Director: Walter Forde. Producer: Michael Balcon. Cast: Jimmy O'Dea, Betty Driver, Sonnie Hale. Man heads to London for radio singing job, ends up on quiz show.

Some Like It Hot, aka *Rhythm Romance* (1939, Paramount Pictures). 65 min. Director: George Archainbaud. Producer: William C. Thomas. Cast: Bob Hope, Shirley Ross, Una Merkel. Sideshow barker gets and loses announcing job, loses and gets girl.

Colorado Sunset (1939, Republic Pictures). 65 min. Director: George Sherman. Producer: Harry Grey. Cast: Gene Autry, Smiley Burnette, June Storey. Outlaws send secret messages via radio broadcasts.

Mexicali Rose (1939, Republic Pictures). 59 min. Director: George Sherman. Producer: Harry Grey. Cast: Gene Autry, Smiley Burnette, Noah Beery. Radio sponsors are actually crooks trying to bilk orphanage.

East Side of Heaven (1939, Universal Pictures). 88 min. Director: David Butler. Producers: David Butler, Herbert Polesie. Cast: Bing Crosby, Joan Blondell. Singing cab driver looks after missing baby while dodging radio reporter.

The Cowboy Quarterback (1939, Warner Bros.). 56 min. Director: Noel M. Smith. Producers: Bryan Foy, Mark Hellinger. Cast: Bert Wheeler, Marie Wilson. Play-by-play broadcasts when hick becomes football star.

Hell's Kitchen (1939, Warner Bros.). 82 min. Director: Lewis Seiler. Producer: E.A. Dupont. Cast: Billy Halop, Grant Mitchell, Ronald Reagan. Play-by-play of hockey game between reform school and orphanage teams.

Band Waggon (1940, Gainsborough Pictures, Britain). 85 min. Director: Marcel Varnel. Producer: Edward Black. Cast: Arthur Askey, Richard Murdoch. Wannabe radio performers discover undercover German TV station in "haunted" castle.

Up in the Air (1940, Monogram Pictures). 62 min. Director: Howard Bretherton. Producer: Lindsley Parsons. Cast: Frankie Darro, Marjorie Reynolds, Mantan Moreland. Radio singer is murdered while on air.

Who Killed Aunt Maggie? (1940, Republic Pictures). 70 min. Director: Arthur Lubin. Producer: Albert Cohen. Cast: John Hubbard, Wendy Barrie, Edgar Kennedy. Radio play murder becomes reality.

The Leather Pushers (1940, Universal Pictures). 64 min. Director: John Rawlins. Producer: Ben Pivar. Cast: Richard Arlen, Andy Devine, Astrid Allwyn. Blow-by-blow descriptions when female sports reporter wins boxer in raffle.

Melody Ranch (1940, Republic Pictures). 84 min. Director: Joseph Santley. Producer: Sol C. Siegel. Cast: Gene Autry, Jimmy Durante, Ann Miller. Gene Autry returns home for radio broadcast, tangles with bad guys.

Radio Ranch, aka *Men with Steel Faces* (1940, Mascot Pictures). 70 min. Directors: Otto Brower, B. Reeves Eason. Producer: Nat Levine. Cast: Gene Autry, Frankie Darro. Gene Autry discovers ranch he broadcasts from sits atop advanced civilization. Feature version of 1935 serial *The Phantom Empire*.

Buck Benny Rides Again (1940, Paramount Pictures). 82 min. Director-Producer: Mark Sandrich. Cast: Jack Benny, Eddie Anderson, Ellen Drew. Radio comedian goes west as publicity stunt, ends up fighting rustlers.

Hit Parade of 1941 (1940, Republic Pictures). 88 min. Director: John H. Auer. Producer: Sol C. Siegel. Cast: Kenny Baker, Frances Langford, Hugh Herbert. Failing radio station adds TV service so sponsor's daughter can attract viewers.

Village Barn Dance (1940, Republic Pictures). 74 min. Director: Frank McDonald. Producer: Armand Schaefer. Cast: Richard Cromwell, Doris Day, George Barbier. Locals try to save barn dance radio show.

*The Fatal Hour (1940, Monogram Pictures). 68 min. Director: William Nigh. Producer: Scott Dunlap. Cast: Boris Karloff, Grant Withers, Marjorie Reynolds. Radio broadcast gunshot is used to mask murder.

*Music in My Heart (1940, Columbia Pictures). 70 min. Director: Joseph Santley. Producer: Irving Starr. Cast: Tony Martin, Rita Hayworth, Edith Fellows. Singer about to be deported appears on radio show.

Grand Ole Opry (1940, Republic Pictures). 67 min. Director: Frank McDonald. Producer: Armand Schaefer. Cast: Leon Weaver, Frank Weaver, June Weaver. Imprisoned governor broadcasts from jail about controversial farm bill.

*Charter Pilot (1940, Twentieth Century-Fox). 70 min. Director: Eugene Forde. Producer: Sol M. Wurtzel. Cast: Lloyd Nolan, Lynn Bari, Arleen Whelan. Pilot whose exploits are plot of radio show marries show's writer but can't keep promise to give up flying.

*Christmas in July (1940, Paramount Pictures). 67 min. Director: Preston Sturges. Producers: Paul Jones, Buddy G. DeSylva. Cast: Dick Powell, Ellen Drew, Raymond Walburn. Office clerk's co-workers trick him into thinking he won radio contest.

*Nobody's Children (1940, Columbia Pictures). 64 min. Director: Charles Barton. Producer: Jack Fier. Cast: Edith Fellows, Billy Lee, Georgia Caine. Radio show helps orphaned children find new homes.

*A Little Bit of Heaven (1940, Universal Pictures). 87 min. Director: Andrew Marton. Producer: Joe Pasternak. Cast: Gloria Jean, Robert Stack, Hugh Herbert. Child becomes star after singing for street broadcast of radio show.

*Hullabaloo (1940, MGM). 78 min. Director: Edwin L. Marin. Producer: Louis K. Sidney. Cast: Frank Morgan, Virginia Grey, Dan Dailey. Ex-vaudevillian wants radio career.

*City for Conquest (1940, Warner Bros.). 104 min. Director-Producer: Anatole Litvak. Cast: James Cagney, Ann Sheridan, Anthony Quinn. Blow-by-blow account of championship fight.

*Charlie Chan at the Wax Museum (1940, Twentieth Century-Fox). 63 min. Director: Lynn Shores. Producers: Ralph Dietrich, Walter Morosco. Cast: Sidney Toler, Victor Sen Yung. Broadcast from wax museum is intended to kill detective.

*Underground (1941, Warner Bros.). 95 min. Director: Vincent Sherman. Producer: Bryan Foy. Cast: Jeffrey Lynn, Philip Dorn, Kaaren Verne. German underground broadcasts anti–Nazi propaganda.

*Knockout (1941, Warner Bros.). 73 min. Director: William Clemens. Producer: Bryan Foy. Cast: Arthur Kennedy, Olympe Bradna, Anthony Quinn. Blow-by-blow accounts as fighter's career disintegrates.

*Hi, Gang! (1941, Gainsborough Pictures, Britain). 100 min. Director: Marcel Varnel. Producer: Edward Black. Cast: Bebe Daniels, Ben Lyon, Vic Oliver. Soon-to-be-divorced announcers try to outdo each other on rival stations.

*The Great American Broadcast (1941, Twentieth Century-Fox). 90 min. Director: Archie Mayo. Producer: Darryl F. Zanuck. Cast: Alice Faye, John Payne. World War I vets start radio station.

*The Bride Came C.O.D. (1941, Warner Bros.). 92 min. Director: William Keighley. Producer: Hal B. Wallis. Cast: James Cagney, Bette Davis. Radio reporter becomes involved in kidnapping of heiress.

*Pot O' Gold (1941, (United Artists). 86 min. Director: George Marshall. Producer:

James Roosevelt. Cast: James Stewart, Paulette Goddard. Wealthy young man gets job with band, persuades uncle to let them perform on radio show.

Uncle Joe (1941, Wilding Picture Productions). 51 min. Directors: Raymond E. Swartly, Howard M. Railsback. Cast: Gale Storm, Slim Summerville, ZaSu Pitts. Socialite goes to live with eccentric uncle, helps win radio contest to save widow's home.

Playmates (1941, RKO Radio Pictures). 96 min. Director-Producer: David Butler. Cast: John Barrymore, Kay Kyser, Patsy Kelly. Shakespearean actor with financial problems joins bandleader on new radio show.

In the Navy (1941, Universal Pictures). 86 min. Director: Arthur Lubin. Producer: Alex Gottlieb. Cast: Bud Abbott, Lou Costello, Dick Powell. Radio star who tries to enlist in Navy incognito is pursued by reporter.

Freedom Radio (1941, Two Cities Films, Britain). 95 min. Director: Anthony Asquith. Producer: Mario Zampi. Cast: Clive Brook, Diana Wynyard, Raymond Huntley. British patriots start underground station to broadcast anti–Nazi messages after Germany wins World War II.

International Lady (1941, Edward Small Productions). 102 min. Director: Tim Whelan. Producer: Edward Small. Cast: George Brent, Ilona Massey, Basil Rathbone. Music broadcast on radio contains Nazi codes.

Puddin' Head (1941, Republic Pictures). 80 min. Director: Joseph Santley. Producer: Albert Cohen. Cast: Judy Canova, Francis Lederer. New York station discovers land under new headquarters building is owned by Arkansas hillbillies.

Lucky Devils (1941, Universal Pictures). 62 min. Director: Lew Landers. Producer: Ben Pivar. Cast: Richard Arlen, Andy Devine, Dorothy Lovett. Newsreel reporters get secretary a radio news reporting job.

Melody Lane (1941, Universal Pictures). 60 min. Director: Charles Lamont. Producer: Ken Goldsmith. Cast: Judd McMichael, Ted McMichael, Joe McMichael, Mary Lou Cook. Iowa musicians are recruited for New York radio show.

Swing It Soldier (1941, Universal Pictures). 66 min. Director: Harold Young. Producer: Joseph Gershenson. Cast: Ken Murray, Frances Langford, Don Wilson. Soldier returns to civilian life as radio executive.

Whistling in the Dark (1941, MGM). 78 min. Director: S. Sylvan Simon. Producer: George Haight. Cast: Red Skelton, Conrad Veidt, Ann Rutherford. First of three films with radio detective Wally "The Fox" Benton.

Where Did You Get That Girl? (1941, Universal Pictures). Director: Arthur Lubin. Producer: Joseph Gershenson. Cast: Leon Errol, Helen Parrish, Charles Lang. Struggling composer and struggling musician become stars when their record is stolen and eventually played on radio.

Too Many Blondes (1941, Universal Pictures). 60 min. Director: Thornton Freeland. Producer: Joseph Gershenson. Cast: Rudy Vallee, Helen Parrish, Lon Chaney, Jr. Marital problems threaten breakup of radio singing group.

Rise and Shine (1941, Twentieth Century-Fox). 92 min. Director: Allan Dwan. Producer: Mark Hellinger. Cast: Jack Oakie, George Murphy, Walter Brennan. Play-by-play accounts of football games with star player who's not too bright.

Whistling in Dixie (1942, MGM). 74 min. Director: S. Sylvan Simon. Producer: George Haight. Cast: Red Skelton, Ann Rutherford, George Bancroft. Second of three films with radio detective Wally "The Fox" Benton.

The Lady Has Plans (1942, Paramount Pictures). 77 min. Director: Sidney Lanfield. Producer: Fred Kohlmar. Cast: Ray Milland, Paulette Goddard. Radio reporters get mixed up with Nazi spies.

Who Done It? (1942, Universal Pictures). 77 min. Director: Erle C. Kenton. Producer: Alex Gottlieb. Cast: Bud Abbott, Lou Costello. Radio mystery writers play detective when station president is murdered.

Men of San Quentin (1942, Producers Releasing Corporation). 80 min. Director: William Beaudine. Producers: Max King, Martin Mooney. Cast: J. Anthony Hughes, Eleanor Stewart, Dick Curtis. New warden tries to rehabilitate prisoners by staging radio variety show that from prison to show some inmates want to make good.

Murder in the Big House (1942, Warner Bros.). 59 min. Director: B. Reeves Eason. Producer: William Jacobs. Cast: Van Johnson, Faye Emerson, George Meeker. Convict is electrocuted by headphones while listening to radio.

What's Cookin'? (1942, Universal Pictures). 69 min. Director: Edward F. Cline. Producer: Ken Goldsmith. Cast: The Andrews Sisters, Jane Frazee, Robert Paige. Sponsor wants to update music on show but runs into opposition from wife.

Rio Rita (1942, MGM). 91 min. Director: S. Sylvan Simon. Producer: Pandro S. Berman. Cast: Bud Abbott, Lou Costello. Bumblers end up thwarting Nazi broadcasting plans.

Once Upon a Honeymoon (1942, RKO Radio Pictures). 117 min. Director-Producer: Leo McCarey. Cast: Cary Grant, Ginger Rogers. American radio reporter in Europe becomes involved with woman suspected of working for Nazis.

Sherlock Holmes and the Voice of Terror (1942, Universal Pictures). 65 min. Director: John Rawlins. Producer: Howard Benedict. Cast: Basil Rathbone, Nigel Bruce. Detective investigates Nazi propaganda broadcasts.

Manila Calling (1942, Twentieth Century-Fox). 81 min. Director: Herbert I. Leeds. Producer: Sol M. Wurtzel. Cast: Lloyd Nolan, Carole Landis, Cornel Wilde. American soldiers in Philippines plan to capture Japanese radio station.

You're Telling Me (1942, Universal Pictures). 60 min. Director: Charles Lamont. Producer: Ken Goldsmith. Cast: Hugh Herbert, Anne Gwynne. Woman gets eccentric nephew job at radio station.

Ridin' Down the Canyon (1942, Republic Pictures). 55 min. Director: Joseph Kane. Producer: Harry Grey. Cast: Roy Rogers, George "Gabby" Hayes. Rustlers use radio show to transmit information about next target.

Sweetheart of the Fleet (1942, Columbia Pictures). 65 min. Director: Charles Barton. Producer: Jack Fier. Cast: Joan Davis, Jinx Falkenburg, Joan Woodbury. Complications arise when models are hired to impersonate radio singers to aid Navy recruiting.

Madame Spy (1942, Universal Pictures). 63 min. Director: Roy William Neill. Producer: Marshall Grant. Cast: Constance Bennett, Don Porter, John Litel. Wife of patriotic radio commentator may be Nazi spy.

Stand By All Networks (1942, Columbia Pictures). 65 min. Director: Lew Landers. Producer: Jack Fier. Cast: John Beal, Florence Rice. Nazi agents impersonate radio reporter to spread propaganda.

Berlin Correspondent (1942, Twentieth Century-Fox). 70 min. Director: Eugene Forde. Producer: Bryan Foy. Cast: Dana Andrews, Virginia Gilmore, Martin Kosleck. Reporter in Berlin transmits secret Nazi information via radio newscasts.

A Tragedy at Midnight (1942, Republic Pictures). 53 min. Director: Joseph Santley. Producer: Robert North. Cast: John Howard, Margaret Lindsay, Roscoe Karns. Radio detective finds woman's body in his bed.

Whispering Ghosts (1942, Twentieth Century-Fox). 75 min. Director: Alfred L. Werker. Producer: Sol M. Wurtzel. Cast: Milton Berle, Brenda Joyce. Radio detective tries to solve old murder case.

Pride of the Yankees (1942, Samuel Goldwyn Company). 128 min. Director: Sam Wood. Producer: Samuel Goldwyn. Cast: Gary Cooper, Teresa Wright, Walter Brennan. Bill Stern does play-by-play in Lou Gehrig biopic.

It Happened in Flatbush (1942, Twentieth Century-Fox). 80 min. Director: Ray McCarey. Producer: Walter Morosco. Cast: Lloyd Nolan, Carole Landis. Broadcast of Brooklyn-St. Louis championship baseball game.

Sunday Punch (1942, MGM). 76 min. Director: David Miller. Producer: Irving Starr. Cast: William Lundigan, Jean Rogers, Dan Dailey. Two boxers fall in love with same girl.

I Live on Danger (1942, Pine-Thomas Productions). 73 min. Director: Sam White. Producers: William H. Pine, William C. Thomas. Cast: Chester Morris, Jean Parker, Elisabeth Risdon. Radio reporter tries to clear man wrongly accused of murder.

Stardust on the Sage (1942, Republic Pictures). 64 min. Director: William Morgan. Producer: Harry Grey. Cast: Gene Autry, Smiley Burnette, William Henry. Mining stock promoter edits Gene Autry interview to make it seem he favors dubious mine venture.

Don't Get Personal (1942, Universal Pictures). 60 min. Director: Charles Lamont. Producer: Ken Goldsmith. Cast: Hugh Herbert, Mischa Auer, Jane Frazee. Real-life couple substitutes for stars of radio show to fool sponsor.

Road to Happiness (1942, Monogram Pictures). 84 min. Director: Phil Rosen. Producer: Scott R. Dunlap. Cast: John Boles, Mona Barrie, Billy Lee. Divorced opera singer takes job on children's radio show to support son.

Unforgotten Crime, aka *The Affairs of Jimmy Valentine* (1942, Republic Pictures). 72 min. Director: Bernard Vorhaus. Producer: Leonard Fields. Cast: Dennis O'Keefe, Ruth Terry. Radio contest leads to uncovering of old crimes and to new murders.

Whistling in Brooklyn (1943, MGM). 87 min. Director: S. Sylvan Simon. Producer: George Haight. Cast: Red Skelton, Ann Rutherford, Jean Rogers. Third film with radio detective Wally "The Fox" Benton.

Hi, Buddy (1943, Universal Pictures). 66 min. Director: Harold Young. Producer: Joseph Gershenson. Cast: Dick Foran, Harriet Hilliard, Marjorie Lord. Radio singer helps raise money to save boys' club.

Mystery Broadcast (1943, Republic Pictures). 53 min. Director-Producer: George Sherman. Cast: Ruth Terry, Frank Albertson, Wynne Gibson. Radio mystery writer risks life by reopening old murder case.

Reveille with Beverly (1943, Columbia Pictures). 78 min. Director: Charles Barton. Producer: Sam White. Cast: Ann Miller, William Wright. Two soldiers compete for affections of female DJ.

We'll Meet Again (1943, Columbia British Pictures, Britain). 84 min. Director: Philip Brandon. Producer: Ben Henry. Lead actor: Vera Lynn. Biopic of Vera Lynn includes rise to fame on BBC.

Spotlight Scandals, aka *Spotlight Revue* (1943, Banner Productions). 79 min. Director: William Beaudine. Producers: Jack Dietz, Sam Katzman. Cast: Billy Gilbert, Frank Fay, Bonnie Baker. Vaudeville team eventually finds radio success.

Jive Junction (1943, Producers Releasing Corporation). 62 min. Director: Edgar G. Ulmer. Producer: Leon Fromkess. Cast: Dickie Moore, Tina Thay. High school band plans to enter national radio contest until sheriff seizes their instruments.

Campus Rhythm (1943, Monogram Pictures). 63 min. Director: Arthur Dreifuss. Producer: Lindsley Parsons. Cast: Johnny Downs, Gale Storm, Robert Lowery. Singer tries to give up radio career to return to college.

Here Comes Elmer (1943, Republic Pictures). 74 min. Director: Joseph Santley. Producer: Armand Schaefer. Cast: Al Pearce, Dale Evans, Frank Albertson. Entertainers try to get radio jobs back after parrot's on-air comment gets them fired.

Salute for Three (1943, Paramount Pictures). 74 min. Director: Ralph Murphy. Producer: Walter MacEwen. Cast: Betty Jane Rhodes, Macdonald Carey, Marty May. Returning soldier becomes involved with radio singer.

Hoosier Holiday (1943, Republic Pictures). 72 min. Director: Frank McDonald. Producer: Armand Schaefer. Cast: George Byron, Dale Evans, Thurston Hall, the Hoosier Hot Shots. The Hoosier Hot Shots find it's not easy to quit radio show to join army.

Swing Out the Blues (1943, Columbia Pictures). 73 min. Director: Malcolm St. Clair.

Producer: Sam White. Cast: Bob Haymes, Lynn Merrick. Musical combo concocts story to get radio sponsor.

True to Life (1943, Paramount Pictures). 94 min. Director: George Marshall. Producer: Paul Jones. Cast: Mary Martin, Franchot Tone, Dick Powell. Seeking inspiration for radio show, writer moves in with middle-class family to secretly note daily antics.

Appointment in Berlin (1943, Columbia Pictures). 77 min. Director: Alfred E. Green. Producer: Samuel Bischoff. Cast: George Sanders, Marguerite Chapman, Onslow Stevens. RAF officer infiltrates Nazis by broadcasting German propaganda.

National Velvet (1944, MGM). 123 min. Director: Clarence Brown. Producer: Pandro S. Berman. Cast: Elizabeth Taylor, Mickey Rooney, Anne Revere. Radio description of girl winning Grand National Steeplechase.

The Black Parachute (1944, Columbia Pictures). 68 min. Director: Lew Landers. Producer: Jack Fier. Cast: John Carradine, Osa Massen, Larry Parks. Nazis use actor to impersonate king of small country on radio but American reporter helps free real king to broadcast the truth.

Hi, Good Lookin' (1944, Universal Pictures). 62 min. Director: Edward C. Lilley. Producer: Frank Gross. Cast: Harriet Hilliard, Eddie Quillan, Kirby Grant. Radio station usher pretends to be executive to help girl become singer.

Ever Since Venus (1944, Larry Darmour Productions). 74 min. Director: Arthur Dreifuss. Producer: Larry Darmour. Cast: Ina Ray Hutton, Hugh Herbert, Ann Savage. Cook writes song that wins radio contest.

Meet Miss Bobby Socks (1944, Columbia Pictures). 68 min. Director: Glenn Tryon. Producer: Ted Richmond. Cast: Bob Crosby, Lynn Merrick, Louise Erickson. Teen starts fan club for favorite radio singer.

My Gal Loves Music (1944, Universal Pictures). 60 min. Director-Producer: Edward C. Lilley. Cast: Bob Crosby, Grace McDonald. Woman fakes her way onto radio contest and wins.

Twilight on the Prairie (1944, Universal Pictures). 62 min. Director: Jean Yarbrough. Producer: Warren Wilson. Cast: Johnny Downs, Vivian Austin, Leon Errol. Radio cowboys head to Hollywood but movie plans are sidetracked when plane makes emergency landing in Texas.

Hot Rhythm (1944, Monogram Pictures). 79 min. Director: William Beaudine. Producer: Lindsley Parsons. Cast: Dona Drake, Robert Lowery. Radio commercial jingle writers use fake song to get recording contract for singer.

Sing, Neighbor, Sing (1944, Republic Pictures). 70 min. Director: Frank McDonald. Producer: Donald H. Brown. Cast: Stanley Brown, Ruth Terry, Roy Acuff. Young man creates fake radio psychologist persona.

Take It or Leave It (1944, Twentieth Century-Fox). 70 min. Director: Benjamin Stoloff. Producer: Bryan Foy. Cast: Phil Baker, Edward Ryan, Madge Meredith. Complications arise when sailors appear on radio quiz show.

The Ghost That Walks Alone (1944, Columbia Pictures). 63 min. Director: Lew Landers. Producer: Jack Fier. Cast: Arthur Lake, Janis Carter, Lynne Roberts. Radio show cast becomes involved in murder.

The National Barn Dance (1944, Paramount Pictures). 76 min. Director: Hugh Bennett. Producer: Walter MacEwen. Cast: Jean Heather, Charles Quigley, The Hoosier Hot Shots. WLS Chicago starts hillbilly program.

I'm from Arkansas (1944, Kleinert-Vershel Productions). 70 min. Director: Lew Landers. Producers: E.H. Kleinert, Irving Vershel. Cast: Slim Summerville, Bruce Bennett, Iris Adrian. Western band broadcasts from small town to save farm.

A Menina da Radio (1944, Companhia Portuguesa de Filmes, Portugal). 106 min. Director: Arthur Duarte. Cast: Antonio Silva, Maria Eugenia, Fernando Ribeiro. Businessmen start community radio station, with unanticipated results.

Charlie Chan in the Scarlet Clue (1945, Monogram Pictures). 65 min. Director: Phil Rosen. Producer: James S. Burkett. Cast: Sidney Toler, Mantan Moreland. Detective investigates murder in radio station building.

The Frozen Ghost (1945, Universal Pictures). 61 min. Director: Harold Young. Producer: Will Cowan. Cast: Lon Chaney, Jr., Evelyn Ankers, Milburn Stone. Radio hypnotist believes his power can kill.

It's a Pleasure (1945, MGM). 90 min. Director: William A. Seiter. Producer: David Lewis. Cast: Sonja Henie, Michael O'Shea. Play-by-play of hockey game opens film with thin plot about figure skaters.

There Goes Kelly (1945, Monogram Pictures). 61 min. Director: Phil Karlson. Producer: William Strohbach. Cast: Jackie Moran, Wanda McKay, Sidney Miller. Station pages solve murder when singer is killed.

I'll Remember April (1945, Universal Pictures). 63 min. Director: Harold Young. Producer: Gene Lewis. Cast: Gloria Jean, Kirby Grant, Milburn Stone. Girl who tries to get radio singing job becomes involved in murder.

On Stage Everybody (1945, Universal Pictures). 75 min. Director: Jean Yarbrough. Producer: Warren Wilson. Cast: Jack Oakie, Peggy Ryan, Johnny Coy. Former vaudevillian finally accepts radio.

Senorita from the West (1945, Universal Pictures). 63 min. Director: Frank R. Strayer. Producer: Philip Cahn. Cast: Allan Jones, Bonita Granville. Girl leaves desert home to become radio singer.

Eve Knew Her Apples (1945, Columbia Pictures). 64 min. Director: Will Jason. Producer: Wallace MacDonald. Cast: Ann Miller, William Wright. A radio singing star, who is believed to have been kidnapped, is really on vacation.

Rhythm Round-up (1945, Columbia Pictures). 66 min. Director: Vernon Keays. Producer: Colbert Clark. Cast: Ken Curtis, Cheryl Walker, The Hoosier Hot Shots. Radio show helps woman save hotel.

Sagebrush Heroes (1945, Columbia Pictures). 54 min. Director: Benjamin H. Kline. Producer: Jack Fier. Cast: Charles Starrett, Dub Taylor, Constance Worth. Radio cowboys discover boys' home is front for rustlers.

Radio Stars on Parade (1945, RKO Radio Pictures). 69 min. Director: Leslie Goodwins. Producers: Benjamin Stoloff. Cast: Wally Brown, Alan Carney, Frances Langford. Talent agents take clients to audition for radio shows.

Blonde from Brooklyn (1945, Columbia Pictures). 65 min. Director: Del Lord. Producer: Ted Richmond. Cast: Bob Haymes, Lynn Merrick, Thurston Hall. Woman pretends to be Southern belle to land radio job.

The Horn Blows at Midnight (1945, Warner Bros.). 78 min. Director: Raoul Walsh. Producer: Mark Hellinger. Cast: Jack Benny, Alexis Smith. Radio orchestra trumpet player dreams about end of world.

Swingin' on a Rainbow (1945, Republic Pictures). 72 min. Director: William Beaudine. Producer: Armand Schaefer. Cast: Jane Frazee, Stanley Brown, Harry Langdon. Nebraska songwriter goes to New York to find man who has stolen her songs and is playing them on radio.

I'll Tell the World (1945, Universal Pictures). 61 min. Director: Leslie Goodwins. Producer: Edward Dodds. Cast: Lee Tracy, Brenda Joyce. Talkative man lands job as sportscaster, tries to get radio singing gig for girlfriend.

Here Come the Co-eds (1945, Universal Pictures). 90 min. Director: Jean Yarbrough. Producer: John Grant. Cast: Bud Abbott, Lou Costello, Peggy Ryan. Play-by-play description of basketball game between rival colleges.

No Leave, No Love (1946, MGM). 119 min. Director: Charles Martin. Producer: Joe Pasternak. Cast: Van Johnson, Keenan Wynn, Patricia Kirkwood. Mix-up occurs when Marines appear on radio show.

The Inner Circle (1946, Republic Pictures). 57 min. Director: Philip Ford. Producer: William J. O'Sullivan. Cast: Adele Mara, Warren Douglas. Radio commentator is killed to prevent him from naming members of society involved with criminals.

Tokyo Rose (1946, Pine-Thomas Productions). 69 min. Director: Lew Landers. Producer: William H. Pine. Cast: Byron Barr, Osa Massen, Donald Douglas. Escaped American POW joins Japanese underground in plot to kill Japanese broadcaster.

The People's Choice (1946, Planet Pictures). 67 min. Director: Harry L. Fraser. Producer: Ray Collins. Cast: Bill Kennedy, Louise Arthur, George Meeker. Complications arise when boy gets announcing job, jokingly claims to be bank robber.

Lone Star Moonlight (1946, Columbia Pictures). 67 min. Director: Ray Nazarro. Producer: Colbert Clark. Cast: Ken Curtis, Joan Barton, Guy Kibbee, The Hoosier Hot Shots. Returning soldier finds father has let family radio station fall into ruins.

Freddie Steps Out (1946, Monogram Pictures). 75 min. Director: Arthur Dreifuss. Producer: Sam Katzman. Cast: Freddie Stewart, June Preisser, Warren Mills. High school student impersonates retired radio singing heartthrob.

Breakfast in Hollywood (1946, Golden Pictures). 90 min. Director: Harold D. Schuster. Producer: Robert Golden. Cast: Tom Breneman, Bonita Granville, Beulah Bondi. Stories of those who appear on Tom Breneman's morning show.

People Are Funny (1946, Pine-Thomas Productions). 93 min. Director: Sam White. Producer: Sam White. Cast: Jack Haley, Helen Walker, Rudy Vallee. Producers compete to come up with original idea for new show.

Cuban Pete (1946, Universal Pictures). 60 min. Director: Jean Yarbrough. Producer: Howard Welsch. Cast: Desi Arnaz, Joan Shawlee. Advertising executive persuades Cuban bandleader to star on New York radio show.

Stars on Parade (1946, All-American News). 42 min. Director: Joseph Seiden. Producer: E.M. Glucksman. Cast: Milton Wood, Francine Everett, Jane Cooley. All-black cast in story about returning vet who rounds up big-name talent for radio show to save station.

Genius at Work (1946, RKO Radio Pictures). 61 min. Director: Leslie Goodwins. Producer: Herman Schlom. Cast: Wally Brown, Alan Carney, Anne Jeffreys. Radio detectives go up against real-life killer.

Smash-up: The Story of a Woman (1947, Universal International Pictures). 103 min. Director: Stuart Heisler. Producer: Walter Wanger. Cast: Susan Hayward, Lee Bowman. Former singer who can't handle husband's success as radio star descends into alcoholism.

Louisiana (1947, Monogram Pictures). 85 min. Director: Phil Karlson. Producer: Lindsley Parsons. Cast: Jimmie Davis, Margaret Lindsay, John Gallaudet. Biopic of Jimmie Davis, singer who became radio star, then Louisiana governor.

The Fabulous Dorseys (1947, Charles R. Rogers Productions, Embassy Productions). 88 min. Director: Alfred E. Green. Producer: Charles R. Rogers. Cast: Tommy Dorsey, Jimmy Dorsey. First radio performance by Dorsey Brothers ends in music squabbles.

Hollywood Barn Dance (1947, Screen Guild Productions). 72 min. Director: Bernard B. Ray. Producer: Jack Schwarz. Cast: Ernest Tubb, Helen Boice, Earle Hodgins. Ernest Tubb hosts radio show.

Ladies' Man (1947, Paramount Pictures). 91 min. Director: William D. Russell. Producer: Daniel Dare. Cast: Eddie Bracken, Cass Daley, Virginia Welles. Man becomes rich striking oil, heads to New York, meets radio interviewer.

Blondie in the Dough (1947, Columbia Pictures). 69 min. Director: Abby Berlin. Producer: Burt Kelly. Cast: Penny Singleton, Arthur Lake. Dagwood becomes radio engineer, accidently airs commercial for Blondie's cookies on show sponsored by cookie company.

The Hucksters (1947, MGM). 115 min. Director: Jack Conway. Producer: Arthur Hornblow, Jr. Cast: Clark Gable, Deborah Kerr, Sydney Greenstreet. War vet becomes disenchanted with radio advertising industry.

The Unsuspected (1947, Warner Bros.). 103 min. Director: Michael Curtiz. Producers: Michael Curtiz, Charles Hoffman. Cast: Joan Caulfield, Claude Rains. Radio crime show host becomes involved in murder.

Something in the Wind (1947, Universal International Pictures). 94 min. Director: Irving Pichel. Producer: Joseph Sistrom. Cast: Deanna Durbin, John Dall, Donald O'Connor. DJ is mistaken for her aunt by millionaire's grandson.

Killer McCoy (1947, MGM). 104 min. Director: Roy Rowland. Producer: Sam Zimbalist. Cast: Mickey Rooney, Brian Donlevy, Ann Blyth. Blow-by-blow accounts as street pug becomes boxer and kills opponent in ring.

The Babe Ruth Story (1948, Allied Artists). 106 min. Director-Producer: Roy Del Ruth. Cast: William Bendix, Claire Trevor. Play-by-play broadcasts of slugger's memorable games.

I Surrender Dear (1948, Columbia Pictures). 67 min. Director: Arthur Dreifuss. Producer: Sam Katzman. Cast: Gloria Jean, David Street, Don McGuire. DJ is fired, replaced by daughter's boyfriend.

Song of Idaho (1948, Columbia Pictures). 67 min. Director: Ray Nazarro. Producer: Colbert Clark. Cast: Kirby Grant, June Vincent, The Hoosier Hotshots. Plans to produce radio show from Idaho ranch hit numerous snags.

Lady at Midnight (1948, John Sutherland Productions). 62 min. Director: Sam Newfield. Producer: John Sutherland. Cast: Richard Denning, Frances Rafferty, Lora Lee Michel. Radio newsman becomes involved in child adoption case and murder.

Docks of New Orleans (1948, Monogram Pictures). 64 min. Director: Derwin Abrahams. Producer: James S. Burkett. Cast: Roland Winters, Virginia Dale, Mantan Moreland. Killer broadcasts music at specific frequency to shatter radio tube, releasing poison gas.

Brass Monkey, aka *Lucky Mascot* (1948, United Artists). 100 min. Director: Thornton Freeland. Producer: Nat A. Bronsten. Cast: Carroll Levis, Carole Landis, Herbert Lom. Radio singer gets involved in murder and search for valuable brass monkey.

The Story of Seabiscuit (1949, Warner Bros.). 98 min. Director: David Butler. Producer: William Jacobs. Cast: Barry Fitzgerald, Shirley Temple, Lon McCallister. Radio sportscaster comments on famous horse.

My Dream Is Yours (1949, Warner Bros.). 101 min. Director-Producer: Michael Curtiz. Cast: Jack Carson, Doris Day, Lee Bowman. Singer becomes radio star in musical with Bugs Bunny dream sequence.

A Woman's Secret (1949, RKO Radio Pictures). 84 min. Director: Nicholas Ray. Producer: Herman J. Mankiewicz. Cast: Maureen O'Hara, Melvyn Douglas, Gloria Grahame. Former singing star confesses to shooting death of protégé.

Blondie Hits the Jackpot (1949, Columbia Pictures). 66 min. Director: Edward Bernds. Producer: Ted Richmond. Cast: Penny Singleton, Arthur Lake, Larry Simms. Blondie wins radio quiz show.

A Letter to Three Wives (1949, Twentieth Century-Fox). 103 min. Director: Joseph L. Mankiewicz. Producer: Sol C. Siegel. Cast: Jeanne Crain, Linda Darnell, Ann Sothern. Soap opera writer is one of three women receiving letter from friend announcing she is eloping with one of their husbands.

Champion (1949, Stanley Kramer Productions). 99 min. Director: Mark Robson. Producer: Stanley Kramer. Cast: Kirk Douglas, Marilyn Maxwell. Rise and fall of boxing champ includes fight broadcasts.

Ringside (1949, Lippert Pictures). 68 min. Director: Frank McDonald. Producer: Ron Ormond. Cast: Don Barry, Tom Brown. Blow-by-blow account of match in which pianist turned fighter avenges brother's blinding in ring.

The Kid from Cleveland (1949, Herbert Kline Productions). 89 min. Director: Herbert Kline. Producer: Walter Colmes. Cast: Russ Tamblyn, George Brent. Sportscaster befriends runaway boy.

Make Believe Ballroom (1949, Columbia Pictures). 79 min. Director: Joseph Santley. Producer: Ted Richmond. Cast: Al Jarvis, Jerome Courtland, Ruth Warrick. DJ stages dance concert to help teens start club.

The Sickle or the Cross (1949, Roland Reed Productions). 74 min. Director: Frank R. Strayer. Producer: Roland D. Reed. Cast: Kent Taylor, Gloria Holden, Gene Lockhart. Communists sneak agent into U.S. to broadcast propaganda.

Home in San Antone (1949, Columbia Pictures). 62 min. Director: Ray Nazarro. Producer: Colbert Clark. Lead actor: Roy Acuff. Band enters radio contest, becomes involved with robbers.

Father Was a Fullback (1949, Twentieth Century-Fox). 84 min. Director: John M. Stahl. Producer: Fred Kohlmar. Cast: Fred MacMurray, Maureen O'Hara, Betty Lynn. Play-by-play account of a game that beleaguered college coach must win.

It Happens Every Spring (1949, Twentieth Century-Fox). 87 min. Director: Lloyd Bacon. Producer: William Perlberg. Cast: Ray Milland, Jean Peters, Paul Douglas. Broadcasts of games in which batters can't hit doctored ball.

Kill the Umpire (1950, Columbia Pictures). 78 min. Director: Lloyd Bacon. Producer: John Beck. Cast: William Bendix, Ray Collins. Man who hates umps becomes one in games broadcast on radio.

The Next Voice You Hear ... (1950, MGM). 83 min. Director: William A. Wellman. Producer: Dore Schary. Cast: James Whitmore, Nancy Davis, Gary Gray. God's voice begins coming from radios around the world.

No Trace (1950, Tempean Films, Britain). 76 min. Director: John Gilling. Producers: Robert S. Baker, Monty Berman. Cast: Hugh Sinclair, Dinah Sheridan, John Laurie. Writer becomes blackmail victim after broadcasting crime stories.

David Harding, Counterspy (1950, Columbia Pictures). 71 min. Director: Ray Nazarro. Producer: Milton Feldman. Cast: Willard Parker, Audrey Long, Howard St. John. Radio commentator's broadcasts are used as counter-espionage tool in film based on long-running radio series.

The Jackpot (1950, Twentieth Century-Fox). 85 min. Director: Walter Lang. Producer: Samuel G. Engel. Cast: James Stewart, Barbara Hale, James Gleason. Man's life turns upside down when he wins radio quiz show.

My Blue Heaven (1950, Twentieth Century-Fox). 96 min. Director: Henry Koster. Producer: Sol C. Siegel. Cast: Betty Grable, Dan Dailey, David Wayne. Radio songsters begin television careers, try to adopt child.

Hit Parade of 1951 (1950, Republic Pictures). 85 min. Director-Producer: John H. Auer. Cast: John Carroll, Marie McDonald, Estelita Rodriguez. Radio crooner becomes involved with gambler who is his exact double.

The Jackie Robinson Story (1950, Legend Films). 76 min. Director: Alfred E. Green. Producer: Mort Briskin. Cast: Jackie Robinson, Ruby Dee, Minor Watson. Play-by-play broadcasts of baseball star's memorable moments.

To Please a Lady (1950, MGM). 91 min. Director-Producer: Clarence Brown. Cast: Clark Gable, Barbara Stanwyck. Radio description of Indy 500 race.

Angels in the Outfield (1951, MGM). 99 min. Director-Producer: Clarence Brown. Cast: Paul Douglas, Janet Leigh, Donna Corcoran. Sports announcer feuds with baseball manager, then angels become involved.

The Harlem Globetrotters (1951, Columbia Pictures). 78 min. Director: Phil Brown. Producer: Buddy Adler. Cast: Thomas Gomez, Billy Brown, Dorothy Dandridge. Radio accounts of famous team's games.

A Millionaire for Christy (1951, Bert E. Friedlob Productions). 91 min. Director: George Marshall. Producer: Bert E. Friedlob. Cast: Fred MacMurray, Eleanor Parker, Richard Carlson. Secretary tries to seduce millionaire radio announcer.

Disc Jockey (1951, Allied Artists Pictures). 77 min. Director: Will Jason. Producer:

Maurice Duke. Cast: Ginny Simms, Tom Drake, Jane Nigh. Article in *Variety* about influence of television on radio ratings leads announcers to make star of unknown singer.

Queen for a Day (1951, Robert Stillman Productions). 107 min. Director: Arthur Lubin. Producer: Robert Stillman. Cast: Jack Bailey, Jim Morgan, Ford Pearson. Stories behind three contestants on popular radio show.

The Prowler (1951, Horizon Pictures). 92 min. Director: Joseph Losey. Producer: Sam Spiegel. Cast: Van Heflin, Evelyn Keyes, John Maxwell. Cop investigates prowler complaint at DJ's home, then has affair with his wife.

Radio tekee murron, aka *The Radio Burglary* (1951, Suomen Filmiteollisuus, Finland). 91 min. Director: Matti Kassila. Producer: T.J. Sarkka. Cast: Hannes Hayrinen, Ritva Arvelo, Kullervo Kalske. Radio reporter breaks into museum as a stunt, then real burglars show up.

The Ring (1952, King Brothers Productions). 79 min. Director: Kurt Neumann. Producers: Frank King, Maurice King, Herman King. Cast: Lalo Rios, Rita Moreno. Broadcast of championship fight.

With a Song in My Heart (1952, Twentieth Century-Fox). 117 min. Director: Walter Lang. Producer: Lamar Trotti. Cast: Susan Hayward, Rory Calhoun. Singer Jane Froman is crippled in plane crash but continues to entertain troops.

We're Not Married! (1952, Twentieth Century-Fox). 86 min. Director: Edmund Goulding. Producer: Nunnally Johnson. Cast: Ginger Rogers, Fred Allen, Victor Moore. Morning show team discovers they're not husband and wife.

The Pride of St. Louis (1952, Twentieth Century-Fox). 93 min. Director: Harmon Jones. Producer: Jules Schermer. Cast: Dan Dailey, Joanne Dru. The "Dizzy" Dean story includes sportscasting career.

The Winning Team (1952, Warner Bros.). 98 min. Director: Lewis Seiler. Producer: Bryan Foy. Cast: Ronald Reagan, Doris Day. Biopic of pitcher Grover Cleveland Alexander includes game broadcasts.

The Kid from Left Field (1953, Twentieth Century-Fox). 80 min. Director: Harmon Jones. Producer: Leonard Goldstein. Cast: Dan Dailey, Billy Chapin, Anne Bancroft. Play-by-play descriptions when kid becomes baseball team's manager.

White Lightning (1953, Monogram Pictures). 61 min. Director: Edward Bernds. Producer: Ben Schwalb. Cast: Stanley Clements, Barbara Bestar, Steve Brodie. Play-by-play accounts of hockey games in which gamblers bribe players.

Champ for a Day (1953, Republic Pictures). 90 min. Director-Producer: William A. Seiter. Cast: Alex Nicol, Audrey Totter. Blow-by-blow accounts when heavyweight gets mixed up with gamblers.

The All American (1953, Universal International Pictures). 83 min. Director: Jesse Hibbs. Producer: Aaron Rosenberg. Cast: Tony Curtis, Lori Nelson, Richard Long. Star quarterback has problems when he changes schools.

Little Boy Lost (1953, Paramount Pictures). 95 min. Director: George Seaton. Producer: William Perlberg. Cast: Bing Crosby, Claude Dauphin, Christian Fourcade. American radio reporter searches for child he fathered with French radio singer.

Amor sobre ruedas (1954, C.E.A., Spain). 87 min. Director: Ramon Torrado. Cast: Alicia Altabella, Matilde Artero, Pepe Blanco. Singing taxi driver enters radio talent contest.

Roogie's Bump (1954, Republic Pictures). 71 min. Director: Harold Young. Producer: John Bash. Cast: Robert Marriott, Ruth Warrick, Robert F. Simon. Play-by-play when kid becomes pitcher for Brooklyn Dodgers.

Historias de la radio (1955, Chapalo Films S. A., Spain). 95 min. Director: Jose Luis Saenz de Heredia. Cast: Carlos Acevedo, Alicia Altabella. Five stories illustrate radio's importance to Spain in early 1950s.

Love Me or Leave Me (1955, MGM). 122 min. Director: Charles Vidor. Producer:

Joe Pasternak. Cast: Doris Day, James Cagney. Biopic of singer Ruth Etting includes radio performances.

The Great Man (1956, Universal International Pictures). 98 min. Director: Jose Ferrer. Producer: Aaron Rosenberg. Cast: Jose Ferrer, Dean Jagger, Keenan Wynn. Few people have good things to say about radio commentator after his death.

Journey to Freedom (1957, Republic Pictures). 60 min. Director: Robert C. Dertano. Producer: Stephen C. Apostolof. Cast: Jacques Scott, Genevieve Aumont. Bulgarian journalist uses Radio Free Europe and Voice of America for anti–Communist broadcasts.

A Face in the Crowd (1957, Newtown Productions). 125 min. Director-Producer: Elia Kazan. Cast: Andy Griffith, Patricia Neal, Walter Matthau. Hayseed gains stardom on radio and TV, becomes political megalomaniac.

Jamboree, aka *Disc Jockey Jamboree* (1957, Vanguard Productions). 71 min. Director: Roy Lockwood. Producers: Max Rosenberg, Milton Subotsky. Cast: Kay Medford, Bob Pastine, Paul Carr. Thin plot features DJs introducing singing stars. Dick Clark's movie debut as telethon host.

Mister Rock and Roll (1957, Aurora Productions). 86 min. Director: Charles S. Dubin. Producers: Howard B. Kreitsek, Ralph B. Serpe. Cast: Alan Freed, Teddy Randazzo, Lois O'Brien. Alan Freed biopic consists mainly of musical performances.

Sing Boy Sing (1958, Twentieth Century-Fox). 90 min. Director-Producer: Henry Ephron. Cast: Tommy Sands, Edmond O'Brien. DJs help create singing star who comes to hate teen idol lifestyle.

The Beast of Budapest (1958, Barlene Corporation). 72 min. Director: Harmon Jones. Producer: Archie Mayo. Cast: Gerald Milton, Michael Mills. Anti-Communist protestors take over government radio station.

*Another Time, Another Plac*e (1958, Paramount Pictures). 91 min. Director: Lewis Allen. Producer: Joe Kaufmann. Cast: Lana Turner, Sean Connery, Barry Sullivan. American journalist gets involved with BBC radio war correspondent.

Go, Johnny, Go! (1959, Hal Roach Studios). 75 min. Director: Paul Landres. Producer: Alan Freed. Cast: Alan Freed, Jimmy Clanton, Sandy Stewart. DJ searches for mysterious singer of new hit song.

The Young Ones, aka *Wonderful to Be Young!* (1961, Associated British Pictures Corporation, Britain). 108 min. Director: Sidney J. Furie. Producer: Kenneth Harper. Cast: Cliff Richard, Robert Morley. Teens raise money to save club by starting pirate station.

The Gleiwitz Case, aka *Der Fall Gleiwitz* (1961, Deutsche Film, East Germany). 70 min. Director: Gerhard Klein. Cast: Hannjo Hasse, Herwart Grosse. Nazis posing as Poles attack German radio station to justify invading Poland.

The Courtship of Eddie's Father (1963, MGM). 118 min. Director: Vincente Minnelli. Producer: Joe Pasternak. Cast: Glenn Ford, Shirley Jones, Ron Howard. Radio program director deals with rapscallion DJ and son who wants to find him new wife.

How to Be Loved, aka *Jak byc kochana* (1965, WFF Wroclaw, Poland). 110 min. Director: Wojciech Has. Producer: Jozef Krawkowski. Cast: Barbara Krafftowna, Zbigniew Cybulski. Actress recalls career on stage and radio, including tragic love affair.

Disk-O-Tek Holiday, aka *Just For You* (1966, Delmore-Canterbury Productions, Britain/US). 72 min. Directors: Douglas Hickox, Vince Scarza. Producers: Jacques De Lane Lea, Frank C. Slay. Cast: Katherine Quint, Casey Paxton. Singers harass DJs to get song played on the air.

My Dog, the Thief (1969, Walt Disney Productions). 88 min. Director: Robert Stevenson. Producer: Ron Miller. Cast: Dwayne Hickman, Mary Ann Mobley. TV movie in which kleptomaniac dog boosts traffic reporter's ratings, helps nab robbers.

The Dirty Mind of Young Sally (1970, Boxoffice International Pictures). 95 min. Director-Producer: Bethel Buckalew. Cast: Sharon Kelly, George "Buck" Flower. Sexy pirate radio host operates from van.

WUSA (1970, Paramount Pictures). 115 min. Director: Stuart Rosenberg. Producers: John Foreman, Paul Newman. Cast: Paul Newman, Joanne Woodward, Anthony Perkins. Liberal drifter gets DJ job at conservative radio station.

Play Misty for Me (1971, Universal Pictures, Malpaso Company). 102 min. Director: Clint Eastwood. Producers: Robert Daley, Jennings Lang. Cast: Clint Eastwood, Jessica Walter, Donna Mills. Obsessive listener tries to kill DJ and his girlfriend.

Vanishing Point (1971, Cupid Productions). 99 min. Director: Richard C. Sarafian. Producer: Norman Spencer. Cast: Barry Newman, Cleavon Little. Blind DJ helps former race car driver elude police while taking car from Colorado to California.

Melinda (1972, MGM). 109 min. Director: Hugh A. Robertson. Producer: Pervis Atkins. Cast: Calvin Lockhart, Rosalind Cash, Vonetta McGee. Fast-talking DJ avenges death of girlfriend at hands of white mobsters.

Tout le monde il est beau, tout le monde il est gentil (1972, Belstar, Cine Qua Non, IDI Cinematografica, France). 105 min. Director: Jean Yanne. Producers: Jean-Pierre Rassam, Jean Yanne. Cast: Jean Yanne, Bernard Blier, Michel Serrault. Satire of current events set in commercial radio station.

The King of Marvin Gardens (1972, BBS Productions). 103 min. Director-Producer: Bob Rafelson. Cast: Jack Nicholson, Bruce Dern, Ellen Burstyn. Quiet air personality becomes embroiled in get-rich-quick scheme with fast-talking brother.

Lady Sings the Blues (1972, Motown Productions, Furie Productions). 144 min. Director: Sidney J. Furie. Producers: Brad Dexter, Jay Weston, James S. White. Cast: Diana Ross, Billy Dee Williams, Richard Pryor. Billie Holiday's network radio debut is cancelled because Southern stations won't carry it.

Slipstream (1973, Pacific Rim Films, Canada). 93 min. Director: David Acomba. Producer: James Margellos. Cast: Luke Askew, Patti Oatman. DJ broadcasts from farmhouse, clashes with management over music, becomes involved with woman who arrives unexpectedly.

Birds of Prey (1973, Tomorrow Entertainment). 81 min. Director: William A. Graham. Producer: Alan A. Armer. Cast: David Janssen, Ralph Meeker, Elayne Heilveil. Traffic reporter engages bank robbers in aerial dogfight over Utah.

Tenafly (1973, Universal TV). 90 min. Director: Richard A. Colla. Producer: Jon Epstein. Cast: James McEachin, Ed Nelson, David Huddleston. Pilot for short-lived TV series in which detective investigates murder of talk show host's wife.

American Graffiti (1973, Lucasfilm, The Coppola Company, Universal Pictures). 110 min. Director: George Lucas. Producer: Francis Ford Coppola. Cast: Richard Dreyfuss, Ron Howard, Paul Le Mat. DJ Wolfman Jack rocks California teenagers in 1960.

The Night That Panicked America (1975, Paramount Television). 92 min. Director-Producer: Joseph Sargent. Cast: Paul Shenar, Vic Morrow, John Ritter. TV dramatization of *The War of the Worlds*, showing how sound effects were produced and show's impact.

Fear on Trial (1975, Alan Landsburg Productions). 100 min. Director: Lamont Johnson. Producer: Stanley Chase. Cast: George C. Scott, William Devane, Dorothy Tristan. TV biopic of radio-TV personality John Henry Faulk, who won libel suit against CBS after 1950s blacklist.

That's the Way of the World (1975, Sig Shore Productions). 100 min. Director-Producer: Sig Shore. Cast: Harvey Keitel, Ed Nelson, Cynthia Bostick. Record company uses interview with lecherous New York DJ to help promote singing group.

A Cry for Help (1975, Universal TV). 73 min. Director: Daryl Duke. Producer: Howie Horwitz. Cast: Robert Culp, Elayne Heilveil, Ken Swofford. TV movie in which abusive talk show host asks listeners to help find suicidal caller.

The Disappearance of Aimee (1975, Hallmark Hall of Fame Productions). 100 min. Director: Anthony Harvey. Producer: Paul Leaf. Cast: Faye Dunaway, Bette Davis, James Woods. TV biopic of radio evangelist Aimee Semple McPherson focuses on mysterious disappearance to Mexico.

*__Bound for Glory__ (1976, United Artists). 147 min. Director: Hal Ashby. Producers: Robert F. Blumofe, Harold Leventhal. Cast: David Carradine, Ronny Cox, Melinda Dillon. Woody Guthrie begins singing career on radio.

__Redneck Miller__ (1977, Nu-South Films). Director: John Clayton. Producer: W. Henry Smith. Cast: Geoffrey Land, Sydney Rubin. Country music DJ tries to recover stolen motorcycle used to transport drugs.

*__Slap Shot__ (1977, Kings Road Entertainment, Pan Arts, Universal Pictures). 123 min. Director: George Roy Hill. Producers: Stephen J. Friedman, Robert J. Wunsch. Cast: Paul Newman, Strother Martin. Charlestown Chiefs' play-by-play announcer also interviews players and coach.

*__Outlaw Blues__ (1977, Sequoia Productions). 100 min. Director: Richard T. Heffron. Producer: Steve Tisch. Cast: Peter Fonda, Susan Saint James, John Crawford. Ex-con again on the lam has hit record he promotes with radio interviews while dodging police.

*__Anurodh__ (1977, Samanta Enterprises, India). 147 min. Director: Shakti Samanta. Producer: Girija Samanta. Cast: Rajesh Khanna, Vinod Mehra, Ashok Kumar. Young man disobeys father, leaves home to pursue career as radio singer.

*__FM__ (1978, Universal Pictures). 104 min. Director: John A. Alonzo. Producer: Rand Holston. Cast: Michael Brandon, Eileen Brennan. DJs take over station to protest program changes. This film is thought to have inspired the TV series __WKRP in Cincinnati.__

*__American Hot Wax__ (1978, Paramount Pictures). 91 min. Director: Floyd Mutrux. Producer: Art Linson. Cast: Tim McIntire, Fran Drescher, Jay Leno. Alan Freed biopic.

*__Thank God It's Friday__ (1978, Casablanca Filmworks). 89 min. Director: Robert Klane. Producer: Rob Cohen. Cast: Ray Vitte, Donna Summer, Jeff Goldblum. DJ encounters problems while doing remote broadcast from disco.

__Bud and Lou__ (1978, Bob Banner Associates). 98 min. Director: Robert C. Thompson. Producers: Clyde Phillips, Robert C. Thompson. Cast: Harvey Korman, Buddy Hackett. TV biopic about careers of Abbott and Costello in radio and film.

*__Ring of Passion__ (1978, 20th Century-Fox Television). 100 min. Director: Robert Michael Lewis. Producer: Lou Morheim. Cast: Bernie Casey, Stephen Macht, Britt Ekland. TV movie in which American and German announcers cover Louis-Schmeling fights.

*__The Prize Fighter__ (1979, TriStar Pictures). 99 min. Director: Michael Preece. Producers: Lang Elliott, Wanda Dell. Cast: Don Knotts, Tim Conway. Broadcasts of bumbling boxer's fights.

*__On the Air Live with Captain Midnight__ (1979, Sebastian International). 90 min. Directors-Producers: Beverly Sebastian, Ferd Sebastian. Cast: Tracy Sebastian, John Ireland. Teenagers operate pirate station from van.

*__The Warriors__ (1979, Paramount Pictures). 92 min. Director: Walter Hill. Producers: Laurent Bouzereau, Freeman A. Davies, Lawrence Gordon, Walter Hill. Cast: Michael Beck, James Remar. DJ comments on gang's journey to home turf in New York City.

*__The Kid from Left Field__ (1979, Gary Coleman Productions). 100 min. Director: Adell Aldrich. Producer: David Vreeland. Cast: Gary Coleman, Robert Guillaume, Gary Collins. TV remake of 1953 movie includes play-by-play broadcasts of games in which kid becomes manager of San Diego Padres.

*__Marciano__ (1979, ABC Circle Films). 104 min. Director: Bernard L. Kowalski. Producer: John G. Stephens. Cast: Tony Lo Bianco, Belinda Montgomery, Vincent Gardenia. TV biopic of heavyweight champ with blow-by-blow fight broadcasts.

*__The Fog__ (1980, AVCO Embassy Pictures). 89 min. Director: John Carpenter. Producer: Debra Hill. Cast: Adrienne Barbeau, Jamie Lee Curtis. DJ helps seaside town residents escape zombies.

__Cma,__ aka __The Moth__ (1980, Film Polski, Poland). 100 min. Director: Tomasz Zygadlo. Cast: Roman Wilhelmi, Anna Seniuk, Iwona Bielska. Talk show host has mental problems that eventually make him lose control.

Radio On (1980, British Film Institute, Britain). 104 min. Director: Christopher Petit. Producer: Keith Griffiths. Lead actor: David Beames. London DJ drives to Bristol to investigate death of brother, listening to radio and encountering disparate characters along the way.

Times Square (1980, Robert Stigwood Organization, Butterfly Valley Productions). 111 min. Director: Allan Moyle. Producers: Jacob Brackman, Robert Stigwood. Cast: Tim Curry, Trini Alvarado, Robin Johnson. DJ helps runaway girls become cult heroes.

The Great American Traffic Jam, aka *Gridlock* (1980, Ten-Four Productions). 100 min. Director: James Frawley. Producers: Dave Hackel, Steve Hattman, Arthur E. McLaird. Cast: Desi Arnaz, Jr., John Beck, Noah Beery, Jr. TV movie in which unseen DJ comments on massive traffic jam.

Don't Answer the Phone! (1980, Scorpion). 94 min. Director: Robert Hammer. Producers: Michael D. Castle, Robert Hammer. Cast: James Westmoreland, Ben Frank, Flo Lawrence. Vietnam vet strangles women, calls radio psychologist, then stalks her.

Raging Bull (1980, United Artists). 129 min. Director: Martin Scorsese. Producers: Robert Chartoff, Irwin Winkler. Cast: Robert De Niro, Cathy Moriarty, Joe Pesci. Biopic of boxer Jake LaMotta includes Don Dunphy radio fight description.

Don't Look Back: The Story of Leroy "Satchel" Paige (1981, Satie Productions). 98 min. Director: Richard A. Colla. Producers: Jimmy Hawkins, Stanley Rubin. Lead actor: Louis Gossett, Jr. Play-by-play descriptions in TV biopic of pitcher.

Kings and Desperate Men (1981, Kineversal Productions, Canada). 118 min. Director-Producer: Alexis Kanner. Cast: Patrick McGoohan, Alexis Kanner, Andrea Marcovicci. Talk show host is taken hostage by terrorists demanding on-air trial for convicted comrade.

Gas (1981, Filmplan International, Canada). 94 min. Director: Les Rose. Producer: Claude Heroux. Cast: Donald Sutherland, Susan Anspach, Howie Mandel, Sterling Hayden. DJ does show from helicopter in spoof about 1970s gas shortages.

Behind Glass, aka *Achter glas* (1981, Netherlands). 70 min. Director: Ab van Ieperen. Producer: Frans Rasker. Cast: Joop Admiraal, Ria Beckers, Wim Bloemendaal. Radio reporter becomes involved with window washer.

Man of Iron, aka *Czlowiek z zelaza* (1981, Film Polski, Poland). 140 min. Director: Andrzej Wajda. Cast: Marian Opania, Jerzy Radziwilowicz, Krystyna Janda. Alcoholic radio reporter covering Gdansk shipyard strike runs afoul of authorities by becoming sympathetic to strikers.

Fatty Girl Goes to New York, aka *Cicciabomba* (1982, Emme R. T. Cinematografica, Italy). 92 min. Director: Umberto Lenzi. Cast: Donnatella Rettore, Dario Caporaso, Anita Ekberg. Overweight DJ wins contest, goes to New York, becomes glamour girl, returns home to take revenge on those who teased her.

Girls Nite Out (1982, Concepts Unlimited). 96 min. Director: Robert Deubel. Producer: Anthony N. Gurvis. Cast: Julia Montgomery, James Carroll, Suzanne Barnes. Killer in bear suit calls college station with clues about sorority girl murders.

Rosie: The Rosemary Clooney Story (1982, Alan Sacks Productions). 100 min. Director-Producer: Jackie Cooper. Cast: Sondra Locke, Kevin McCarthy. TV biopic includes singer's start at WLW Cincinnati.

Vasika... kalispera sas (1982, Giorgos Karagiannis & Co., Greece). 90 min. Director-Producer: Giannis Dalianidis. Cast: Stathis Psaltis, Panos Mihalopoulos, Stamatis Gardelis. Teenagers start competing pirate stations.

Piratene (1983, Norsk Film, Norway). 93 min. Director: Morten Kolstad. Producer: Harald Ohrvik. Cast: Trond Peter Stamse Munch, Kristian Figenschow, Guri Johnson. Boys start pirate station that becomes popular with everyone but police.

Born in Flames (1983). 80 min. Director-Producer: Lizzie Borden. Cast: Honey, Adele Bertei, Jeanne Satterfield. Feminists use underground radio stations to fight "the system."

Tiger Town (1983, Walt Disney Productions). 95 min. Director: Alan Shapiro. Producer: Susan B. Landau. Cast: Roy Scheider, Justin Henry. Ernie Harwell does play-by-play when boy becomes enamored with Detroit Tigers player.

Dempsey (1983, Chuck Fries Productions). 100 min. Director: Gus Trikonis. Producer: Jay Benson. Cast: Treat Williams, Sally Kellerman, Victoria Tennant. TV movie with blow-by-blow broadcasts of heavyweight championship fights.

The Escapist (1983, Min-America Promotions). 87 min. Director: Eddie Beverly, Jr. Producers: Ron Hostetler, Stephen Meyers, Eddie Beverly, Jr. Cast: Bill Shirk, Christopher Milburn, Peter Lupus. Station owner performs death-defying escapes to save station.

Love Letters (1983, Adams Apple Film Company, Nu Image Millenium Films). 98 min. Director: Amy Holden Jones. Producer: Roger Corman. Cast: Jamie Lee Curtis, Bonnie Bartlett, Matt Clark. DJ's discovery that deceased mother had affair triggers disastrous relationship of her own.

A Christmas Story (1983, MGM). 93 min. Director: Bob Clark. Producers: Bob Clark, Rene Dupont. Cast: Peter Billingsley, Melinda Dillon, Darren McGavin. Recollections of Christmases past include boy's obsession with *Little Orphan Annie* radio show decoder ring.

Choose Me (1984, Tartan Productions). 106 min. Director: Alan Rudolph. Producers: David Blocker, Carolyn Pfeiffer. Cast: Genevieve Bujold, Keith Carradine, Lesley Ann Warren. Radio sex therapist with personality problems becomes involved with listeners.

Night of the Comet (1984, Film Development Fund, Atlantic 9000). 95 min. Director: Thom Eberhardt. Producers: Wayne Crawford, Andrew Lane. Cast: Robert Beltran, Catherine Mary Stewart, Kelli Maroney. Valley Girls use radio station to get help when comet unleashes zombies.

Comfort and Joy (1984, Kings Road Entertainment, Lake Film Productions, Thorn EMI, Britain). 106 min. Director: Bill Forsyth. Producers: Davina Belling, Clive Parsons. Cast: Bill Paterson, Eleanor David, Clare Grogan. Glasgow DJ becomes involved in battle between ice cream companies.

Breakfast with Les and Bess (1985, Public Broadcasting Service). 90 min. Director-Producer: Perry Rosemond. Cast: Shaun Cassidy, Mark Humphrey, Bill Kemp. TV biopic about talk show team who broadcast from apartment in 1960s.

La Radio Folla (1986, Opalo Films, Spain). 95 min. Director: Francesc Bellmunt. Producer: Jose Antonio Perez Giner. Cast: Carme Ballesteros, Jose Maria Canete. Sex comedy in which DJ turns listeners on.

Trick or Treat (1986, De Laurentiis Entertainment Group). 98 min. Director: Charles Martin Smith. Producers: Michael S. Murphey, Joel Soisson. Cast: Marc Price, Tony Fields, Lisa Orgolini. DJ gives troubled teen record containing backward-recorded Satanic messages, then the singer comes to life.

The Gladiator (1986, Walker Brothers Productions). 104 min. Director: Abel Ferrara. Producer: Robert Lovenheim. Cast: Ken Wahl, Nancy Allen, Robert Culp. TV movie in which talk show host becomes involved with mechanic, unaware he's vigilante looking for brother's killer.

Haunted Honeymoon (1986, Orion Pictures). 82 min. Director: Gene Wilder. Producer: Susan Ruskin. Cast: Gilda Radner, Gene Wilder, Dom DeLuise. Stars of *Manhattan Mystery Theater* radio show are married in haunted house.

The Texas Chainsaw Massacre 2 (1986, Cannon Films). 89 min. Director: Tobe Hooper. Producers: Yoram Globus, Menahem Golan, Tobe Hooper. Cast: Dennis Hopper, Caroline Williams, Jim Siedow. DJ broadcasts tape of murders to help police catch killer, then becomes target herself.

Murrow (1986, Titus Productions, TvS Entertainment). 114 min. Director: Jack Gold. Producers: Dickie Bamber, Robert Berger. Cast: Daniel J. Travanti, Stephen Churchett, Robert Vaughn. TV biopic begins with wartime radio broadcasts.

City in Panic (1986, Trans World Entertainment, Canada). 85 min. Director: Robert Bouvier. Producer: Andreas Schneider. Cast: David Adamson, Lee Ann Nestegard, Ed Chester. Talk show host helps police catch psycho who kills homosexuals.

Open House (1987, Intercontinental Releasing Corporation). 95 min. Director: Jag Mundhra. Producer: Sandy Cobe. Cast: Joseph Bottoms, Adrienne Barbeau, Rudy Ramos. Psycho who kills real estate agents also threatens radio psychologist.

Good Morning, Vietnam (1987, Touchstone Pictures). 121 min. Director: Barry Levinson. Producers: Larry Brezner, Mark Johnson. Cast: Robin Williams, Forest Whitaker, Tung Thanh Tran. Biopic of Armed Forces Radio DJ Adrian Cronauer.

Radio Days (1987, Orion Pictures). 88 min. Director: Woody Allen. Producer: Robert Greenhut. Cast: Mike Starr, Paul Herman, Don Pardo. Radio influences young man growing up in 1940s.

Sexy Radio (1987, Mya Communication, Italy). 99 min. Director: Antoni Verdaguer. Cast: Laura Conti, Carme Callol. Talk show host likes to talk about sex.

Rachel River (1987, American Playhouse). 85 min. Director: Sandy Smolan. Producer: Timothy Marx. Cast: Nick Benedict, Ailene Cole, Don Cosgrove. Divorced DJ tries to put her life together in small town as she investigates death of old woman.

La Bamba (1987, Columbia Pictures). 108 min. Director: Luis Valdez. Producers: Bill Borden, Taylor Hackford. Cast: Lou Diamond Philips, Esai Morales. DJ helps propel Ritchie Valens to stardom by playing record.

Midnight Magic (1987, Blackthorn Productions, Canada). 90 min. Director: George Mihalka. Producer: Stewart Harding. Cast: James Wilder, Jennifer Dale, Stuart Gillard. TV movie in which talk show psychologist becomes involved with younger student.

Break of Dawn (1988, Cinewest Entertainment). 100 min. Director: Isaac Artenstein. Producer: Jude Pauline Eberhard. Cast: Oscar Chavez, Maria Rojo. TV biopic about Pedro Gonzales, first Hispanic LA DJ.

The Couch Trip (1988, Orion Pictures). 97 min. Director: Michael Ritchie. Producer: Lawrence Gordon. Cast: Dan Aykroyd, Walter Matthau, Charles Grodin. Mental institution escapee becomes radio psychologist.

Talk Radio (1988, Cineplex-Odeon Films). 110 min. Director: Oliver Stone. Producers: A. Kitman Ho, Edward R. Pressman. Cast: Eric Bogosian, Ellen Greene, Leslie Hope. Based on death of Denver talk show host Allen Berg, killed by neo-Nazis in 1984.

Betrayed (1988, Winkler Films, Sundown Productions). 127 min. Director: Costa-Gavras. Producer: Irwin Winkler. Cast: Debra Winger, Tom Berenger, John Heard. Murder of talk show host leads undercover FBI agent to white supremacists.

Freeway (1988, Gower Street Pictures). 91 min. Director: Francis Delia. Producers: Peter S. Davis, William N. Panzer. Cast: Darlanne Fluegel, James Russo, Billy Drago. Killer calls radio psychiatrist from car while cruising for more victims.

Zombi 3, aka *Zombie Flesh Eaters 2* (1988, Flora Film, Italy). 84 min. Director: Lucio Fulci. Producer: Franco Gaudenzi. Cast: Deran Sarafian, Beatrice Ring. DJ tries to help island residents avoid zombies, then becomes one.

Frequent Death, aka *Frequence meurtre*, aka *Murder Rate* (1988, AAA Production Company, Capac Productions, Films A2, Les Productions de la Gueville, Soprofilms, France). 103 min. Director: Elisabeth Rappeneau. Producers: Daniele Delorme, Yves Robert. Cast: Catherine Deneuve, Andre Dussollier, Martin Lamotte. Talk show psychologist is harassed by caller.

Fakelos Polk Ston Aera, aka *Polk File on the Air* (1988, Greek Films Center, Cinegroup, ERT-1, Greece). 153 min. Director: Dionysus Gregoratos. Cast: Costas Hazoudas, Nikos Hytas. Lives of current CBS radio reporters are endangered when they investigate 1948 death of colleague.

Do the Right Thing (1989, 40 Acres & A Mule Filmworks). 120 min. Director-

Producer: Spike Lee. Cast: Danny Aiello, Ossie Davis, Ruby Dee. DJ provides running commentary on street action in Brooklyn's Bedford-Stuyvesant district.

Columbo: Sex and the Married Detective (1989, Universal Television Entertainment). 120 min. Director: James Frawley. Producer: Stanley Kallis. Cast: Peter Falk, Lindsay Crouse, Stephen Macht. TV movie in which detective investigates death of radio psychologist's assistant.

Major League (1989, Mirage Enterprises). 107 min. Director: David S. Ward. Producers: Chris Chesser, Irby Smith. Cast: Tom Berenger, Charlie Sheen, Bob Uecker. Play-by-play announcer faces challenges when Cleveland Indians' owner tries to field worst possible team.

Radio Corbeau (1989, Cine 5, Saris, Sara Film, France). 95 min. Director: Yves Boisset. Producer: Alain Sarde. Cast: Claude Brasseur, Pierre Arditi, Christine Boisson. Townspeople are upset when pirate station begins broadcasting their secrets in updated version of 1943 film *Le Corbeau.*

Psycho IV: The Beginning (1990, Smart Money Productions). 96 min. Director: Mick Garris. Producers: George Zaloom, Les Mayfield. Cast: Anthony Perkins, Henry Thomas, Olivia Hussey. TV movie in which Norman Bates calls radio psychologist.

Pump Up the Volume (1990, New Line Cinema). 102 min. Director: Allan Moyle. Producers: Rupert Harvey, Sandy Stern. Cast: Christian Slater, Annie Ross. FCC moves to shut down high school pirate DJ after listener commits suicide.

A Matter of Degrees (1990, Backbeat Productions). 88 min. Director: W. T. Morgan. Producers: Randall Poster, Roy Kissin. Cast: Za Za Dupre, Arye Gross, Tom Sizemore. Student disrupts graduation ceremonies when corporation tries to take over college radio station.

Tune in Tomorrow.... (1990, Odyssey Entertainment Group). 107 min. Director: Jon Amiel. Producers: John Fiedler, Mark Tarlov. Cast: Peter Falk, Keanu Reeves, Barbara Hershey. Radio soap opera writer counsels lovesick young man in 1950s New Orleans.

The Adventures of Ford Fairlane (1990, Silver Pictures). 104 min. Director: Renny Harlin. Producers: Joel Silver, Steve Perry. Cast: Andrew Dice Clay, Wayne Newton, Gilbert Gottfried. On-air death of DJ leads private eye to recording industry scam.

Spaced Invaders (1990, Silver Screen Partners IV). 100 min. Director: Patrick Read Johnson. Producer: Luigi G. Cingolani. Cast: Douglas Barr, Royal Dano. Real Martians land during fiftieth anniversary broadcast of famous *War of the Worlds* program.

Invasion of the Space Preachers (1990, Big Pictures Entertainment). 100 min. Director: Daniel Boyd. Producers: Daniel Boyd, A.U. Gallagher, David Wohl. Cast: Jim Wolfe, Guy Nelson. Aliens pose as radio evangelists.

Zoo Radio (1990, Wells Entertainment Group). 90 min. Director: M. Jay Roach. Producers: Jesse Wells, Romero Akrawi. Cast: John Benjamin Martin, Doug Mears. Brothers engage in ratings war to win father's inheritance.

Rafales, aka *Blizzard* (1990, Aska Films, National Film Board of Canada, Canada). 88 min. Director: Andre Melancon. Producers: Yuri Yoshimura-Gagnon, Claude Gagnon. Cast: Marcel Leboeuf, Denis Bouchard. Thief takes radio reporter hostage after department store robbery.

False Identity (1990, Pavilion Pictures). 93 min. Director: James Keach. Producer: James Shavick. Cast: Stacy Keach, Genevieve Bujold. DJ seeks owner of Purple Heart found at garage sale.

The Fisher King (1991, Columbia Pictures). 137 min. Director: Terry Gilliam. Producers: Debra Hill, Lynda Obst. Cast: Jeff Bridges, Robin Williams. Former shock jock develops relationship with homeless man.

Young Soul Rebels (1991, British Film Institute, Britain). 105 min. Director: Isaac Julien. Producer: Nadine Marsh-Edwards. Cast: Valentine Nonyela, Mo Sesay, Dorian Healy. Pirate station operators look for friend's killer.

Barocco (1991, Globe Films, Italy). 94 min. Director: Claudio Sestieri. Producers: Pietro Innocenzi, Pier Francesco Aiello. Cast: Massimo Venturiello, Cristina Marsillach. Art student becomes involved with late night DJ.

*Straight Talk (1992, Hollywood Pictures). 91 min. Director: Barnet Kellman. Producers: Robert Chartoff, Fred Berner. Cast: Dolly Parton, James Woods. Woman leaves Arkansas for Chicago, accidentally becomes talk show host.

*The Babe (1992, Universal Pictures). 115 min. Director: Arthur Hiller. Producer: John Fusco. Cast: John Goodman, Kelly McGillis. Babe Ruth biopic includes play-by-play broadcasts.

*Bad Channels (1992, Full Moon Entertainment). 88 min. Director: Ted Nicolaou. Producer: Keith Payson. Cast: Robert Factor, Martha Quinn. Alien uses DJ to attract women to station, shrink and capture them in bottles, but listeners think it's part of DJ's schtick.

*Laser Moon (1992, Fitzgerald Film Corporation). 91 min. Director: Douglas K. Grimm. Producer: Mark Paglia. Lead actor: Traci Lords. Talk show host helps police solve murders committed with laser because killer calls him after every crime.

*Vintage Model, aka *Modelo antiguo* (1992, Aries Films, Mexico). 95 min. Director: Raul Araiza. Producers: Alejandro Petayo, Miguel Necoechea. Cast: Silvia Pinal, Alonso Echanove. Aging announcer with little time to live forms relationship with cab driver.

*Night Rhythms (1992, Axis Films International). 99 min. Director: A. Gregory Hippolyte. Producer: Andrew Garroni. Cast: Martin Hewitt, David Carradine. Host of talk show about sex must prove innocence when body is found in studio.

*Body Chemistry 2: Voice of a Stranger (1992, Concorde-New Horizons). 84 min. Director: Adam Simon. Producer: Alida Camp. Cast: Lisa Pescia, Gregory Harrison. Radio psychologist with problems of her own and a shady past encourages caller's sexual fantasies.

*Sexual Response (1992, Vision International). 90 min. Director: Yaky Yosha. Producer: Ashok Amritraj. Lead actor: Shannon Tweed. TV movie in which talk show sexologist has affair with sculptor who has as much a dominance problem as her husband.

*Ring of the Musketeers (1992, Motion Picture Corporation of America). 86 min. Director: John Paragon. Producers: Brad Krevoy, Steve Stabler. Cast: Thomas Gottschalk, Cheech Marin, Alison Doody, David Hasselhoff. TV update of *The Three Musketeers*, one of whom is blond radio love doctor.

*Sleepless in Seattle (1993, TriStar Pictures). 105 min. Director: Nora Ephron. Producer: Gary S. Foster. Cast: Tom Hanks, Meg Ryan, Ross Malinger, Rob Reiner. Boy calls talk show to get widowed father new mate and listener decides to meet him.

*Finale in Blood, aka *Da nao guang chang long* (1993, Fortune Star Pictures, Paragon Films, Hong Kong). 94 min. Director: Fruit Chan. Cast: David Wu, Chikako Aoyama. Announcer constructs radio program from visit of ghost.

Perry Mason: The Case of the Telltale Talk Show Host (1993, Dean Hargrove Productions). 96 min. Director: Christian I. Nyby II. Producers: Barry Steinberg, Billy Ray Smith. Cast: Raymond Burr, Barbara Hale, William R. Moses. TV movie in which talk show host is accused of murdering station owner.

*Radioland Murders (1994, Lucasfilm). 112 min. Director: Mel Smith. Producers: Rick McCallum, Fred Roos. Cast: Brian Benben, Mary Stuart Masterson, Ned Beatty. In 1939, cast members begin dying when new radio network starts up.

*Dead Air (1994, Alan Barnette Productions). 91 min. Director: Fred Walton. Producer: Oscar L. Costo. Cast: Gregory Hines, Debrah Farentino. TV movie in which DJ is targeted by listener who may be his girlfriend's killer.

*Major League II (1994, Warner Bros.). 105 min. Director: David S. Ward. Producers: David S. Ward, James G. Robinson. Cast: Charlie Sheen, Tom Berenger, Corbin Bernsen. More play-by-play challenges in second film with Bob Uecker as Harry Doyle.

Columbo: Butterflies in Shades of Grey (1994, Universal TV). 120 min. Director: Dennis Dugan. Producer: Christopher Seiter. Cast: Peter Falk, William Shatner, Molly Hagan. TV movie in which detective suspects talk show host of murder.

***Black Bomber**, aka *Crni bombarder*, aka *Strawberry Switchblade* (1994, D.P. FIVET, Kikinda, Yugoslavia). 113 min. Director: Darko Bajic. Producer: Raka Dokic. Cast: Dragan Bjelogrlic, Anica Dobra. Pirate DJ dodges police and psycho listener with machine gun.

***Airheads** (1994, Twentieth Century-Fox). 92 min. Director: Michael Lehmann. Producers: Robert Simonds, Mark Burg. Cast: Brendan Fraser, Steve Buscemi, Adam Sandler, Joe Mantegna. Rock band takes radio station hostage to get airplay for song.

***Dangerous Touch** (1994, Trimark Pictures). 97 min. Director: Lou Diamond Phillips. Producer: Lisa M. Hansen. Cast: Kate Vernon, Lou Diamond Phillips. Radio sex therapist's promiscuous behavior leads to blackmail and murder.

***Acts of Contrition**, aka *Original Sins* (1995, Courage Productions). 86 min. Director: Jan Egleson. Producer: John Landgraf. Cast: Mark Harmon, Julianne Phillips. TV movie in which talk show host asks callers to reveal secrets and one admits to murder.

***On the Air**, aka *En el aire* (1995, C-Produccciones, Mexico). 86 min. Director: Juan Carlos de Llaca. Producer: Gonzalo Infante. Cast: Daniel Gimenez Cacho, Angelica Aragon, Marta Aura. Aging Mexican hippie and classic rock DJ reflects on his life as station shuts down and marriage fails.

***Magic in the Water** (1995, Oxford Film Company, Canada). 101 min. Director: Rick Stevenson. Producers: Rick Stevenson, Matthew O'Connor, William Stevenson. Cast: Mark Harmon, Sarah Wayne, Joshua Jackson. Divorced radio psychologist with problems takes kids on vacation and they encounter lake monster.

***When the Dark Man Calls** (1995, Power Pictures). 89 min. Director: Nathaniel Gutman. Producers: Nathaniel Gutman, Julian Marks. Cast: Joan Van Ark, Chris Sarandon. TV movie in which talk show host is stalked by husband's killer.

***Halloween: The Curse of Michael Myers** (1995, Halloween VI Productions). 88 min. Director: Joe Chappelle. Producer: Paul Freeman. Cast: Donald Pleasence, Paul Rudd, George P. Wilbur. Homicidal maniac doesn't appreciate DJ's remote broadcast from house he used to live in.

***Midnight Confessions** (1995, Fa Kessler Heinlein). 81 min. Director: Allan Shustack. Producers: David B. Kravis, Babi Walz. Cast: Callie Michael, Steve Michael, Carol Hoyt. Host of sex talk show becomes target of psycho who kills prostitutes.

Stadtgesprach, aka *Talk of the Town* (1995, Buena Vista Pictures, Germany). 93 min. Director: Rainer Kaufmann. Producers: Bettina Reitz, Dirk R. Duwel, Henrik Meyer. Cast: Katja Riemann, August Zirner. Talk show host looks for Mr. Right.

Radio.doc (1995, RTV Slovenia, Slovenia). 85 min. Director: Miran Zupanic. Lead actor: Natasa Matjasec. TV movie in which woman investigates death of father in Yugoslavia by taking job at radio station where he worked.

***Rude** (1995, Conquering Lion Productions, Canada). 89 min. Director: Clement Virgo. Producers: Damon D'Oliveira, Karen A. King. Lead actor: Sharon Lewis. Female pirate DJ broadcasts tales about urban life in Toronto.

***Power 98** (1996, Bergman Lustig Productions). 89 min. Director: Jaime Hellman. Producers: Dana Lustig, Ram Bergman, Carol Curb Nemoy. Cast: Eric Roberts, Jason Gedrick. TV movie in which psycho killer becomes regular talk show caller.

***Eddie** (1996, Hollywood Pictures). 100 min. Director: Steve Rash. Producers: Mark Burg, David Permut. Cast: Whoopi Goldberg, Frank Langella, Dennis Farina. Limo driver's call to sports talk show results in her becoming coach of New York Knicks.

***Love Serenade** (1996, Australian Film Finance Corporation, Australia). 101 min. Director: Shirley Barrett. Producer: Jan Chapman. Cast: Mirnada Otto, Rebecca Frith, George Shevtsov. Small town sisters become involved with new DJ.

***The Truth About Cats and Dogs** (1996, Twentieth Century-Fox). 97 min. Director:

Michael Lehmann. Producer: Cari-Esta Albert. Cast: Uma Thurman, Janeane Garofalo, Ben Chaplin. Host of talk show for pet lovers becomes involved with listener.

Mother Night (1996, Fine Line Features). 114 min. Director: Keith Gordon. Producers: Keith Gordon, Robert B. Weide. Cast: Nick Nolte, Sheryl Lee, Alan Arkin. Expatriate Nazi radio propagandist tries to resume normal life after war.

Pie in the Sky (1996, Fine Line Features). 95 min. Director: Bryan Gordon. Producers: Alan Mindel, Denise Shaw. Cast: Josh Charles, Anne Heche, John Goodman. Young man idolizes radio traffic reporter.

The Fan (1996, Mandalay Entertainment). 116 min. Director: Tony Scott. Producer: Wendy Finerman. Cast: Robert De Niro, Wesley Snipes, Ellen Barkin. Psycho baseball fan calls sports talk show.

Private Parts (1997, Paramount Pictures). 109 min. Director: Betty Thomas. Producer: Ivan Reitman. Cast: Howard Stern, Robin Quivers. Howard Stern biopic.

Vanishing Point (1997, Fox Television Network). 91 min. Director: Charles Robert Carner. Producer: Alan C. Blomquist. Cast: Viggo Mortensen, Jason Priestley. TV remake of 1971 film, without blind DJ.

The Fifth Element (1997, Gaumont Production Company). 126 min. Director: Luc Besson. Producer: Patrice Ledoux. Cast: Bruce Willis, Gary Oldman, Ian Holm. DJ is caught in crossfire during alien invasion.

Telling Lies in America (1997, Banner Entertainment). 101 min. Director: Guy Ferland. Producers: Ben Myron, Fran Rubel Kuzui. Cast: Kevin Bacon, Brad Renfro. Teen idolizes DJ who befriends him but both get caught in web of lies.

Grosse Pointe Blank (1997, Hollywood Pictures). 107 min. Director: George Armitage. Producers: Susan Arnold, Donna Roth, Roger Birnbaum. Cast: John Cusack, Minnie Driver, Dan Aykroyd. Hit man on assignment runs into former girlfriend, now DJ.

Welcome Back, Mr. McDonald, aka *Rajio no jikan* (1997, Fuji Television Network, Japan). 103 min. Director: Koki Mitani. Producers: Takashi Ishihara, Kanjiro Sakura, Hisao Masuda, Chiaki Matsushita. Cast: Toshiaki Karasawa, Kyoka Suzuki. Things spin out of control due to script changes during live broadcast of radio play.

Kokkuri (1997, Nikkatsu Corporation, Hrs Funai Company). 87 min. Director: Takahisa Zeze. Producers: Minoru Yokote, Shigehiro Arake. Cast: Ayumi Yamatsu, Hiroko Shimada, Moe Ishikawa. Teenage DJ and friends conjure up spirit.

99.9 — The Frequency of Terror (1997, Origen P. C.S.A., Impala S.A., Spain). 106 min. Director: Agustin Villaronga. Producer: Antonio Cardenal. Lead actor: Maria Barranco. Host of talk show dealing with psychic phenomena investigate a friend's mysterious death, possibly caused by supernatural forces.

The Apostle (1997, Butcher's Run Films). 134 min. Director: Robert Duvall. Producer: Rob Carliner. Lead actor: Robert Duvall. Itinerant preacher running from law uses small town station to start new ministry.

Levitation (1998, Tenth Muse Productions). 100 min. Director: Scott D. Goldstein. Producers: Shelly Strong, Scott D. Goldstein. Cast: Sarah Paulson, Ernie Hudson, Jeremy London. Blues DJ meets orphaned teen who can levitate.

The Night Caller (1998, Image Organization). 94 min. Director: Robert Malenfant. Producer: Pierre David. Cast: Shanna Reed, Tracy Nelson, Mary Crosby. Listener obsessed with radio psychologist goes on killing spree in order to meet her.

Major League: Back to the Minors (1998, Morgan Creek Productions). 100 min. Director: John Warren. Producer: James G. Robinson. Cast: Scott Bakula, Corbin Bernsen. Bob Uecker as Harry Doyle in final film in trilogy.

Shattered Illusions (1998, Best Pictures). 90 min. Director: Becky Best. Producers: James Bradley, Daniel Hirsch. Cast: Colette O'Connell, Leland Crooke, Morgan Fairchild. Talk show host with psychological problems has a stalker.

Urban Legend (1998, Original Film, Studio Canal, USA/France). 99 min. Director:

Jamie Blanks. Producers: Neal H. Moritz, Gina Matthews, Michael McDonnell. Cast: Jared Leto, Alicia Witt. College DJ is victim of homicidal maniac.

Possums (1998, HSX Films). 97 min. Director: Max Burnett. Producer: Leanna Creel. Cast: Mac Davis, Cynthia Sikes, Andrew Prine. Announcer broadcasts fictitious games after high school football program is canceled.

High Freakquency, aka *Da Station* (1998, Urban Film Productions). 90 min. Director: Tony Singletary. Producer: Cassius Vernon Weathersby. Cast: John Witherspoon, Marcus Chong. TV movie involving antics at urban format station.

Winchell (1998, Fried Films). 105 min. Director: Paul Mazursky. Producer: Stanley J. Wlodkowski. Lead actor: Stanley Tucci. TV biopic about crusading radio reporter.

The Day Silence Died (1998, Pegaso Producciones, Bolivia). 108 min. Director: Paolo Agazzi. Producer: Martin Proctor. Lead actor: Dario Grandinetti. Some residents are upset when DJ sets up loudspeakers in town square and broadcasts local gossip.

Trampa Para un Gato (1998, Producciones Jota Y Joropodo, Bolivar Films, Venezuela). 88 min. Director: Manuel de Pedro. Producer: Marco Antonio Perez. Cast: Alberto Alcala, Simon Ayala. Filmmaker and radio station operator broadcast anti-government programs.

Radiofreccia (1998, Fandango, Italy). 112 min. Director: Luciano Ligabue. Producer: Domenico Proacci. Cast: Stefano Accorsi, Luciano Federico. Five friends start radio station.

Outside Ozona (1998, Millenium Films). 100 min. Director: J. S. Cardone. Producers: Scott Einbinder, Carol Kottenbrook. Cast: Robert Forster, Kevin Pollak, Taj Mahal, Meatloaf. Future victims of killer listen to all-night DJ.

Dil se.. (1998, India Talkies, India). 163 min. Director: Mani Ratnam. Producers: Shekhar Kapur, Ram Gopal Varma, Mani Ratnam. Cast: Sharukh Kahn, Manisha Koirala, Preity Zinta. Reporter for All India Radio is smitten with beautiful woman, discovers she's a terrorist.

Les Gens qui s'aiment (1999, Artemis Productions, France). 90 min. Director: Jean-Charles Tacchella. Producer: Gerard Jourd'hui. Cast: Richard Berry, Jacqueline Bisset, Julie Gayet, Bruno Putzulu. Relationships affect life of talk show host.

Der Vulkan (1999, Lichtblick Film, Ottokar Runze Filmproduktion, Germany). 103 min. Director: Ottokar Runze. Producers: Michael Beier, Ottokar Runze. Cast: Nina Hoss, Christian Nickel. In 1937, German émigrés in Paris broadcast anti–Nazi propaganda.

Late Show (1999, Diana Films, Germany). 111 min. Director: Helmut Dietl. Producers: Helmut Dietl, Alfred Hurmer. Cast: Thomas Gottschalk, Harald Schmidt. TV program director tries to bolster show's ratings by hiring radio DJ as host.

Mr. Rock 'n' Roll: The Alan Freed Story (1999, Von Zerneck-Sertner Films). 88 min. Director: Andy Wolk. Producers: Rick Arredondo, Randy Sutter. Cast: Judd Nelson, Madchen Amick. TV biopic.

Rocky Marciano (1999, Winkler Films). 99 min. Director: Charles Winkler. Producer: Rob Cowan. Cast: Jon Favreau, George C. Scott. TV biopic with blow-by-blow account of Marciano-Louis fight.

Requiem for Murder (1999, Allegro Films, Canada). 95 min. Director: Douglas Jackson. Producers: Robert Wertheimer, Stefan Wodoslawsky. Cast: Molly Ringwald, Christopher Heyerdahl. TV movie in which DJ's listeners are killed.

Dill Scallion (1999, Brady Oil Entertainment, Pedestrian Films). 91 min. Director: Jordan Brady. Producers: Jennifer Amerine, Joe Blake, Kimberly Jacobs. Cast: Billy Burke, Lauren Graham, Henry Winkler. Country singer is upset when DJ plays bootlegged version of his song.

Captive Audience (1999, Corporate Sucker Films). 70 min. Directors: Mike Gioscia, Kurt St. Thomas. Producers: Kurt St. Thomas, Mike Gioscia. Cast: Michael Kevin Walker, Kat Corbett, Mike Gloscia. Late night talk show host is taken hostage.

Dead Air (1999, Bianco Scott Productions). 90 min. Director: Craig Simmons. Cast: John Marlo, Elisabeth Adwin. Shock jock's ratings improve when colleagues are murdered, then he's also threatened.

Entre las piernas, aka *Between Your Legs* (1999, Bocaboca Producciones, Spain). 120 min. Director: Manuel Gomez Pereira. Producers: Manuel Pereira, Alejandro Vazquez, Joaquin Oristrell. Cast: Victoria Abril, Javier Bardem, Carmelo Gomez. Talk show call screener with sex addiction becomes involved with screenwriter and murder.

El chacotero sentimental: La Pelicula (1999, Cebra Producciones, Chile). 87 min. Director: Cristian Galaz. Producer: Alejandro Castillo. Lead actor: Roberto Artiagoitia. Listeners reveal personal details of lives on air.

Kalozok, aka *You or Me* (1999, Axis Plusz, Poland). 98 min. Director: Tamas Sas. Producer: Gyorgy Budai. Cast: Attila Kiraly, Viktor Bodo, Karina Kecskes. Youngsters operate pirate station from van to play favorite songs.

Jakob the Liar (1999, TriStar Pictures). 120 min. Director: Peter Kassovitz. Producers: Marsha Garces Williams, Steven Haft. Cast: Robin Williams, Alan Arkin, Hannah Taylor-Gordon. Fictitious radio news reports have unforeseen consequences in Polish ghetto.

O Brother, Where Art Thou? (2000, Touchstone Pictures). 106 min. Director: Joel Coen. Producer: Roderick Jaynes. Cast: George Clooney, John Turturro, Tim Blake Nelson. Escaped convicts become radio singers while looking for buried loot.

What I Like About You (2000, Warner Bros.). 90 min. Director: Jeff Stolhand. Producer: Tony Hewett. Cast: Ryan Wickerham, Marie Black. Fired DJ falls in love with bookstore owner about to lose store.

Women of the Night (2000, The Zalman King Company). 97 min. Director: Zalman King. Producer: Jordan Leibert. Cast: Shawnee Free Jones, Sally Kellerman, James Farentino. Blind female DJ broadcasts tales of lust and betrayal from 18-wheeler.

Militia (2000, HBO Entertainment). 89 min. Director: Jim Wynorski. Producer: Paul Hertzberg. Cast: Dean Cain, Jennifer Beals, Stacy Keach. TV movie in which talk show host leads militia group planning to attack U.S. with anthrax.

The Ladies Man (2000, SNL Studios). 84 min. Director: Reginald Hudlin. Producer: Lorne Michaels. Lead actor: Tim Meadows. Fired talk show host looks for old flame while dodging cuckolded husbands.

Attraction (2000, Capital Arts Entertainment). 95 min. Director: Russell Degrazier. Producers: Jonathan Krauss, Mike Elliott. Cast: Matthew Settle, Gretchen Mol. Talk show host stalks ex-girlfriend, becomes involved with her friend.

Bare Deception (2000, Ambrosia Productions). 67 min. Director: Eric Gibson. Producer: Debra Nichols. Cast: Tane McClure, Daniel Anderson. TV movie in which talk show host's ratings skyrocket when listener is killed.

The Midnight Hour, aka *Tell Me No* Lies (2000, Santelmo Entertainment). 91 min. Director: Emmanuel Itier. Producer: Scarlet Pettyjohn. Cast: Amber Smith, Byron Bay. Woman gets job as college DJ to find sister's killer but becomes potential victim herself.

Radio Free Steve (2000, Ugh Films). 82 min. Directors: Jules Beesley, Lars Von Biers. Producer: Amy Raymond. Lead actor: Ryan Junell. Radio pirate dodges FCC pursuers.

The Night Watchman (2000, Night Watchman Productions, Canada). 103 min. Director: Scott Eldridge. Producers: Jeffrey Caulfield, Scott Eldridge. Cast: Cory Diamond, Christopher Healey. Acerbic talk show host finds personal life playing out on air when he takes call from suicidal girlfriend.

Jinx'd (2000, Nomad Pictures). 90 min. Director: Damon Wood. Producers: Joy Chapman, Debbie Pagell. Lead actor: Ryan Cameron. Black DJ gets stand-up comedy gig, discovers it's for crowd of redneck white supremacists.

You Belong to Me (2001, Lucky Day Productions, Filmtime Productions, Canada). 95 min. Director: Paolo Barzman. Producer: Lisa Parasyn. Cast: Lesley-Anne Down, Daniel

Morgenroth. TV movie based on Mary Higgins Clark novel in which talk show psychologist helps police track serial killer and also becomes target.

*__Summer Catch__ (2001, Warner Bros.). 108 min. Director: Michael Tollin. Producers: Brian Robbins, Michael Tollin, Sam Weisman. Cast: Freddie Prinze, Jr., Jessica Biel, Fred Ward. Curt Gowdy does play-by-play of college baseball games.

*__Rare Birds__ (2001, Pope Productions, Big Pictures Entertainment, Canada). 101 min. Director: Sturla Gunnarsson. Producers: Paul Pope, Janet York. Cast: William Hurt, Andy Jones, Molly Parker. Call to talk show about fake rare bird sighting has unintended consequences.

__Radyo__, aka __Radio__ (2001, Viva Films, Philippines). 95 min. Director: Yam Laranas. Cast: Rufa Mae Quinto, Jeffrey Quizon. DJ is targeted for death by suicidal listener whose song was ridiculed on air.

__Drive Time Murders__ (2001, Chesler/Perlmutter Productions). 100 min. Director: Eleanor Lindo. Producer: Paco Alvarez. Cast: Cameron Daddo, Fiona Loewi. TV movie in which morning show team gets involved in theft and murder.

__Frau 2 Sucht HappyEnd__, aka __Female2 Seeks Happy End__ (2001, Tobis, Studio Canal, Germany). 96 min. Director: Edward Berger. Producers: Andreas Eicher, Philipp Homberg. Cast: Isabella Parkinson, Ben Becker. Lonely DJ finds companionship via Internet.

*__One Fine Spring Day__, aka __Bomnaleun Ganda__ (2001, Applause Pictures, South Korea). 106 min. Director: Jin-Ho Hur. Producer: Sun-Ah Kim. Cast: Yeong-ae Lee, Jai-tae Yu. Recording engineer becomes involved with radio announcer.

*__Amy's O__, aka __Amy's Orgasm__ (2001, Catchlight Films). 87 min. Director: Julie Davis. Producers: Julie Davis, Fred Kramer. Cast: Julie Davis, Nick Chinlund. Self-help author reexamines her theories after becoming involved with male chauvinist shock jock.

*__Joe Dirt__ (2001, Columbia Pictures). 91 min. Director: Dennie Gordon. Producer: Robert Simonds. Cast: David Spade, Dennis Miller. Janitor's search for parents is aided by listeners after shock jock ridicules him on air.

*__61*__ (2001, 61* Productions Inc.). 129 min. Director: Billy Crystal. Producer: Robert F. Colesberry. Cast: Barry Pepper, Thomas Jane. TV movie with play-by-play accounts of Roger Maris' quest for 61 home runs in single season.

*__Joe and Max__ (2002, Gemini Film). 109 min. Director: Steve James. Producers: Kelli Konop, Brad Krevoy, Klaus Rettig. Cast: Leonard Roberts, Til Schweiger, Peta Wilson. TV movie with blow-by-blow broadcasts of Joe Louis-Max Schmeling fights.

*__Slap Shot 2: Breaking the Ice__ (2002, Universal Home Entertainment). 82 min. Director: Steve Boyum. Producer: Ron French. Cast: Stephen Baldwin, Jessica Steen, Gary Busey. More play-by-play broadcasts in second film about Charlestown Chiefs.

*__American Nightmare__ (2002, Highland Myst Entertainment). 91 min. Director: Jon Keeyes. Producers: Richard T. Carey, Jon Keeyes. Cast: Debbie Rochon, Brandy Little. DJ invites callers to share nightmares and seven people call in from café, unaware that female psycho lurks nearby to turn them into reality.

*__Mother Ghost__ (2002, It's an Us Thing Production). 76 min. Director: Rich Thorne. Producer: Rodney Montague. Cast: Mark Thompson, Kevin Pollak. Man calls radio psychologist to say he's haunted by mother's ghost.

*__Sinful Desires__ (2002, MRG Entertainment). 71 min. Director: David Nicholas. Producer: Debra Nichols. Cast: Jacy Andrews, Nikita Cash, Craig Field, Tony Tedeschi. Talk show host is stalked by caller.

*__Our America__ (2002, Come Sunday Productions). 95 min. Director: Ernest R. Dickerson. Producer: Eda Godel Hallinan. Cast: Josh Charles, Brandon Hammond, Mykelti Williamson. True story of boys who produce radio documentary about inner-city life and investigate child's death.

*__Radio Samurai__ (2002, Trunk Filmed Entertainment, Australia). 85 min. Director-Producer: Nick Levy. Cast: Nathan Hill, Brooke Satchwell. Fired DJ produces concert to get job back.

*Auto Focus (2002, Focus Puller Inc.). 105 min. Director: Paul Shrader. Producers: Scott Alexander, Alicia Alain, Larry Karaszewski, Todd Rosken, Brian Oliver, Pat Dollard. Cast: Greg Kinnear, Willem Dafoe. Biopic of actor Bob Crane includes start as DJ at KNX Los Angeles.

*Halbe Treppe, aka *Grill Point* (2002, Peter Rommel Productions, Germany). 106 min. Director: Andreas Dresen. Producer: Peter Rommel. Cast: Steffi Kuhnert, Gabriela Maria Schmeide, Thorsten Merten. DJ's affair with friend's wife changes all their lives.

*Cherish (2002, 3 Ring Circus Films). 99 min. Director: Finn Taylor. Producers: Johnny Wow, Mark Burton. Cast: Brad Hunt, Robin Tunney, Tim Blake Nelson. Teenager who listens to KXCH Cherish Radio is stalked by DJ.

Uma Onda No Ar (2002, Chimera Films, Brazil). 92 min. Director: Helvecio Ratton. Producer: Simone Magalhaes. Cast: Alexandre Moreno, Bubu Santana, Adolfo Moura, Benjamim Abras. Four friends start shantytown pirate station.

*Deranged, aka *The Rose Technique* (2002, Forsyth Films). 97 min. Director: Jon Scheide. Producer: Ray Stroeber. Lead actor: JoBeth Williams. Radio psychologist becomes scissors-wielding psycho when show is cancelled.

*Vivir Mata, aka *Life Kills* (2002, Instituto Mexicao de Cinematografia, Mexico). 92 min. Director: Nicolas Echevarria. Producer: Matthias Ehrenberg. Cast: Daniel Gimenez Cacho, Susana Zabaleta. Traffic reporter pretending to be journalist becomes involved with toymaker pretending to be author.

*Na Tum Jaano Na Hum (2002, PFH Entertainment, India). 159 min. Director: Arjun Sablock. Producer: Vivek Singhania. Cast: Saif Ali Khan, Hrithik Roshan, Esha Deol. Young man's call to DJ sparks unusual romance.

*Eight Legged Freaks (2002, Warner Bros.). 90 min. Director: Ellory Elkayem. Producers: Dean Devlin, Bruce Berman. Cast: David Arquette, Scarlett Johansson. Paranoid announcer helps battle bloodthirsty mutant spiders.

*8 Mile (2002, Imagine Entertainment). 110 min. Director: Curtis Hanson. Producers: Brian Grazer, Curtis Hanson, Jimmy Iovine. Cast: Eminem, Kim Basinger. Rapper struggles to make it in Detroit.

*First Time Caller (2002, Erimus Films, Canada). 80 min. Director: Alex Zavaglia. Producer: Anthony Ciardulli. Cast: John Catucci, Catherine Rossini. Heartbroken young man calls talk show for advice.

*Seabiscuit (2003, Universal Pictures). 141 min. Director: Gary Ross. Producers: Kathleen Kennedy, Frank Marshall, Gary Ross, Jane Sindell. Cast: Jeff Bridges, Chris Cooper, William H. Macy. Tick Tock McGlaughlin does horse racing broadcasts.

*Night Owl (2003, Morgan Hill Films). 91 min. Director: Matthew Patrick. Producer: Julian Marks. Lead actor: Jennifer Beals. TV movie in which mysterious female DJ takes over air waves of New York station, causing male listeners to commit suicide.

*The Republic of Love (2003, Dan Films, Canada). 95 min. Director: Deepa Mehta. Producers: Anna Stratton, Julie Baines. Cast: Bruce Greenwood, Kate Lynch. Talk show host has little success finding true love.

*Love Chronicles (2003, Melee Entertainment). 78 min. Director: Tyler Maddox-Simms. Producer: Monica R. Cooper. Cast: Terrence Howard, Caroline Whitney Smith. Talk show co-hosts explore love lives of different callers, and their own.

*Mad Song (2003, C.O.D. Productions). 93 min. Director: David Roy. Producers: Stephen L. Cross, Ric Eisman. Lead actor: Kandeyce Jordan. Talk show therapist tries to help Goth rock singer.

*Men Cry in the Dark (2003, I'm Ready Productions). 140 min. Director: Je'Caryous Johnson. Producers: Gary Guidry, Je'Caryous Johnson. Cast: Rhonna Bennett, Allen Payne, Richard Roundtree. Filmed stage play in which magazine publisher's talk show appearance changes his life.

*Wash It Up (2003, 2 A's Films). 80 min. Directors: Nahala Johnson, Frederick C.

Alexander. Producers: Nahala Johnson, Frederick C. Alexander. Cast: Danielle Small, Erika Cameron. Rap DJ's entertain car wash girls.

*__Made in Estonia__ (2003, Ruut Pictures, Estonia). 100 min. Director: Rando Pettai. Producers: Tonis Haavel, Kaupo Karelson. Cast: Henrik Normann, Madis Milling. Improvised radio soap operas spin out of control.

*__Diario de una Pasante__ (2003, Cre-Accion Films, Spain). 100 min. Director: Josecho San Mateo. Producer: Rodolfo Montero de Palacio. Cast: Daniela Costa, Carlos Baleztena, Antonio Hortelano. Radio station interns cope with job pressures and lecherous bosses.

*__Sexphone & the Girl Next Door__ (2003, Yoho Film, Thailand). 113 min. Directors: Heman Chetamee, Chalermpol Bunnak. Producers: Pattira Palawatvichai, Chaiyong Kosolpotisub, Heman Chetamee. Cast: Punlapa Taylor, Kawee Tanjararak. Girl calls sex talk show, not realizing host is her unfriendly neighbor.

*__Burning Annie__ (2004, Armak Productions). 95 min. Director: Van Flesher. Producer: Randy Mack. Cast: Gary Lundy, Sara Downing. College DJ finds obsession with Woody Allen film detrimental to his love life.

*__The J-K Conspiracy__ (2004, Clear Channel). 72 min. Director: Cookie "Chainsaw" Randolph. Producer: Mike Daly. Cast: Dave Rickards, Shelly Dunn, Cookie "Chainsaw" Randolph. Morning crew of KGB San Diego in film with thin plot.

*__Friday Night Lights__ (2004, Universal Pictures). 118 min. Director: Peter Berg. Producer: Brian Grazer. Lead actor: Billy Bob Thornton. Radio play-by-play creates ambience in tale of high school football team's season.

*__Naughty or Nice__ (2004, Rhi Entertainment, Von Zerneck-Sertner Films, Timpano Productions, Frank & Bob Films II, Canada). 90 min. Director: Lane Laneuville. Producers: Karen Moore, Randy Sutter. Cast: George Lopez, Lisa Vidal, James Kirk. TV movie in which life of abrasive sports talk show host is changed by call from dying teen.

*__In My Country__, aka _Country of My Skull_ (2004, Phoenix Pictures, USA-Britain-Ireland). 105 min. Director: John Boorman. Producers: Robert Chartoff, Mike Medavoy, John Boorman, Kieran Corrigan, Lynn Hendee. Cast: Samuel L. Jackson, Juliette Binoche. African American reporter becomes involved with white radio reporter while covering South Africa's Truth and Reconciliation Commission Hearings.

*__Escuela de seduccion__ (2004, Troto Intl. S.A., Spain). 119 min. Director: Javier Balaguer. Producer: Manuel Ramirez. Cast: Victoria Abril, Javier Veiga. Ratings for feminist talk show host jump due to sexist caller.

__Lavorare con Lentezza__, aka _Working Slowly_ (2004, Medusa Film, Fandango, Italy). 111 min. Director: Guido Chiesa. Producer: Domenico Procacci. Cast: Jacopo Bonvicini, Claudia Pandolfi, Marco Luisi. Youths become involved with college station.

*__The Life and Death of Peter Sellers__ (2004, DeMann Entertainment Company Pictures, USA-Britain). 122 min. Director: Stephen Hopkins. Producer: Simon Bosanquet. Lead actor: Geoffrey Rush. TV biopic begins with production of radio's _The Goon Show_.

__Master of Airwaves__, aka _Lord of the Ether_ (2004, Tsentrnauchfilm, Russia). 83 min. Director: Ekaterina Kalinina. Producer: Sergei Zernov. Cast: Cyril Tetenkin, Maria Shalaev, Aleksey Kortnev. DJ invites callers to share love stories on air.

__Communication Breakdown__ (2004, Bang Productions). Director: Richard O'Sullivan. Producers: Fred Hueston, John Michael Burgess. Cast: Dan Lashley, William V. Repoley. Small station is sold to big corporation, to distress of employees.

*__The Booth__, aka _Busu_ (2005, Pony Canyon, Japan). 73 min. Director: Yoshihiro Nakamura. Lead actor: Maiko Asano. Strange things happen when talk show originates from studio in which DJ committed suicide several years before.

*__El Vacilon: The Movie__ (2005, Babylegs Entertainment). 94 min. Director: Agustin. Producers: Agustin, Darryl Neverson. Cast: Luis Jimenez, Moonshadow. Antics of Hispanic New York DJs.

Love Talk, aka *Reobeu tokeu* (2005, LJ Film Corporation, South Korea). 118 min. Director: Yoon Gee Lee. Producer: Il Joung Yun. Cast: Silvana Warnes, Chong-ok Bae, Ban-ya Choi. Talk show host offers advice about romantic relationships while struggling with her own problems.

McBride: Tune In for Murder (2005, Alpine Medien Productions). 88 min. Director: Stephen W. Bridgewater. Producers: Brian J. Gordon, Erik Olson. Cast: John Larroquette, Marta DuBois, Matt Lutz. TV movie about murder of hated talk show host.

salaam namaste (2005, Yash Raj Films, India). 158 min. Director: Siddharth Raj Anand. Producer: Aditya Chopra. Cast: Saif Ali Khan, Preity Zinta, Arshad Warsi. Female DJ becomes involved with chef in Melbourne.

Sueno (2005, El Camino Pictures). 108 min. Director: Renee Chabria. Producers: Eric Kopeloff, Robert Ortiz, Marc Forster. Cast: John Leguizamo, Ana Claudia Talancon. Mexican immigrant gets chance at stardom by entering radio talent contest.

The Upside of Anger (2005, Media 8 Entertainment). 118 min. Director: Mike Binder. Producers: Jack Binder, Alex Gartner, Sammy Lee. Cast: Kevin Costner, Joan Allen. Woman deserted by husband becomes involved with sportscaster.

The Urban Demographic, aka *K-HIP Radio* (2005, Con Communications). 97 min. Director: Theron K. Cal. Producers: Pam Gibson, Theron K. Cal, Will Conley. Cast: Christopher Roosevelt, Rico E. Anderson. Advertiser boycott ensues when classical music station changes format to Urban Contemporary.

Ski Trippin' (2005, Maverick Entertainment). 82 min. Director: Paul Janitis. Cast: Eddy Hustle, Joey Zaza. Urban youths win radio station ski trip contest.

Midnight My Love, aka *Cherm* (2005, Saha Mongkul Film Production, Thailand). 100 min. Director: Kongdej Jaturanrasmee. Producer: Somsak Jaturanrasmee. Lead actor: Petchtai Wongkamlao. Cab driver whose passion is radio soap operas and oldies songs becomes involved with prostitute.

Daddy Long Legs, aka *Kidari ajeossi* (2005, Wellmade Entertainment Company, South Korea). 99 min. Director: Jeong-sik Kong. Producer: Hyeong-jun Kim. Cast: Bo-ra Geum, Bin Hyeon. Radio station writer becomes involved in co-worker's love life.

A Lover's Revenge (2005, Lion Tropical Productions, Canada). 94 min. Director: Douglas Jackson. Producers: Stefan Wodoslawsky, Neil Bregman. Cast: Alexandra Paul, William R. Moses. TV movie in which radio psychologist becomes target of man whose wife followed her advice to end abusive relationship.

The F Word (2005, DitLev Films). 85 min. Director: Jed Weintrob. Producers: Christian D. Bruun, Nicholas Goldfarb, Jed Weintrob. Lead actor: Josh Hamilton. Talk show host losing show due to indecency fines does final broadcast from Republican National Convention.

The Fog (2005, Revolution Studios). 100 min. Director: Rupert Wainwright. Producers: David Foster, Debra Hill, John Carpenter. Cast: Tom Welling, Maggie Grace, Selma Blair. Remake of 1980 John Carpenter zombie film.

Keep Your Distance (2005, Blue & Grey Film Ventures). 94 min. Director: Stu Pollard. Producers: Stu Pollard, Christina Varotsis. Cast: Gil Bellows, Jennifer Westfeldt. Talk show host with marital problems gets involved with another woman; stalkers complicate matters.

Private Moments (2005, Metro Film Corporation, Britain). 85 min. Director: Jag Mundhra. Producer: Sunanda Murali Manhohar. Cast: Aruna Shields, Catalina Guirado, Natasja Vermeer. To boost sagging ratings, talk show host takes calls about sexual experiences.

Piter FM (2006, Igor Tolstunov Production Company, Russia). 85 min. Director: Oksana Bychkova. Producers: Elena Glikman, Igor Tolstunov, Alexandr Rodnyansky. Cast: Yekaterina Fedulova, Yevgeni Tsyganov. DJ becomes involved with architect on eve of her marriage.

Johnny Was (2006, Ben Katz Productions, Ireland). 93 min. Director: Mark Hammond. Producers: Patrick J. FitzSymons, Brendan Foley, Tom Maguire, Paul Largan, Lars Hermann, Ira Besserman. Cast: Vinnie Jones, Patrick Bergin, Lennox Lewis. Pirate radio Rasta DJ becomes involved with drug dealers.

Lage Raho Munna Bhai (2006, Vinod Chopra Productions, India). 144 min. Director: Rajkumar Hirani. Producer: Vidhu Vinod Chopra. Cast: Sanjay Dutt, Arshad Warsi, Vidya Balan. Gangster poses as professor to woo female DJ.

False Prophets (2006, Tabula Rasa Films). 85 min. Director: Robert Kevin Townsend. Producers: Brian Arbuckle, Brian Frederick. Cast: Lori Heuring, Clayne Crawford. Pregnant woman meets radio preacher who also runs gas station.

Facing the Giants (2006, Sherwood Pictures). 111 min. Director: Alex Kendrick. Producers: Alex Kendrick, Stephen Kendrick. Cast: Alex Kendrick, Shannen Fields. Broadcasts of high school football games.

3 Guys, 1 Girl, 2 Weddings (2006, Picture This! Entertainment, France). 90 min. Director: Stephane Clavier. Producers: Catherine Burniaux, Francois Charlent. Cast: Olivier Sitruk, Arnaud Giovaninetti. Host of sex talk show host decides to get married.

The Night Listener (2006, Hart-Sharp Entertainment). 82 min. Director: Patrick Stettner. Producers: John N. Hart, Jeff Sharp, Robert Kessel, Jill Footlick. Cast: Robin Williams, Toni Collette. Talk show host investigates claims of parental abuse by young listener.

I'm Reed Fish (2006, Squared Foot Productions). 93 min. Director: Zackary Adler. Producer: Bader Alwazzan. Cast: Jay Baruchel, Alexis Bledel. DJ's life unravels when former girlfriend returns on eve of his marriage.

Under the Mistletoe (2006, Insight Film Studios, Canada). Director: George Mendeluk. Producer: Kirk Shaw. Cast: Michael Shanks, Jaime Ray Newman, Conan Graham. TV movie in which dead talk show host's son talks to him about his mother's dates.

A Prairie Home Companion (2006, Picturehouse Entertainment). 105 min. Director: Robert Altman. Producers: Robert Altman, Wren Arthur, Joshua Astrachan, Tony Judge, David Levy. Cast: Garrison Keillor, Kevin Kline, Meryl Streep, Lily Tomlin. Altman's last film, based on NPR program.

Statistics (2006, Rebel Image Productions). 104 min. Director: Frank Robak. Producers: Scott Rudolph, David Michaels, Kent Harper, Frank Robak. Lead actor: Kent Harper. After fire destroys his home, talk show host turns program into diatribe against the ills of urban life.

Radio Star, aka *Rado seuta* (2006, Achim Pictures, South Korea). 115 min. Director: Joon-Ik Lee. Producers: Jun-Ik Lee, Seung-Hye Jeong. Cast: Sung-Ki Ahn, Joong-Hoon Park, Jeong-Yun Choi. Ex-rock star becomes small-town DJ to resurrect singing career.

Lo Mejor de Mi, aka *The Best of Me* (2007, Escandalo Films, Spain). 85 min. Director: Roser Aguilar. Producers: Sergi Casamitjana, Aintza Serra. Cast: Marian Alvarez, Juan Sanz. Relationship between radio reporter and athlete runs into problems.

Talk to Me (2007, Sidney Kimmel Entertainment). 118 min. Director: Kasi Lemmons. Producers: Mark Gordon, Sidney Kimmell, Joe Fries, Josh McLaughlin. Cast: Don Cheadle, Chiwetel Ejiofor, Martin Sheen. Biopic of "Petey" Greene, ex-con who gets talk show at WOL Washington and becomes community activist.

Sister Aimee: The Aime Semple McPherson Story (2006, Richard Rossi Productions). 110 min. Director-Producer: Richard Rossi. Lead actor: Mimi Michaels. Biopic of woman radio evangelist.

We Are Marshall (2006, Warner Bros.). 131 min. Director: Joseph McGinty Nichol. Producer: Basil Iwanyk. Cast: Matthew McConaughey, David Strathairn. Play-by-play accounts of Marshall University's football season following plane crash.

Glory Road (2006, Walt Disney Pictures). 118 min. Director: James Gartner. Producer: Jerry Bruckheimer. Lead actor: Josh Lucas. Play-by-play broadcasts of Texas Western's championship basketball season.

Cosmic Radio (2007, Cosmic Productions). 90 min. Director: Stephen Savage. Producer: Ryan Johnson. Cast: Jonathan Sachar, Michael Madsen, Wes Studi. Station verging on bankruptcy becomes voice of movement to save forest.

Blue Chip Mint (2007, Demah Films). Director: Rodney C. Folmar. Producers: Rodney C. Folmar, Deanna Hodges. Lead actor: William Majors. Conservative talk show host has to adjust to new liberal co-host.

*****The Brave One*** (2007, Warner Bros.). 122 min. Director: Neil Jordan. Producers: Joel Silver, Susan Downey. Cast: Jodie Foster, Terrence Howard. Announcer is victim of brutal street attack, buys gun to seek revenge, becomes vigilante.

*****I'll Believe You***, aka *First Time Caller* (2007, 19th Hole Entertainment). 82 min. Director: Paul Francis Sullivan. Producer: Ted Sullivan. Lead actor: David Alan Basche. Talk show host receives call that could be from extraterrestrial.

*****Election Day***, aka *Den' Vyborov* (2007, STAR-T, Russia). 122 min. Director: Oleg Fomin. Producer: Nikolai Ulyanov. Cast: Leonid Barats, Rotislav Khait. Oligarch tries to bribe station owner to support candidate in regional elections.

***Radiopiraten*e** (2007, Nordisk Film, Norway). 87 min. Director: Stig Svendsen. Lead actor: Anders Hermann Clausen. Children start pirate station.

*****The Final Season*** (2007, Final Season Incorporated). 119 min. Director: David M. Evans. Producers: Steven Schott, Michael Wasserman, Hershel Weingrod, D. Parker Widemire, Jr., Tony Wilson. Cast: Powers Boothe, Sean Astin. Play-by-play broadcasts in true story of high school baseball team's last season.

*****A Valentine Carol*** (2007, Insight Film Studios, Canada). 90 min. Director: Mark Jean. Producer: Kirk Shaw. Cast: Emma Caulfield, Barbara Niven. TV movie in which talk show host learns about true love by visiting past boyfriends.

Radio Day, aka *Den' Radio* (2008, Central Partnership, Russia). 100 min. Director: Dmitry Dyachenko. Cast: Rotislav Khait, Mikhail Kozyrev. Station sensationalizes news story to get more listeners.

*****Radio Cape Cod*** (2008, Silver Production). 88 min. Director: Andrew Silver. Producers: Andrew Silver, Thomas Casaretto, Michael Spindler. Cast: Tamzin Outhwaite, Tamzin Merchant, Olatunde Fagbenle. Talk show host copes with loss of husband.

*****Slap Shot 3: The Junior League*** (2008, Universal Pictures). 90 min. Director: Richard Martin. Producer: Connie Dolphin. Lead actor: Leslie Nielsen. Father-son team does play-by-play in third *Slap Shot* movie.

*****Leatherheads*** (2008, Casey Silver Productions). 114 min. Director: George Clooney. Producers: George Clooney, Grant Heslov, Casey Silver. Lead actors: George Clooney, Renee Zellweger, John Krasinski. Play-by-play description of early NFL game.

*****The Express*** (2008, Davis Entertainment). 130 min. Director: Gary Fleder. Producer: John Davis. Cast: Rob Brown, Dennis Quaid. Ernie Davis biopic with play-by-play of Syracuse football games.

*****Flick*** (2008, Monster Films, Wales). 96 min. Director: David Howard. Producer: Rik Hall. Cast: Hugh O'Conor, Faye Dunaway. One-armed cop tracks teenage killer brought back to life after forty years by pirate radio broadcasts.

Il mattino ha l'oro in bocca (2008, Rodeo Drive, Italy). 100 min. Director: Francesco Patierno. Producer: Marco Poccioni. Cast: Elio Germano, Laura Chiatt. Biopic of DJ Marco Baldini.

*****Carnera: The Walking Mountain*** (2008, Domino Film, Italy). 125 min. Director-Producer: Renzo Martinelli. Cast: Andrea Laia, Anna Valle. Radio accounts of heavyweight champ's fights.

Radio Love (2008, Today Films, Spain). 110 min. Director: Leonardo Armas. Producers: Carmen Ruiz, Txesma Lasa. Lead actor: Beatriz Rico. Aging talk show host tries to recapture her youth.

*****Radio Dayz***, aka Ra-deui-o De-i-jeu (2008, Sidus Pictures, South Korea). 111 min.

Director: Gi-ho Ha. Producers: Cha Sung-jai, Kim Mi-hee. Lead actor: Seung-beom Ryu. Producers create programming for Korea's first radio station.

45 RPM (2008, Nomadic Pictures, Canada). 91 min. Director: Dave Schultz. Producers: Michael Frislev, Chad Oakes. Cast: Jordan Gavaris, Justine Banszky, Michael Madsen. Saskatchewan youngsters pick up signal of New York station, plot to win its contest to escape small town life.

Pontypool (2008, Ponty Up Pictures, Canada). 96 min. Director: Bruce McDonald. Producers: Ambrose Roche, Jeffrey Coghlan. Lead actor: Stephen McHattie. Radio station staff discovers that a virus turns people into zombies.

Quid Pro Quo (2008, HDNet Films). 82 min. Director: Carlos Brooks. Producers: Sarah Pillsbury, Midge Sanford. Lead actor: Nick Stahl. Wheelchair-bound radio reporter investigates underground sect of people who want to be disabled.

The Aquarium, aka *Genenet al asmak* (2008, Archipel 33 Production Co., Egypt). 90 min. Director: Yousry Nasrallah. Producers: Gabriel Khoury, Denis Freyd, Karl Baumgartner. Lead actor: Laila Samy. Listeners discuss personal lives on late night talk show.

Ba Bai Bang, aka *Letters from Death Row* (2008, Dream Machine Pictures, China). 93 min. Director: Kevin Feng Ke. Cast: Yeuming Di, Su Li. Inmate becomes involved with female prison radio announcer.

Speeding Scandal, aka *Kwasok Scaendeul*, aka *Scandal Makers* (2008, Toilet Pictures, DCG Plus, South Korea). 109 min. Director: Hyeong-cheol Kang. Producer: Ahn Byung Ki. Cast: Bao-young Park, Tae Hyun Cha, Seok Hyun Wang. Talk show host discovers he has daughter and grandson when they suddenly show up on his doorstep.

Day of the Dead (2008, Millenium Films). 86 min. Director: Steve Miner. Producers: James Glenn Dudelson, Randall Emmett, George Furla, M. Dal Walton III, Boaz Davidson. Lead actor: Ving Rhames. Radio station becomes refuge from zombies.

Cadillac Records (2008, Parkwood Pictures, Sony Music Film). 109 min. Director: Darnell Martin. Producers: Andrew Lack, Sofia Sondervan. Cast: Adrien Brody, Jeffrey Wright, Beyonce Knowles. Chess Records story, in which DJs help popularize blues and rock 'n' roll.

Sugar (2008, Journeyman Pictures, HBO Films). 120 min. Directors: Anna Boden, Ryan Fleck. Producers: Paul S. Mezey, Jamie Patricof, Jeremy Kipp Walker. Lead actor: Algenis Perez Soto. Play-by-play broadcasts when Latino baseball player starts career in Iowa.

The Accidental Husband (2008, Blumhouse Productions). 90 min. Director: Griffin Dunne. Producers: Jason Blum, Uma Thurman, Suzanne Todd, Jennifer Todd, Bob Yari. Cast: Uma Thurman, Colin Firth, Jeffrey Dean Morgan. Talk show host preparing for wedding discovers prank has already made her a married woman.

College Radio Sucks (2008, Radar Scope Reworked). 70 min. Director-Producer: Greg Bradley. Cast: Bobby August, Jr., Riley Kempton. Student DJs try to win radio contest to get real DJ jobs.

Changeling (2008, Imagine Entertainment). 141 min. Director: Clint Eastwood. Producers: Ron Howard, Clint Eastwood, Brian Grazer, Robert Lorenz. Cast: Angelina Jolie, Walter Collins, John Malkovich. Radio preacher takes on LAPD in missing child case.

Dead Signal: The Jonathon Moon Chronicles (2008, Moon House Studios). 95 min. Director: Robert Diaz Leroy. Producers: Richard Hays, Al Gomez, Karen Kolling. Cast: J. Scott Shonka, Victoria Lauture. Aliens try to use radio signal to attack talk show host.

Billy: The Early Years of Billy Graham (2009, Solex Productions). 87 min. Director: Robbie Benson. Producers: William Paul McKay, Lawrence Mortoff, Martin Shiel. Cast: Armie Hammer, Marin Landau, Kristoffer Polaha. Evangelist uses radio to start career.

Dead Air (2009, Antibody Films, Team Cherokee Productions). 93 min. Director: Corbin Bernsen. Producers: Corbin Bernsen, Jesse Lawler, Chris Aronoff. Cast: Bill Moseley, David Moscow, Corbin Bernsen. Radio station is attacked by zombies.

Me and Orson Welles (2009, CinemaNX). 114 min. Director: Richard Linklater. Producers: Ann Carli, Richard Linklater, Marc Samuelson. Cast: Zac Efron, Christian McKay, Claire Danes. Includes depiction of live radio broadcast.

*****The Boat That Rocked***, aka *Pirate Radio* (2009, Universal Pictures). 135 min. Director: Richard Curtis. Producers: Tim Bevan, Eric Fellner, Richard Curtis, Hilary Bevan Jones. Cast: Bill Nighy, Philip Seymour Hoffman, Kenneth Branagh. Hijinks aboard 1960s pirate radio ship.

Forever Waiting (2009, Fair Films, Spain). 118 min. Director: Francisco Avizanda. Producers: Francisco Avizanda, Elisabeth Perello-Santandreu. Cast: Carolina Bona, Jesus Noguero. Radio writer becomes involved in clandestine anti-government activities.

Special Correspondents, aka *Envoyes tres speciaux* (2009, Les Films Manuel Munz, France). 93 min. Director: Frederic Auburtin. Producer: Manuel Munz. Cast: Gerard Lanvin, Gerard Jugnot. Radio reporters with problems in Iraq file fake reports from Paris.

Kung Fu Assassins (2009, All Colorz Entertainment). 98 min. Director: Stan Derain. Producers: John Lim, Bodo Holst, Maribell Komashko. Cast: Nadia Dawn, David Marc, Stan Derain. Beautiful female martial artists take revenge on shock jock.

*****Radio: Love on Air*** (2009, Plus Entertainment Pvt. Ltd., India). 106 min. Director: Ishaan Trivedi. Producer: Ravi Agarwal. Cast: Himesh Reshammiya, Shehnaz Treasurywala, Sonal Sehgal. Divorce throws DJ's life into turmoil.

*****More Than Blue***, aka *Seulpeumboda Deo Seulpeun lyagi* (2009, Core Contents Media, South Korea). 103 min. Director: Tae-yeon Won. Producers: Won-Jang Cho, Chang-Ryul Kim. Cast: Sang-woo Kwon, Beom-soo Lee, Bo-young Lee. TV movie in which radio producer with cancer looks for someone to marry his fiancée.

Hello My Love (2009, Aim High Productions, South Korea). 95 min. Director: Aaron Kim. Producer: Seong-ho Choi. Cast: Jo An, Oh Min-Seok, Ryu Sang-Wook. DJ discovers that her boyfriend is gay.

Protektor (2009, Negativ S.R.O., Czech Republic). 102 min. Director: Marek Najbrt. Producers: Pavel Strnad, Milan Kuchynka. Cast: Marek Daniel, Jana Plodkov. Radio journalist collaborates with Nazis to survive in World War II Czechoslovakia.

*****Big Fan*** (2009, Big Fan Productions). 86 min. Director: Robert D. Siegel. Producers: Elan Bogarin, Jean Kouremetis. Lead actor: Patton Oswalt. Football fan obsessed with sports talk radio finds life changed by violent encounter with player.

*****2012*** (2009, Columbia Pictures). 158 min. Director: Roland Emmerich. Producers: Roland Emmerich, Harald Kloser, Larry Franco. Cast: John Cusack, Amanda Peet. Talk show host meets spectacular end when Yellowstone Park erupts in balls of fire.

Hikidashi no Naka no Love Letter, aka *Listen to My Heart* (2009, Shochika Company, Japan). 119 min. Director: Shinichi Mishiro. Producers: Naoya Narita, Yumi Suzuki. Cast: Takako Tokiwa, Kento Hayashi. DJ shares feelings about dead father with listeners.

Comedown (2010, Serotonin Films, Britain). 90 min. Director: Menhaj Huda. Producers: Dominic Norris, Gareth Wiley. Cast: Martin Comptson, Adam Deacon, Geoff Bell. Teens encounter psychopath while trying to set up pirate station transmitter.

Nice Guy Johnny (2010, Wild Ocean Films). 89 min. Director: Edward Burns. Producer: Aaron Lubin. Cast: Matt Bush, Max Baker, Edward Burns. Complications develop when sports talk show host quits job to please fiancé.

The King's Speech (2010, See-Saw Films, Britain) 118 min. Director: Tom Hooper. Producers: Iain Canning, Emile Sherman, Gareth Unwin. Cast: Colin Firth, Geoffrey Rush. Speech therapist helps King George VI overcome stutter to deliver radio speech.

Chapter Notes

Chapter One

1. Gerald Nachman, *Raised on Radio* (New York: Pantheon, 1998), p. 4.
2. Michele Hilmes, *Radio Voices: American Broadcasting, 1922–1952* (Minneapolis: University of Minnesota Press, 1997), p. 58.
3. Nachman, p. 4.
4. Stanley Elkin, *The Dick Gibson Show* (New York: Dutton, 1970), p. 4.
5. Wes Smith, *The Pied Pipers of Rock 'n' Roll: Radio Deejays of the 50s and 60s* (Atlanta: Longstreet, 1989).
6. George H. Douglas, *The Early Days of Radio Broadcasting* (Jefferson, NC: McFarland, 1987), p. 1.
7. Daniel J. Czitrom, *Media and the American Mind* (Chapel Hill: University of North Carolina Press, 1982), Chapter 3.
8. Douglas, p. 86.
9. Erik Barnouw, *The Golden Web* (New York: Oxford University Press, 1968).
10. For example, see Mitchell E. Shapiro, *Radio Network Prime Time Programming, 1926–1960* (Jefferson, NC: McFarland, 2002). Also see J. Fred MacDonald, *Don't Touch That Dial!: Radio Programming in American Life, 1920–1960* (Chicago: Nelson-Hall, 1979).
11. Steve Craig, *Out of the Dark: A History of Radio and Rural America* (Tuscaloosa: University of Alabama Press, 2009), p. 65.
12. Peter Fornatale and Joshua E. Mills, *Radio in the Television Age* (Woodstock: Overlook, 1980), p. 3.
13. Marshall McLuhan, *Understanding Media: The Extensions of Man* (New York: Signet, 1966), p. 267.
14. Barnouw, p. 219.
15. *Ibid.*, p. 217.
16. Douglas, p. 53.
17. Arnold Passman, *The Deejays* (New York: Macmillan, 1991), p. 22.
18. Laurence W. Etling, "Al Jarvis: Pioneer Disc Jockey." *Popular Music and Society* 23.3 (1999): 41–52.
19. "Result is Official: Jock's in Webster!" *Billboard* 14 May 1949: 3.
20. Passman, p. 10.
21. Elkin, p. 19.
22. William H. Kenney, *Recorded Music in American Life: The Phonograph and Popular Memory, 1890–1945* (New York: Oxford University Press, 1999), p. 188.
23. RCA Mfg. Co. v. Whiteman, 2 Cir., 1940, 114 F.2d 86, 88. 311 U.S. 712 (1940).
24. Fornatale and Mills, p. 18.
25. *Ibid.*, p. 18.
26. McLuhan, p. 264.
27. Eric Rothenbuhler and Tom McCourt, "Radio Redefines Itself, 1947–1962," in *Radio*

Reader: Essays in the Cultural History of Radio, ed. Michele Hilmes and Jason Loviglio (New York: Routledge, 2002), 367–387, p. 378.

28. Jim Dawson and Steve Propes, *45 RPM: The History, Heroes, and Villains of a Pop Music Revolution* (San Francisco: Backbeat, 2003), p. 34.

29. *Ibid.,* p. 6.

30. Fornatale and Mills, p. 41.

31. *Ibid.,* p. 42.

32. *Ibid.,* Chapter 3.

33. Michele Hilmes, *Hollywood and Broadcasting: From Radio to Cable* (Urbana: University of Illinois Press, 1990), p. 34.

34. "Art Mix." Accessed 11 Mar. 2010. <http://www.imdb.com/name/nm0594283/>

35. "*The Radio King.*" Accessed 11 Mar. 2010. <http://www.imdb.com/title/tt0013527/>

36. Arthur B. Reeve, *The Radio Detective* (New York: Grosset & Dunlap, 1926), p. 14.

37. *Ibid.,* pp. 23–24.

38. "Trivia for *Weary River.*" Accessed 12 Mar. 2010. <http://www.imdb.com/title/tt0019 557/trivia>

39. Nachman, Chapter 8.

40. Bruce Lenthall, "Critical Reception: Public Intellectuals Decry Depression-era Radio, Mass Culture, and Modern America," in *Radio Reader: Essays in the Cultural History of Radio,* ed. Michele Hilmes and Jason Loviglio (New York: Routledge, 2002), 41–62, p. 42.

41. *Ibid.,* p. 51.

42. For example, discussions of various issues are included in *Radio Reader: Essays in the Cultural History of Radio,* ed. Michele Hilmes and Jason Loviglio (New York: Routledge, 2002). Also see *Radio Cultures: The Sound Medium in American Life,* ed. Michael C. Keith (New York: Lang, 2008).

43. Frank D. McConnell, "Leopards and History: The Problem of Film Genre" in *Film Genre: Theory and Criticism,* ed. Barry K. Grant (Metuchen: Scarecrow, 1977), 7–15, p. 9.

44. Edward Buscombe, "The Idea of Genre in the American Cinema" in *Film Genre Reader II,* ed. Barry K. Grant (Austin: University of Texas Press, 1995), 2–25.

45. Barry K. Grant, Introduction to *Film Genre Reader II,* ed. Barry K. Grant (Austin: University of Texas Press, 1995), xv-xx, p. xv.

46. Garry Whannel, "Winning and Losing Respect: Narratives of Identity in Sport Films" in *Sport in Films,* ed. Emma Poulton and Martin Roderick (New York: Routledge, 2009), 79–92, pp. 80–81.

Chapter Two

1. Virginia Wright Wexman, *A History of Film* 7th ed. (New York: Allyn & Bacon, 2010), p. 72.

2. John Belton, *American Cinema/American Culture* 3rd ed. (New York: McGraw-Hill, 2009), p. 165.

3. Douglas Gilbert, *American Vaudeville, its Life and Times* (New York: Dover, 1940), p. 4.

4. *Ibid.,* p. 6.

5. *Ibid.,* p. 8.

6. *Ibid.,* p. 6.

7. Daniel J. Czitrom, *Media and the American Mind* (Chapel Hill: University of North Carolina Press, 1982), p. 71.

8. Stanley Elkin, *The Dick Gibson Show* (New York: Dutton, 1970), p. 42.

9. Marshall McLuhan, *Understanding Media: The Extensions of Man* (New York: Signet, 1966), p. 254.

10. William H. Kenney, *Recorded Music in American Life: The Phonograph and Popular Memory, 1890–1945* (New York: Oxford University Press, 1999), Chapter 3.

11. Robert Sklar, *Movie-Made America* (New York: Random House, 1975), p. 68.

12. George H. Douglas, *The Early Days of Radio Broadcasting* (Jefferson, NC: McFarland, 1987), p. 184.

13. Sklar, Chapter 15.

14. 47 U.S.C. § 301 of the Communications Act of 1934, as amended, 47 U.S.C. § 151 et seq.

15. Edward Mitchell, "Apes and Essences: Some Sources of Significance in the American Gangster Film" in *Film Genre Reader II* ed. Barry K. Grant (Austin: University of Texas Press, 1995), 203–212, p. 207.

16. "Plot Summary for *Radio Free Steve*." Accessed 30 Apr. 2010. <http://www.imdb.com/title/tt0274748/plotsummary>

17. Jamie Russell, *Book of the Dead: The Complete History of Zombie Cinema* (Surrey: FAB, 2005), p. 9.

18. *Ibid.*, p. 298.

19. David Miller and Mark Gatiss, *They Came from Outer Space!: Alien Encounters in the Movies* (London: Visual Imagination Ltd., 1996).

Chapter Three

1. Marshall McLuhan, *Understanding Media: The Extensions of Man* (New York: Signet, 1966), p. 264.

2. Arnold Passman, *The Deejays* (New York: Macmillan, 1991), p. 7.

3. McLuhan, p. 260.

4. Wes Smith, *The Pied Pipers of Rock 'n' Roll: Radio Deejays of the 50s and 60s* (Atlanta: Longstreet, 1989), p. 24.

5. Peter Fornatale and Joshua E. Mills, *Radio in the Television Age* (Woodstock: Overlook, 1980), p. 38.

6. "Alan Freed Biography." Accessed 15 Dec. 2009. <http://www.alanfreed.com/wp/biography/>

7. Leonard Maltin, *Leonard Maltin's 2007 Movie Guide* (New York: Penguin, 2006), p. 1426.

8. George H. Douglas, *The Early Days of Radio Broadcasting* (Jefferson, NC: McFarland, 1987), p. 66.

9. Donna L. Halper, *Invisible Stars: A Social History of Women in American Broadcasting* (Armonk: Sharpe, 2001), p. 11.

10. *Ibid.*, p. 61.

11. Douglas, p. 65.

12. Smith, p. 23.

13. Halper, pp. 145–147.

14. Passman, 1971.

15. Charles F. Ganzert, "All-Women's Radio: WHER-AM in Memphis," *Journal of Radio Studies* 10.1 (2003): 80–92.

16. "*False Identity.*" Accessed 20 Dec. 2009. <http://www.imdb.com/title/tt0099541/>

17. Eric Rothenbuhler and Tom McCourt, "Radio Redefines Itself, 1947–1962 in *Radio Reader: Essays in the Cultural History of Radio*, ed. Michele Hilmes and Jason Loviglio (New York: Routledge, 2002), 367–387, p. 370.

18. Fornatale and Mills, p. 69.

19. J. Fred MacDonald, *Don't Touch That Dial!: Radio Programming in American Life, 1920–1960* (Chicago: Nelson-Hall, 1979), p. 366.

20. Maltin, p. 1447.

21. Walter Hill, "The Warriors: The Beginning," in *The Warriors: Ultimate Director's Cut* (Paramount Pictures, 1979), DVD.

21. *Ibid.*, "The Warriors: The Phenomenon," in *The Warriors: Ultimate Director's Cut* (Paramount Pictures, 1979), DVD.

22. "*Levitation.*" Accessed 21 Dec. 2009. <http://www.imdb.com/title/tt0119525/>

23. Joseph E. Baudino, and John M. Kittross, "Broadcasting's Oldest Stations: An Examination of Four Claimants," *Journal of Broadcasting* 21.1 (1977): 61–83, p. 72.

24. John E. Conklin, *Campus Life in the Movies* (Jefferson, NC: McFarland, 2008).

25. *Random House Webster's Unabridged Dictionary* 2nd ed. (New York: Random House, 2001), p. 1352.
26. Billy Weber, "Warriors: The Phenomenon," in *The Warriors: Ultimate Director's Cut* (Paramount Pictures, 1979), DVD.

Chapter Four

1. Shirl J. Hoffman, *Good Game: Christianity and the Culture of Sport* (Waco: Baylor University Press, 2010), p. 2.
2. Michael Novak, "The Natural Religion," in *Sport and Religion,* ed. Shirl J. Hoffman (Champagne: Human Kinetics, 1992), 35–42.
3. Hoffman, 2010.
4. James Michener, *Sports in America* (New York: Random House, 1976), p. 386.
5. Hoffman, 2010.
6. *Ibid.*, p. 14.
7. Tona J. Hangen, "Speaking of God, Listening for Grace: Christian Radio and its Audiences," in *Radio Cultures: The Sound Medium in American Life*, ed. Michael C. Keith (New York: Lang, 2008). 131–149, p. 145.
8. Jennings Bryant and Andrea M. Holt, "A Historical Overview of Sports and Media in the United States," in *Handbook of Sports and Media*, ed. Arthur A. Raney and Jennings Bryant (Mahwah: Erlbaum, 2006), 21–43, p. 30.
9. Robert W. McChesney, "Media Made Sport: A History of Sports Coverage in the United States," in *Media, Sports, & Society*, ed. Lawrence A. Wenner (Newbury Park: Sage, 1989), 49–69, p. 49.
10. Michele Hilmes, *Radio Voices: American Broadcasting, 1922–1952* (Minneapolis: University of Minnesota Press, 1997), p. 68.
11. George H. Douglas, *The Early Days of Radio Broadcasting* (Jefferson, NC: McFarland, 1987), p. 114.
12. Benjamin G. Rader, *In its Own Image: How Television has Transformed Sports* (New York: Macmillan, 1984), p. 26.
13. Michener, p. 309.
14. Bryant and Holt, p. 30.
15. Gerald Nachman, *Raised on Radio* (New York: Pantheon, 1998), p. 428.
16. Rader, p. 31.
17. Nora Sayre, "Winning the Weepstakes: The Problems of American Sports Movies," in *Film Genre: Theory and Tradition,* ed. Barry K. Grant (Metuchen: Scarecrow, 1977), 182–194, p. 183.
18. Austin E. Weir, *The Struggle for National Broadcasting in Canada* (Toronto: McClelland and Stewart, 1965), p. 10.
19. William Leggett, "Friday — and No Fight," *Sports Illustrated* 11 July 1960: 24–25.
20. Leonard Maltin, *Leonard Maltin's 2007 Movie Guide* (New York: Penguin, 2006), p. 70.
21. *Stories true and false.* (n.d.). Web. 17 Mar. 2010. <http://baberuthcentral.com/legends/>
22. Jack M. Dempsey, "Sign-On," in *Sports-Talk Radio in America: Its Context and Culture*, ed. Jack M. Dempsey (New York: Haworth, 2006), 1–14, pp. 8–9.

Chapter Five

1. Quentin J. Schultze, "Evangelical Radio and the Rise of the Electronic Church, 1921–1948," *Journal of Broadcasting and Electronic Media* 12.3 (1988): 289–306.
2. Edith L. Blumhofer, *Aimee Semple McPherson: Everybody's Sister* (Grand Rapids: Erdmans, 1993), p. 266.
3. Daniel J. Czitrom, *Media and the American Mind* (Chapel Hill: University of North Carolina Press, 1982), p. 79.

4. Steve Craig, *Out of the Dark: A History of Radio and Rural America* (Tuscaloosa: University of Alabama Press, 2009), p. 105.

5. George H. Hill, *Airwaves to the Soul: The Influence and Growth of Religious Broadcasting in America* (Saratoga: R & E, 1983).

6. Tona J. Hangen, "Speaking of God, Listening for Grace: Christian Radio and its Audiences," in *Radio Cultures: The Sound Medium in American Life*, ed. Michael C. Keith (New York: Lang, 2008), 131–149, p. 131.

7. Craig, Chapter Six.

8. Hangen, p. 138.

9. Craig, p. 107.

10. Sheldon Marcus, *Father Coughlin: The Tumultuous Life of the Priest of the Little Flower* (Boston: Little, Brown, 1973).

11 Charley Orbison, "'Fightin' Bob Shuler: Early Radio Crusader," *Journal of Broadcasting* 21.4 (1977): 459–472.

12. Stewart M. Hoover, *Mass Media Religion: The Social Sources of the Electronic Church* (Newbury Park: Sage, 1988), p. 50.

13. Quentin J. Schultze, "Evangelicals' Uneasy Alliance with the Media," in *Religion and Mass Media: Audiences and Adaptations*, ed. Daniel A. Stout and Judith M. Buddenbaum (Thousand Oaks: Sage, 1996), 61–73, p. 69.

14. Hoover, 1988.

15. Robert K. Johnston, *Reel Spirituality: Theology and Film in Dialogue* Rev. ed. (Grand Rapids: Baker Academic, 2006).

16. Michael Medved, *Hollywood vs. America: Popular Culture and the War on Traditional Values* (New York: HarperCollins, 1992), p. 22.

17. *Ibid.*, p. 50.

18. *Ibid.*, p. 55.

19. *Ibid.*, Chapter 1.

20. Blumhofer, p. 83.

21. *Ibid.*, p. 194.

22. *Ibid.*, p. 262.

23. *Ibid.*, p. 267.

24. "Hallmark Hall of Fame: *The Disappearance of Aimee.*" Accessed 15 Feb. 2010. <http://www.imdb.com/title/tt0074411/>

25. Shirl J. Hoffman, *Good Game: Christianity and the Culture of Sport* (Waco: Baylor University Press, 2010), p. 246.

Chapter Six

1. Mary Ellen O'Toole, Sharon S. Smith, and Robert D. Hare, "Psychopathy and Predatory Stalking of Public Figures," in *Stalking, Threatening, and Attacking Public Figures*, ed. J. Reid Meloy, Lorraine Sheridan and Jens Hoffmann (New York: Oxford University Press, 2008), 215–243, pp. 217–218.

2. Paul E. Mullen, Michele Pathe, and Rosemary Purcell, *Stalkers and Their Victims* (New York: Cambridge University Press, 2000), p. 55.

3. Jens Hoffmann and Lorraine Sheridan, "Celebrities as Victims of Stalking," in *Stalking, Threatening, and Attacking Public Figures*, ed. J. Reid Meloy, Lorraine Sheridan and Jens Hoffmann (New York: Oxford University Press, 2008), 195–213, p. 197.

4. Louis V. Schlesinger and V. Blair Mesa, "Homicidal Celebrity Stalkers: Dangerous Obsessions with Nonpolitical Public Figures," in *Stalking, Threatening, and Attacking Public Figures*, ed. J. Reid Meloy, Lorraine Sheridan and Jens Hoffmann (New York: Oxford University Press, 2008), 83–104, p. 85.

5. Frederick S. Calhoun and Stephen W. Weston, "On Public Figure Howlers," in *Stalking, Threatening, and Attacking Public Figures*, ed. J. Reid Meloy, Lorraine Sheridan and Jens Hoffmann (New York: Oxford University Press, 2008), 105–122, p. 105.

6. *Ibid.*, p. 106.

7. John Dunning, *Tune in Yesterday: The Ultimate Encyclopedia of Old-Time Radio, 1925–1976* (Englewood Cliffs: Prentice-Hall, 1976), pp. 242–243.

8. Peter Fornatale and Joshua E. Mills, *Radio in the Television Age* (Woodstock: Overlook, 1980), p. 83.

9. *Ibid.*, p. 82.

10. *Ibid.*, p. 83.

11. Donald Horton and R. Richard Wohl, "Mass Communication and Para-social Interaction: Observations on Intimacy at a Distance," *Psychiatry* 19 (1956): 215–219, p. 215.

12. *Ibid.*, p. 215.

13. Peter Laufer, "Talk Nation: Turn Down Your Radio," in *Radio Cultures: The Sound Medium in American Life*, ed. Michael C. Keith (New York: Lang, 2008), 217–236, p. 221.

14. Phylis Johnson, "The Howl that Could Not Be Silenced: The Rise of Queer Radio," in *Radio Cultures: The Sound Medium in American Life*, ed. Michael C. Keith (New York: Lang, 2008), 95–111, p. 98.

15. Marshall McLuhan, *Understanding Media: The Extensions of Man* (New York: Signet, 1966), p. 261.

16. *Talkers Magazine.* Accessed 30 May 2010. <http://www.talkers.com>

Bibliography

Balk, Alfred. *The Rise of Radio, from Marconi Through the Golden Age*. Jefferson, NC: McFarland, 2006.

Barber, Red. *The Broadcasters*. New York: Dial, 1970.

Barlow, William. *Voice Over: The Making of Black Radio*. Philadelphia: Temple University Press, 1999.

Barnouw, Erik. *The Golden Web*. New York: Oxford University Press, 1968.

Baudino, Joseph E., and John M. Kittross. "Broadcasting's Oldest Stations: An Examination of Four Claimants." *Journal of Broadcasting* 21.1 (1977): 61–83.

Belton, John. *American Cinema/American Culture*. 3d ed. New York: McGraw-Hill, 2009.

Blumhofer, Edith L. *Aimee Semple McPherson: Everybody's Sister*. Grand Rapids: Erdmans, 1993.

Bryant, Jennings, and Andrea M. Holt. "A Historical Overview of Sports and Media in the United States." In *Handbook of Sports and Media*, ed. by Arthur A. Raney and Jennings Bryant. Mahwah: Erlbaum, 2006. 21–43.

Bryant, M. Darrol. "Cinema, Religion, and Popular Culture." In *Religion in Film*, ed. by John R. May and Michael Bird. Knoxville: University of Tennessee Press, 1982. 101–114.

Buscombe, Edward. "The Idea of Genre in the American Cinema." In *Film Genre Reader II*, ed. by Barry K. Grant. Austin: University of Texas Press, 1995. 2–25.

Calhoun, Frederick S., and Stephen W. Weston. "On Public Figure Howlers." In *Stalking, Threatening, and Attacking Public Figures*, ed. by J. Reid Meloy, Lorraine Sheridan and Jens Hoffmann. New York: Oxford University Press, 2008. 105–122.

Conklin, John E. *Campus Life in the Movies*. Jefferson, NC: McFarland, 2008.

Cox, Jim. *American Radio Networks*. Jefferson, NC: McFarland, 2009.

Craig, Steve. *Out of the Dark: A History of Radio and Rural America*. Tuscaloosa: University of Alabama Press, 2009.

Czitrom, Daniel J. *Media and the American Mind*. Chapel Hill: University of North Carolina Press, 1982.

Dawson, Jim, and Steve Propes. *45 RPM: The History, Heroes, and Villains of a Pop Music Revolution*. San Francisco: Backbeat, 2003.

Dempsey, Jack M. "Sign-On." In *Sports-Talk Radio in America: Its Context and Culture*, ed. by Jack M. Dempsey. New York: Haworth, 2006. 1–14.

Douglas, George H. *The Early Days of Radio Broadcasting*. Jefferson, NC: McFarland, 1987.

Douglas, Susan J. *Listening in: Radio and the American Imagination*. Minneapolis: University of Minnesota Press, 2004.

Dunning, John. *Tune in Yesterday: The Ultimate Encyclopedia of Old-Time Radio, 1925–1976*. Englewood Cliffs: Prentice-Hall, 1976.

Elkin, Stanley. *The Dick Gibson Show*. New York: Dutton, 1970.

Enriquez, Jon. "Coverage of Sports." In *American Journalism: History, Principles, Practices*, ed. by W. David Sloan and Lisa Mullikin Parcell. Jefferson, NC: McFarland, 2002. 198–208.

Etling, Laurence W. "Al Jarvis: Pioneer Disc Jockey." *Popular Music and Society* 23.3 (1999): 41–52.

Fisher, Marc. *Something in the Air: Radio, Rock, and the Revolution That Shaped a Generation.* New York: Random House, 2002.

Fornatale, Peter, and Joshua E. Mills. *Radio in the Television Age.* Woodstock: Overlook, 1980.

Ganzert, Charles F. "All-Women's Radio: WHER-AM in Memphis." *Journal of Radio Studies* 10.1 (2003): 80–92.

Gilbert, Douglas. *American Vaudeville, its Life and Times.* New York: Dover, 1940.

Grant, Barry K. Introduction to *Film Genre Reader II*, ed. by Barry K. Grant. Austin: University of Texas Press, 1995. xv–xx.

Halper, Donna L. *Invisible Stars: A Social History of Women in American Broadcasting.* Armonk, NY: Sharpe, 2001.

Hangen, Tona J. *Redeeming the Dial: Radio, Religion, and Popular Culture in America.* Chapel Hill: University of North Carolina Press, 2002.

_____. "Speaking of God, Listening for Grace: Christian Radio and its Audiences." In *Radio Cultures: The Sound Medium in American Life*, ed. by Michael C. Keith. New York: Lang, 2008. 131–149.

Hill, George H. *Airwaves to the Soul: The Influence and Growth of Religious Broadcasting in America.* Saratoga: R & E, 1983.

Hilliard, Robert L. "Band of Hate: Rancor on the Radio." In *Radio Cultures: The Sound Medium in American Life*, ed. by Michael C. Keith. New York: Lang, 2008. 201–215.

Hilmes, Michele. *Hollywood and Broadcasting: From Radio to Cable.* Urbana: University of Illinois Press, 1990.

_____. *Radio Voices: American Broadcasting, 1922–1952.* Minneapolis: University of Minnesota Press, 1997.

Hoffmann, Jens and Lorraine Sheridan. "Celebrities as Victims of Stalking." In *Stalking, Threatening, and Attacking Public Figures*, ed. by J. Reid Meloy, Lorraine Sheridan and Jens Hoffmann. New York: Oxford University Press, 2008. 195–213.

Hoffman, Shirl J., ed. *Sport and Religion.* Champagne: Human Kinetics, 1992.

_____. *Good Game: Christianity and the Culture of Sport.* Waco: Baylor University Press, 2010.

Hoover, Stewart M. *Mass Media Religion: The Social Sources of the Electronic Church.* Newbury Park: Sage, 1988.

Horton, Donald, and R. Richard Wohl. "Mass Communication and Para-social Interaction: Observations on Intimacy at a Distance." *Psychiatry* 19 (1956): 215–219.

Jackson, John A. *The Big Beat: Alan Freed and the Early Years of Rock & Roll.* New York: Schirmer, 1995.

Johnson, Phylis. "The Howl That Could Not Be Silenced: The Rise of Queer Radio." In *Radio Cultures: The Sound Medium in American Life*, ed. by Michael C. Keith. New York: Lang, 2008. 95–111.

Johnston, Robert K. *Reel Spirituality: Theology and Film in Dialogue.* Rev. ed. Grand Rapids: Baker Acad., 2006.

Kenney, William H. *Recorded Music in American Life: The Phonograph and Popular Memory, 1890–1945.* New York: Oxford University Press, 1999.

Ladd, Jim. *Radio Waves: Life and Revolution on the FM Dial.* New York: St. Martin's, 1991.

Laufer, Peter. "Talk Nation: Turn Down Your Radio." In *Radio Cultures: The Sound Medium in American Life*, ed. by Michael C. Keith. New York: Lang, 2008. 217–236.

Laurie, Joe. *Vaudeville: From the Honky-Tonks to the Palace.* New York: Holt, 1953.

Leggett, William. "Friday — and No Fight." *Sports Illustrated* 11 July 1960: 24–25.

Lenthall, Bruce. "Critical Reception: Public Intellectuals Decry Depression-era Radio, Mass Culture, and Modern America." In *Radio Reader: Essays in the Cultural History of Radio*, ed. by Michele Hilmes and Jason Loviglio. New York: Routledge, 2002. 41–62.

MacDonald, J. Fred. *Don't Touch That Dial! Radio Programming in American Life, 1920–1960*. Chicago: Nelson-Hall, 1979.

Maltin, Leonard. *Leonard Maltin's 2007 Movie Guide*. New York: Penguin, 2006.

Marcus, Sheldon. *Father Coughlin: The Tumultuous Life of the Priest of the Little Flower*. Boston: Little, Brown, 1973.

McChesney, Robert W. "Media Made Sport: A History of Sports Coverage in the United States." In *Media, Sports, & Society*, ed. by Lawrence A. Wenner. Newbury Park: Sage, 1989. 49–69.

McConnell, Frank D. "Leopards and History: The Problem of Film Genre." In *Film Genre: Theory and Criticism*, ed. by Barry K. Grant. Metuchen, NJ: Scarecrow, 1977. 7–15.

McLuhan, Marshall. *Understanding Media: The Extensions of Man*. New York: Signet, 1966.

Medved, Michael. *Hollywood vs. America: Popular Culture and the War on Traditional Values*. New York: Harper, 1992.

Michener, James. *Sports in America*. New York: Random House, 1976.

Miller, David, and Mark Gatiss. *They Came from Outer Space!: Alien Encounters in the Movies*. London: Visual Imagination Ltd., 1996.

Miller, Larry. "Underground Radio: Voices from the Purple Haze." In *Radio Culture: The Sound Medium in American Life*, ed. by Michael C. Keith. New York: Lang, 2008. 113–127.

Mitchell, Edward. "Apes and Essences: Some Sources of Significance in the American Gangster Film." In *Film Genre Reader II*, ed. by Barry K. Grant. Austin: University of Texas Press, 1995. 203–212.

Mullen, Paul E., Michele Pathe, and Rosemary Purcell. *Stalkers and Their Victims*. New York: Cambridge University Press, 2000.

Munson, Wayne. *All Talk: The Talkshow in Media Culture*. Philadelphia: Temple University Press, 1993.

Nachman, Gerald. *Raised on Radio*. New York: Pantheon, 1998.

Novak, Michael. "The Natural Religion." In *Sport and Religion.*, ed. by Shirl J. Hoffman. Champagne: Human Kinetics, 1992. 35–42.

Orbison, Charley. "'Fightin' Bob Shuler: Early Radio Crusader." *Journal of Broadcasting* 21.4 (1977): 459–472.

O'Toole, Mary Ellen, Sharon S. Smith, and Robert D. Hare. "Psychopathy and Predatory Stalking of Public Figures." In *Stalking, Threatening, and Attacking Public Figures*, ed. by J. Reid Meloy, Lorraine Sheridan and Jens Hoffmann. New York: Oxford University Press, 2008. 215–243.

Passman, Arnold. *The Deejays*. New York: Macmillan, 1991.

Rader, Benjamin G. *In Its Own Image: How Television Has Transformed Sports*. New York: Macmillan, 1984.

Reeve, Arthur B. *The Radio Detective*. New York: Grosset & Dunlap, 1926.

"Result Is Official: Jock's in Webster!" *Billboard* 14 May 1949: 3.

Rothenbuhler, Eric, and Tom McCourt. "Radio Redefines Itself, 1947–1962." In *Radio Reader: Essays in the Cultural History of Radio*, ed. by Michele Hilmes and Jason Loviglio. New York: Routledge, 2002. 367–387.

Russell, Jamie. *Book of the Dead: The Complete History of Zombie Cinema*. Surrey: FAB, 2005.

Sayre, Nora. "Winning the Weepstakes: The Problems of American Sports Movies." In *Film Genre: Theory and Tradition*, ed. by Barry K. Grant. Metuchen: Scarecrow. 1977. 182–194.

Schlesinger, Louis V., and V. Blair Mesa. "Homicidal Celebrity Stalkers: Dangerous Obsessions with Nonpolitical Public Figures." In *Stalking, Threatening, and Attacking Public Figures*, ed. by J. Reid Meloy, Lorraine Sheridan and Jens Hoffmann. New York: Oxford University Press, 2008. 83–104.

Schultze, Quentin J. "Evangelical Radio and the Rise of the Electronic Church, 1921–1948." *Journal of Broadcasting and Electronic Media* 12.3 (1988): 289–306.

_____. "Evangelicals' Uneasy Alliance with the Media." In *Religion and Mass Media: Audiences and Adaptations*, ed. by Daniel A. Stout and Judith M. Buddenbaum. Thousand Oaks: Sage, 1996. 61–73.

Scott, Gini Graham. *Can We Talk?: The Power and Influence of Talk Shows*. New York: Insight, 1996.

Shapiro, Mitchell E. *Radio Network Prime Time Programming, 1926–1967*. Jefferson, NC: McFarland, 2002.

Sies, Luther F. *Encyclopedia of American Radio, 1920–1960*. 2nd ed. Jefferson, NC: McFarland, 2008.

Silk, Michael, Jaime Schultz, and Brian Bracey. "From Mice to Men: Miracle, Mythology and the 'Magic Kingdom.'" In *Sport in Films*, ed. by Emma Poulton and Martin Roderick. New York: Routledge, 2009. 163–181.

Sklar, Robert. *Movie-Made America*. New York: Random House, 1975.

Smith, Wes. *The Pied Pipers of Rock 'n' Roll: Radio Deejays of the 50s and 60s*. Atlanta: Longstreet, 1989.

Sterling, Christopher H. "The Rise of Radio Studies: Scholarly Books Over Four Decades." *Journal of Radio & Audio Media* 16.2 (2009): 229–250.

Terrace, Vincent. *Radio Programs, 1924–1984*. Jefferson, NC: McFarland, 1999.

Walker, Jesse. *Rebels on the Air: An Alternative History of Radio in America*. New York: New York University Press, 2001.

Warren, Donald. *Radio Priest: Charles Coughlin, the Father of Hate Radio*. New York: Free Press, 1996.

Weir, Austin E. *The Struggle for National Broadcasting in Canada*. Toronto: McClelland and Stewart, 1965.

Wexman, Virginia Wright. *A History of Film*. 7th ed. New York: Allyn & Bacon, 2010.

Whannel, Garry. "Winning and Losing Respect: Narratives of Identity in Sport Films." In *Sport in Films*, ed. by Emma Poulton and Martin Roderick. New York: Routledge, 2009. 79–92.

Index

Radio station call letters listed are those of actual stations, not fictitious film stations. This index does not include references to information in the filmography.

On Stage Everybody 41–42
On the Air Live with Captain Midnight 56, 57, 80, 99
Once Upon a Honeymoon 51
One Hour Late 45
Open House 151, 152, 158
O'Reilly, Bill 33, 153
Our America 37
Outlaw Blues 80–81
Outside Ozona 88–89
Over the Goal 127
Over the Wall 46

Page Miss Glory 45
Paige, Leroy "Satchel" 65, 117, 121, 123–124
The Palmolive Hour (radio show) 16
Palooka 27, 103, 110
Palooka, Joe (comic strip character) 27, 110
Panic on the Air (aka You May be Next) 48
The Paper 29
Paradise 141
Paradise Valley 50
parasocial interaction 153
Passman, Arnold 18, 82
payola 22, 33, 79, 80
People Are Funny 27
The Phantom Broadcast 46
The Phantom Empire 3
Pigskin Parade 126–127
pirate radio 17, 35–36, 54–60
Pirate Radio (aka The Boat That Rocked) 35–36, 57–58, 74
Piratene 59
Piter FM 97, 101, 171
The Planet Man (radio show) 16
play-by-play broadcasting 25, 26, 40, 103–135
Play Misty for Me 7, 74, 86–87, 149, 153, 155, 157
Pontypool 29, 38, 62, 98
Poor Little Rich Girl 27, 45
Possums 104, 129
Pounder, CCH 90, 160
Power 98 16, 168
Pray TV 141
The Pride of St. Louis 122–123
The Pride of the Yankees 104, 118–120
Private Moments 97
Private Parts 4, 34, 79, 92, 99
The Prize Fighter 116
Professional Sweetheart 27
Protektor 54
Psycho IV: The Beginning 90, 159–160
psycho listeners 7, 8, 9, 84, 85, 91, 93, 149, 150–165, 168, 171
public radio 37, 91
Pump up the Volume 57

Queen for a Day 27, 149
Quid Pro Quo 37–38
Quiz Kids (radio show) 16
Quo Vadis 140

Racketeers in Exile 48, 143
Radio Cape Cod 171
Radio Caroline 57
Radio Corbeau 59
radio cowboys 3, 16, 28, 49–51, 149
Radio Days 1, 32, 36
The Radio Detective 25, 46, 48
radio detectives 16, 48–49, 149
Radio Free Steve 57
The Radio King 24
Radio Love 98, 171
Radio: Love on Air 96, 97, 171
radio news 28–29, 37–38, 48
Radio Pirates 58
radio preachers 37, 139–145, 147–148
radio psychologists 151–154, 158, 162, 165–167, 169–171
radio ratings: importance of 15–16, 30, 34, 36, 45, 68, 74, 78, 85, 86, 104, 166, 168
Radio Samurai 96
Radio Star 96
radio stations: ATV London 96; Bayerische Rundfunk Munich 96; BBC London 96; CKEY 96; CKOV 96; KABC 152; KDKA 14, 18, 103; KFWB 18, 19, 67; KGB 79, 98; KGEF 139; KJMZ 89; KLAC 152; KNBR 136; KNX 139; KOLN Munich 96; KPFK 98; KSFG 141; KSJS 93, 98; KYW 44; Mega 97.9 79, 98; Power 99 FM 90, 98; WAOW 139; WDIA 86; WFAN 135; WFNX 98; WHA 91; WHER 82; WIBG 73; WITH 73; WJLB 89, 98; WJR 139; WKMH 86; WLS 51; WLW 44; WNBC 135; WNEW 18; WOL 35, 90; WOR 72; WOV 86; WRIF 98, 136; WSM 44; WTBU 92; WWJ 103; WXOX 13, 91, 98
Radio tekee murron (aka The Radio Burglary) 26
Radioland Murders 47
Radiopiratene (aka The Radio Pirates) 60
Radyo 163
Raging Bull 116
Randle, Bill 72
Ransome, John W. 41
rap music 16, 34–35, 80, 89, 90
Rare Birds 48, 97
Reagan, Ronald 48, 122, 131
Rebecca of Sunnybrook Farm 27
religion and sports 102, 103
Remote Control 48
The Republic of Love 171
Requiem for a Heavyweight 109
Requiem for Murder 84, 156, 157, 162
Reveille with Beverly 18, 26, 28, 67, 69, 82
Rhythm in the Clouds 48, 80
Rhythm Round-up 51
Richard Diamond, Private Eye (radio show) 48
Ridin' Down the Canyon 48, 50
The Ring 109, 114–115
Ring of Passion 65, 115, 116
Ring of the Musketeers 85, 98